A WAR IN DIXIE

ALABAMA V. AUBURN

A WAR

IN DIXIE

Ivan Maisel

and

Kelly Whiteside

HarperCollins*Publishers*

HarperCollins books may be purchased for educational, business, or sales promotional use. For information, please write: Special Markets Department, HarperCollins Publishers Inc., 10 East 53rd Street, New York, NY 10022.

FIRST EDITION

Designed by Elliott Beard

Library of Congress Cataloging-in-Publication Data

Maisel, Ivan.
    A war in Dixie : Alabama v. Auburn / Ivan Maisel and Kelly Whiteside.
      p. cm.
    ISBN 0-06-019800-1
    1. University of Alabama—Football—History. 2. Auburn University—Football—History. I. Whiteside, Kelly.
    GV958.A4 M35   2001
    796.332'63'09761—dc21

                                    2001039318

01 02 03 04 05 06 ❖/RRD 10 9 8 7 6 5 4 3 2 1

"Sure I'd love to beat Notre Dame, don't get me wrong. But nothing matters more than beating that cow college on the other side of the state."
—Paul "Bear" Bryant

"Wait until you whip their ass. You ain't seen nothing yet. It will be a different world."
—former Auburn coach Pat Dye

Contents

Acknowledgments

The idea for this book was more than one year old when Iron Bowl Week 2000 began. In that time the fortunes of Alabama coach Mike DuBose and his staff turned completely around. The coaches lost their jobs. They had to prepare for Auburn. They had to find another job. Despite those circumstances, DuBose and his coaches couldn't have been more accommodating. A special thanks to Dee Gibson and Don Rawson and the Alabama graduate assistants, who allowed me to loiter in their offices when I had nowhere else to be.

Larry White, who runs the Alabama media relations office, couldn't be more professional. His staff is always dependable for assistance with a smile. Leon Ashford, Joe Fine, and Governor Don Siegelman, Rodney Orr of TiderInsider.com, and Craig Silver of *CBS Sports* opened doors to provide insight on various aspects of the rivalry. The following journalists on the Crimson Tide beat filled in the blanks when needed: Ray Melick, Steve Kirk, Gene Duffey, Tom Murphy, Cecil Hurt, David Goodwin, and play-by-play man extraordinaire Eli Gold. Matt Coulter, Scott Griffin, and Ryan Haney of WJOX in Birmingham kept me abreast of public opinion throughout the season by having me on as a guest. Bill Colson and Bobby Clay, my editors at *Sports Illustrated,* showed extreme patience in providing me the leeway to write this book. Thanks to Kelly Whiteside, who asked me to write with her and never dozed off once as I prattled on about my native state. My family never complained when I disappeared into the attic office. Thank you, Meg, Sarah, Max, and Elizabeth.

—*I.M.*

It was the second half of the Iron Bowl and the tension was tight. The Tigers were only ahead, 6–0. I had just finished jostling with a bunch of third-string linemen for some warmth around the portable heaters when linebacker Alex Lincoln caught my eye. "Was any Rutgers game ever like this?" Lincoln said with a smile. I laughed at the crack at my alma mater. Of course not. There is no game, at any level, quite like this one.

I would have never grasped its passion without the help of Lincoln, Ben Leard, Cole Cubelic, Rob Pate, Rodney Crayton, and Rudi Johnson, who graciously allowed me into their lives during Iron Bowl week. The same goes for Coach Tommy Tuberville and his staff, Athletic Director David Housel, and Media-Relations Directors Meredith Jenkins and Kirk Sampson and their staff who made me feel right at home. Thanks to Phillip Marshall of the *Huntsville Times* for his perspective, and to recent Auburn graduates Lorie Johnson and Ryan Powell, and Ty Prim at UAB for their assistance. Tom O'Toole, my editor at *USA Today*, couldn't have been more understanding through it all. And, of course, there couldn't have been a better person to write this book with than Ivan Maisel.

A special thanks to my sister, Nancy Binowski, who transcribed much of the one hundred thousand words of interviews during her maternity leave. Childbirth was surely a less painful process. And to Mike Freeman, who made life easier in every other way during the delivery of this manuscript.

—*K.W.*

Much thanks from the both of us to our editor at HarperCollins, Mauro DiPreta, and his assistant, Joelle Yudin; John Monteleone and the staff of Mountain Lion, Inc.; and to Randy Voorhees, whose idea it was in the first place.

ALABAMA
Foreword by Ken Stabler

From day one, I understood the difference between orange and blue and crimson and white. I could tell an elephant from a tiger. Even today, when I meet somebody and he introduces himself as being from Alabama, one of the first things that pops into my mind is, "I wonder who he pulls for." Unless you're in the middle of the Alabama–Auburn rivalry, or grew up in it, or raised children in it, it's just hard to explain. I tell people it's part of our culture. It's a natural thing. The rivalry is woven into everyday life. My daughters are the same way. They figured out early on which side we were on. I can remember them coming home and saying, "I made this new friend. She's a sweet girl but she goes for Auburn." That's in third and fourth grade.

It starts early, and you have to deal with it if you live here. Nine times out of ten, when you go to the vet here, he's going to be from Auburn. And nine out of ten visits to the dentist, you've got to talk about the quarterback situation at Alabama if you want to get your teeth cleaned. I've got a big mail slot in my office, big enough to drive a car through. Yet my mailman knocks on the door every day: "What's going on in spring ball? What's Coach Fran [new Alabama coach Dennis Franchione] like?"

I'm not criticizing it. Hell, I love it. When I go pick up prescriptions for my daughters or for my wife, Rose, I know the guy handing them to me is from Auburn. They love their school as much as we love ours. I try to see it from their perspective, the way they look at me. We beat the hell out of Auburn when I played. I always thought they appreciated me as a player. It's self-serving to say to them, "You guys scored six points on us in three years." We beat them 30–3, 31–0, and in my senior year, we beat them 7–3.

The Auburn people in Foley, Alabama, tried very hard to recruit me. Their style of playing in 1964 was very appealing. They had a quarterback named Jimmy Sidle who would sprint out and throw or run. That's how I played in high school. It was fun to watch Auburn play. Why, then, did I go to Alabama? Because Alabama won. When I was growing up in the early 1960s, in Foley—which is on the other side of the bay from Mobile—I followed Alabama football. I knew who Pat Trammell was, the great quarterback who died so young of cancer. I'd hear the stories of what it was like to play for Coach Paul "Bear" Bryant. I knew who Harry Gilmer was and Bart Starr and Joe Namath, and I wanted to be a part of that.

I don't remember feeling the intensity of the two teams' rivalry as a player as much as I do now. Maybe Coach Bryant kept us away from it. Don't get me wrong. He made us aware of how important it was to beat Auburn. "You don't have to win," he told us. "But if you don't, you do have to deal with losing." It's not life or death, but it is a helluva lot more fun to deal with winning than to deal with losing. Because it was Auburn, it was awfully important.

We never lost to Auburn but we came awfully close in my senior year. That's the game when I ran 47 yards for a touchdown in the fourth quarter in a terrible rainstorm. We managed to win, 7–3. We had a tight end named Dennis Dixon, and after the game, Coach Ralph "Shug" Jordan of Auburn and Gusty Yearout, their linebacker, both said that Dennis had held Gusty on my run. Well, hell, somebody holds on every play. That's football. Sometimes it gets called. Sometimes it doesn't. I've always said it's no lead-pipe cinch that Gusty would have tackled me, either.

When you have a special play, people are always coming up to you and talking about it. Even after all the plays I made as a pro quarterback, all those games against Pittsburgh when I was at Oakland, winning the Super Bowl, that run in the mud is one of the first things that people bring up. "I was there when the umbrellas were turned inside out," or "Man, I was there at Legion Field." Or, "You know where I was on December 2, 1967?" I always say, "I bet you were wet." I get that a couple of times a month.

That was almost thirty-five years ago. I wish we could play again tomorrow and I wish we could beat them 40–0. After Auburn beat us 9–0 last year—sorry, I just gave away the ending of the book—the pharmacist said, "Tough luck. You still played hard." I said, "Just give me my medicine."

I'm fifty-five years old. You see the intensity of the rivalry and you look back and think about that Auburn game and how they were ahead of us in the fourth quarter and you made one of the great plays in Alabama history. When you do it, you have no idea how much it will mean to so many people. I understand now. If I didn't, all I would have to do is step out on the street. Pretty soon someone would remind me.

Ken Stabler
MOBILE
April 2001

AUBURN
Foreword by Pat Sullivan

Before I went into coaching, I spent six years as the football analyst on the Auburn radio network. I remember visiting with Keith Jackson, the voice of college football, before one Alabama game. He told me that he had called all the great rivalries for ABC but that Auburn–Alabama was the top.

I'm sure he might get an argument in Columbus and Ann Arbor, or at Annapolis and West Point. But unless you've been part of this rivalry, it's hard to understand how intense it is. People take it so personally. When you're close to it, as I was as a player and a coach at Auburn, you have mutual respect for the players and coaches on the other sideline. I was an All-American quarterback for Auburn University from 1969 to 1971. After each of the three games against Alabama, Johnny Musso—an All-American running back for Alabama—and I would always go out together. That might sound like heresy, but we did it for three straight years. We were both from Birmingham. We knew each other in high school, through recruiting. We took our visits together.

The thing is, you have a lot of friends on the other side. The majority of players on both teams are from the state of Alabama. You play against them in high school, or with them in the state high school all-star game. Auburn–Alabama games are like playing basketball in the backyard. It's no-holds-barred, do-anything-to-win football. I'm not talking about dirty football. In fact, Iron Bowls are known for being clean games. But we all know what it's like to play basketball in the backyard against your brother. You hate losing, right? Take that emotion and put it on a football field in front of 85,000 fans. There's so much pressure, whichever side you're on. You're always being compared to the other side. You're always being asked about how you're going to compete. You know the players on the other side are going through the same thing. You develop a mutual respect.

That mutual respect isn't so apparent as far as the fans are concerned. They do take it personally. If you've ever been a part of the game, like I have, people meet you and immediately let you know whether they're Auburn or Alabama. My wife and I got married before my sophomore year at Auburn. Her cousin, Eddie Burg, was twelve or thirteen years old at the time. I can remember eating supper with them and he told me, "Y'all haven't got a chance against Alabama." And I had just married his cousin! That fall we beat Alabama 49–26, and I remember Eddie coming over to the fence behind the Auburn bench with this long, drawn face. "All right, y'all won," Eddie said. "But we're going to get you next year."

If you drive down a rural road in this state and pull into a store or a gas station, you find out real quickly where folks stand. These people bleed that deep loyalty. That's all they want to talk about. It might be in the summer, but the comment would be, "How we going to do against them?" "Them" is not Tennessee or Georgia; it's, how are we going to do against *them*? You know who they mean.

I played against Alabama four times, once in the freshman game— back in 1968, we had them—and three times on the varsity. In those days, the teams had two weeks to prepare and the freshman game would be played on that middle Saturday. Alabama jumped ahead of us 28–0 but we came back and beat them—the first time Auburn had won the freshman or varsity game since 1963. My classmates and I drew on that victory in my junior year. Alabama jumped ahead of us 17–0. I think having come from behind as freshmen gave us the confidence that we could do it again. We came back and beat them 33–28.

In my senior year, both teams were undefeated. Both Johnny and I were candidates for the Heisman. In 1971, the Downtown Athletic Club awarded the Heisman on Thanksgiving night, two days before the Alabama game. When they announced my name, we were all in the coliseum on campus, which was packed with fans. The emotion my teammates and I felt was incredible. The coliseum felt like a locker room after beating Alabama or Tennessee. The next morning, when we had to get on the bus to go to Birmingham to play Alabama, I think we were all spent. Hey, don't get me wrong. Alabama had a great team. I don't know that we would have played any differently without all the fuss. But they beat us 31–7.

I was very close to our head coach, Ralph "Shug" Jordan. In fact, after I left Auburn and went to the NFL, he and I talked every week, usually on Thursday afternoons. The funny thing is, I ended up feeling pretty close to Coach Paul "Bear" Bryant, too. Coach Bryant was bigger than life. I'll never forget broadcasting the Iron Bowl in 1982, Coach Bryant's last year. I used to go to the stadium early to be there on the field to talk with the coaches and players before the game. That year, I got there before either team. I walked down toward the Auburn locker room and sat on a bench outside. Alabama arrived first and filed into its locker room. Coach Bryant came out to smoke a cigarette. He saw me, walked over, and he and I visited for a few minutes. He told me he was thinking about getting out of coaching. He talked to me like I was one of his boys. It was very special.

Two-and-a-half weeks later, he announced he was retiring. I jotted down a note to him, wishing him well against Illinois, and told him I hoped he and his family would have a merry Christmas. A little while later I got a nice two-page, handwritten letter from him thanking me. Within a matter of days, he was gone.

I am the quarterback coach and offensive coordinator at UAB now, so I should have a little distance from the Auburn–Alabama rivalry. The truth is, I still can't help but get caught up in it. But once you decide to live in this state, you can't help it. Folks here wouldn't have it any other way.

Pat Sullivan
Birmingham
April 2001

Introduction
The Elephant v. The Tiger

True story: one afternoon in late July 2000, Tommy Tuberville entertained three guests at the Shoal Creek Golf Club in suburban Birmingham. Tuberville's membership in the exclusive club is a perk of his position as head football coach at Auburn University. The Shoal Creek men's locker room is a large, comfortable haven complete with big shower heads, every conceivable grooming item a man could need (big towels, perfumed talc, sunscreen, even cotton swabs), and a smiling attendant. What it doesn't have is enough lockers for its out-of-town members. Tuberville was somewhat abashed that he and his guests had to become squatters in another man's locker for the afternoon. As Tuberville left the locker room, his guests in tow, his reaction said loads about the nature of the relationship between Auburn and its archrival.

"Guess I'm going to have to beat Alabama before I get my own locker," Tuberville said.

He said it to get a laugh, of course, but Tuberville's comment reveals what Alabama fans believe to be a law of nature: It is Alabama's locker room, Alabama's Birmingham, and Alabama's world. Auburn is not an equal. Far from it. Take this February 2000 exchange on TiderInsider.com, a web site devoted to Alabama athletics:

"What event, if any, made you hate Auburn?"—DBTide
"My birth: I never knew there was a choice."—BamaBrave

Not every Alabama fan hates Auburn. There are plenty that do, yes, and their passion helps fuel this rivalry, not to mention how it fuels scholarship donations, newspaper circulation, the T-shirt industry, and the occasional legendary bumper sticker (namely, the blue-and-orange Punt Bama Punt from Auburn's 17–16 shocker in 1972). That said, the predominant emotion among Alabama fans regarding their archrival is not hate; that would grant to the Auburn community a measure of equality that the Alabama faithful don't believe is warranted.

No, the predominant emotion among the Alabama fans is fear. They don't fear Auburn. Hell, they barely respect Auburn. What Alabama fans fear is losing to Auburn. It's bad enough that every loss to Auburn brings with it a year of barbs from Tiger fans and a year of reliving the one or two plays that went against the Crimson Tide again and again. The loss to Auburn is a public display that Alabama is not better than Auburn. No Crimson Tide partisan ever wants to admit that.

We are talking about good old-fashioned condescension. Never mind that in recent years Auburn's enrollment has well surpassed Alabama's. Auburn had approximately 22,000 students in the 2000–2001 academic year. Alabama had about 19,300. That's right, Auburn is bigger. The Crimson Tide fans take as a law of nature that in the sixty-five-game series between the schools, Alabama leads 37–27–1. Never mind that in the eighteen years since coach Paul "Bear" Bryant died, Alabama is 9–9 against Auburn, or that only three of those games had winning margins greater than 10 points, another indication of how evenly matched the schools are.

You can break out charts and statistics and empirical evidence from now until the next millennium. Auburn University is a land-grant institution that includes well-respected schools of agriculture, veterinary medicine, engineering, pharmacy, and communication. Auburn has sent astronauts into space, for God's sake. Doesn't matter—Alabama fans call it "Aubarn," reveling in the stereotype of the Auburn hayseed.

Auburn fans, or "Barners," are the subject of jokes otherwise used to denigrate blondes or, if you're in the Lone Star state, Texas A&M graduates. For instance, an Auburn man at a cocktail party sees a well-dressed gentleman wearing a graduation ring with a blue stone.

Auburn man: "Whar'd yew go to school?"
Gentleman: "Yale."
Auburn man: "WHAR'D YEW GO TO SCHOOL?"

"In every state, you have the state university and the land-grant university," says Howell Raines, a Birmingham native who is now the executive editor of the *New York Times*. Raines grew up an Alabama fan and earned a graduate degree in Tuscaloosa. "In every state, you see the state university look down upon the land-grant university. You see that handled in social terms. Given the struggles we've had in Alabama, economically and culturally, it seems like [the condescension] is on totally artificial terms. It also goes back to the migration before the Depression from the farm into the city. You look at the figures from the county seat to the towns in the twenties. That was a big watershed. Auburn identified with agriculture and the traditional way of life. Alabama became identified with the new, modern way of life."

Raines has been gone from the state for a generation and is somewhat taken aback at the intensity of the rivalry today. Nevertheless, the Iron Bowl, like the final round of the Masters, is an annual watershed event for him. In 1994, Raines wrote a *Times* editorial in which he described "the impossible task of ceasing to care." He joked, "If there is a moral order in the universe, Alabama will win this year. Next year would be good, too."

Gaining distance from the rivalry, as Raines did, can provide a sense of perspective. So, too, can being closer to it. Neil Callaway played at Alabama in the mid-1970s, coached at Auburn under Pat Dye from 1981–92, then coached for Mike DuBose from 1997 through the 2000 Iron Bowl. While in Auburn, Callaway lived next door to a businessman named Bill Ham Jr. Last November, Ham—a lifelong resident of Auburn, an Auburn graduate, and now the mayor of the city of Auburn—and his family stayed with the Callaway family in

Tuscaloosa for the Iron Bowl. The men's wives, Karen Callaway and Carol Ham are close friends. Their daughters, Kate Callaway and Ashley Ham, remain close. Callaway's teenaged boys, Clay and Russ, look up to Ham's son, Forrest. It never occurred to Callaway to not have the Hams stay with him. "You know how you got three or four guys in your life you could call if you needed them?" Callaway explains. "He's one of them." Ham agrees, although he admits, "The first time I went to visit him in Tuscaloosa," Ham says, "I felt like I had a stomach virus the whole weekend."

Former Auburn linebacker Bill Newton knows the feeling. Newton, the man behind the most famous football moment in Auburn history, the "Punt Bama Punt" game, felt uneasy as he stood on the sideline at Bryant-Denny Stadium at Alabama's 2000 spring game.

"Bill Newton? Aren't yew the one who blocked those two punts? What are yew doin' here?" the man asked, as did many others throughout the day.

"Well, my son's a prospect kicker," Newton told him.

"Well, I'm glad you got smart and got him looking at a good school," the man said. Which is a typical Alabama reaction.

Newton was in enemy territory because his son, Will, was being recruited by the Tide. Will, a standout kicker for Fayette County High School in West Alabama, was invited to A-Day along with the other Tide recruits and their families.

"My wife made me go," says Newton, who now owns a natural gas and oil company. "She told me I needed to go to support my son. So I went down and we went through their meetings. It was a funny feeling looking at the red and white. I couldn't imagine being in that stadium yelling, 'Roll, Tide, Roll,' if he decided to go to Alabama."

For Newton, there was no place to hide that day, not with the name tag on his shirt proclaiming, "Hi, I'm Bill Newton," a name synonymous with one of the most dramatic comebacks in Iron Bowl history.

Second-ranked Alabama brought a 10–0 record into Legion Field to meet the No. 9 Tigers, who were 8–1. Alabama's defense dominated the game, and with 5:30 remaining, the Tide led, 16–3. But then Newton blocked an Alabama punt and David Langner returned it 25 yards for an Auburn touchdown. Three minutes later, it looked like an instant replay. Newton blocked another punt and Langner ran 20 yards for the score. Auburn's 17–16 win spoiled Bama's bid for a national title.

From that moment on, Bill Newton was no longer just Bill Newton. Instead, he became Bill Newton, The Guy Who Blocked Those Two Punts. "I can't associate it with the bombing of Pearl Harbor or anything like that, but in modern-day sports, to people of this state, they have a vivid memory of where they were and what they were doing that day," Newton says. Rarely a day goes by without someone mentioning the game to him.

As for his son, after Alabama signed another kicker in February, Auburn invited Will to walk-on next season. "Deep down in my heart, I hoped he would have an opportunity to go to Auburn because it's the love of my life," says Newton, who also began his career at Auburn as a walk-on. "Everything just fell into place." How serendipitous: the son of the "Punt, Bama, Punt" guy someday kicking punts for Auburn.

If central casting were to look for the quintessential Auburn type, the Newtons would serve as good leading men. The overlooked player who was spurned by Alabama goes on to ruin the Tide's hopes of a national championship. Though that stereotype is not entirely correct, as the Tigers' roster is also smattered with All-Americans, the label perseveres.

It doesn't matter that Auburn dominated the series in the second half of the 1950s, under coach Ralph "Shug" Jordan, winning the school's only national championship in 1957. It doesn't matter that after Bama ruled during the '60s and '70s, there was a shift in power when Alabama's Bear Bryant retired and Pat Dye took over at Auburn in the early '80s. It doesn't matter, because Auburn judges its self-worth through Alabama's looking glass.

Usually the rivalry is called the Alabama–Auburn game, which drives Tigers fans crazy. Why is Alabama always listed first? Why isn't the game called the Auburn–Alabama game?

Though Auburn is now the state's largest university, though it arguably has the prettiest campus in the SEC, and though it's only about a ninety-minute drive away from Atlanta, Auburn will always be the cow college located in a rural part of the state.

"Alabama people got a superiority complex, and Auburn people got an inferiority complex, that's the way it's been," Auburn athletic director David Housel says.

"We're still the stepchildren because they are THE University of Alabama," longtime Auburn equipment manager Frank Cox says. "They're the lawyers and doctors and we're the farmers and vets."

"They are always going to have those twelve national championships, however many All-Americans, whatever record against us, always being so much better," Auburn center Cole Cubelic says.

"It seems that everyone at Alabama believes that they are better than us. Believes they are going to be our bosses in years to come. That is a hard pill to swallow. You don't want them to think that. You want to get the best of them every time you step on the field," Auburn quarterback Ben Leard says.

It doesn't matter that the Tigers have an 8–2 record and the Tide are 3–7 entering Saturday's game, the 2000 Iron Bowl. Auburn still believes that Alabama has the upper hand, because, well, they're Alabama. "Auburn is a little-David team. Going into the Alabama game people would say it is a Goliath team," Housel says. "But it's not in terms of record but in terms of prestige, home field, talent. All the supposed intangibles are on Alabama's side."

No matter how many Rudi Johnsons the Tigers have in their arsenal, Auburn always sees itself as the one toting the sling shot.

The passion of the rivalry can express itself in ways unseen in other parts of the country. In one so-called mixed marriage, the couple agreed that the loser's diploma would hang upside down over a toilet until the next game. When the passion collides with the real world, the result can be unfortunate. For years, Alabama and Auburn left the Saturday before their game open. Walt Pittman, a 1984 Alabama grad and now a real estate appraiser in the Birmingham suburb of Mountain Brook, remembers shrewdly setting his wedding date on that weekend. In 1993, the schools eliminated the off-week. On November 22, 1997, Pittman's anniversary, he stayed home with a buddy to watch the Iron Bowl while their wives went to dinner. "Big mistake," he recalls. "She normally watches the games with me and a group of our friends. She wanted me to choose her over the game. I knew she was going to be upset, but I thought the dinners the night before and after would smooth things out. This was one of those tests that wives like to give and there was only one right answer. I was fairly calm after the game and was very nice to her. When our friends left the house she went to the bedroom and locked the door. I spent my anniversary on the couch. It took a dozen roses and a trip to see the Rolling Stones in Atlanta for my wife to forgive me."

To add insult to injury, Alabama lost that Iron Bowl in the final minute when, with a 17–15 lead, offensive coordinator Bruce Arians called a third-down screen pass rather than have the quarterback put down a knee and punt. Fullback Ed Scissum fumbled the reception and Auburn recovered at the Alabama 33 with :42 to play. Jaret Holmes kicked a 39-yard field goal with :15 left and the Tigers won, 18–17. DuBose fired Arians and three other coaches in a matter of days. "I have still not forgiven Mike DuBose for losing that game," Pittman says.

In the heart of Dixie, as the state is known, loyalty and enmity are passed from one generation to the next like a family heirloom. Senior offensive tackle Colin Sears is the product of a mixed marriage, which, in this state, means he's the offspring of an Auburn fan and an Alabama fan. His mother is an Alabama graduate and his father has always been an Auburn fan. "When I chose to go to Auburn, I knew my dad was going to be proud of me," Sears says, "and my mother, well, she's adjusted."

Phillip Gargis, a reserve cornerback, was raised in the rivalry because his father, Phillip, was the Tigers' quarterback in the mid-'70s and his mother, Scarlotte, was an Auburn majorette. "I was brought up not to hate Alabama but to dislike them just because my dad went through it and my mom went through it. But the dislike is not between the players so much. I mean, the players want to win it, but they can get along. It is the fans that make it this huge."

From birth, babies born during Iron Bowl weekend are given Auburn or Alabama caps in the maternity ward; to death, it is not unusual for fans to be buried with Auburn or Alabama memorabilia in their casket; from love, no one dares to schedule a wedding on the same date as the Iron Bowl; to politics, Auburn fans vote for politicians who went to Auburn and Alabama fans vote for Alabama grads—the rivalry intersects everyday life.

"The best thing about this game is also the worst thing about this game," Cox, the equipment manager, says. "It's too important to too many people."

Outside linebackers coach Phillip Lolley, a longtime high school coach in the state, grew up in Butler, which is not far from Tuscaloosa. Needless to say, the area is Alabama country. "My kin folks are big Alabama fans, so I have to hear it all the time. The rivalry is thicker than blood. They love me, but not as much as the Crimson Tide. Some of my closest friends are Alabama guys, and we don't discuss the game, I mean, because we'll come to blows. We will come to blows, and have before. We just kind of don't discuss it.

"I mean, this is serious business here. Families separate over this game each year. There have been people never the same after this ball game. Family members get killed over this game. Through the years, you get used to it."

On the other hand, Housel thinks the worst of the rivalry—the hatred and the division among the fans—isn't as bad as it used to be. "It's still the most important day of the year. The outcome of this game is something that affects people the year round. People think about it the year round. But it used to be there were families permanently divided. There were relationships broken. Business deals broken. And friendships broken forever. I don't sense as much of that as I used to. And I think that is a maturing process of the people in the state of Alabama. Now, it may be that I don't sense it as much because I have grown older. But I think fans on both sides used to internalize the outcome of this game too much. I think they used to let it affect how they felt about themselves. I'm not sure there's as much of that as there used to be."

Walt Pittman is a subscriber to TiderInsider.com, a web site, started by a Bama grad named Rodney Orr, who junked his desk job in Corpus

Christi, Texas, and moved his family to Tuscaloosa in order to follow his heart. He has more than two thousand subscribers who pay a $36 annual fee to learn what's going on inside the Tide. To help provide any and all information, Orr has a reporter at every practice. He also has a radio show.

Orr, forty, is a recovering Alabama maniac. He says even he understood that the strain put on his marriage by his sulking, furious reaction to the 1993 loss at Auburn was too much. That 22–14 loss concluded Auburn's undefeated season. To Orr and others of his rabid ilk, that Auburn could go 11–0 with first-year coach Terry Bowden, while on NCAA probation, and do so only one year after the Crimson Tide won the national championship, messed with the natural order of life as they understood it.

Now that Orr sees the inside of college football, knows the coaches and the players as people, Alabama football is not life or death to him; it's his bread and butter. But Orr understands the mentality. He caters to the belief of Alabama fans that they are special.

"From Auburn, it's obvious," Orr says. "If you look at it, they've been the little brother. Beating Alabama seems to make their season. Alabama, on the other hand, is scared to death to lose to Auburn. In a way, for Alabama fans, Auburn was just a stepping stone to bigger and better things. Beat Auburn and play for a national championship. Beat Auburn and go to a major bowl game. For Auburn, beating Alabama meant gaining respect. For Alabama, beating Auburn does not mean getting respect."

Orr's subscribers support this theory, and they have a few of their own. Chris Plaster, an Alabama law student, grew up in Virginia but attached himself to the Crimson Tide at an early age because his grandfather respected Bryant. He professes himself mystified by Auburn. "I simply cannot understand how anyone can be that close to greatness, that close to everything good about the South and Southern football," Plaster says, "and choose not only to reject it but to hate it. Jealousy. Jealousy and envy. Nothing more and nothing less. A simple case of little-brother syndrome. Yeah, we lost this year, but it doesn't change the fact that we're still Alabama and they're still Auburn. We're the University of Alabama and they're a university in Alabama."

Terrance Harrington says, "Their greatest claim to fame is living off our coattails, using our glory to drag themselves to a level they neither deserve nor even appreciate. . . . We intend never to recognize them for anything other than a speed bump on the way to another crown, and that galls them all the more."

Milo Dakin, a former journalist and now a lobbyist in Montgomery, says that as a Louisiana State University graduate, he doesn't have a dog in this hunt. "The one thing Auburn has not established, and it still sticks in their craw, is a tradition," he opines. "Alabama has a tradition. Most schools don't. It's a silk-stocking, ivory-tower attitude that Auburn folks resent. I work with both Auburn and Alabama folks. I don't find Alabama folks who like anything from Auburn."

The occasional sallies of public respect paid to Auburn by Crimson Tide coaches and athletes are accepted by the Bama diehards as doing what is necessary to compete. No one else can get away with them. Witness this exchange on TiderInsider.com in the third week of the 2000 season: One Tide fan, after reassuring everyone where he stood ("I'm BAMA through and through") wrote a well-reasoned note of praise for Auburn fullback Heath Evans for "his toughness, effort, and exemplary conduct on the field. . . . I remember a certain coach in houndstooth who would have loved Heath's attitude. His parents should be proud of him and AU fans should be, too. My hat's off to him and I certainly hope that his example is being observed by kids all over the state."

The response to this eloquence came quickly.

"Yeah, the Nazis had some good soldiers, too."

It has been ever thus. Alabama and Auburn played twelve times between 1893 and 1907 before the schools got into a dispute over the per diem that would be allowed for each player. Auburn wanted to splurge and give each player $3.50. The skinflints at Alabama wanted to spend $3.00. It took them forty-one years to come to an agreement to play again. In that period from 1907 to 1948, Alabama became a national power, winning five national championships in a seventeen-year period from 1925 to 1941. During that hiatus, Alabama played in six Rose Bowls, immortalized the game in its fight song ("Remember the

Rose Bowl, we'll win then!"), and sent one of its best players, Johnny Mack Brown, to Hollywood to become a movie-star cowboy. Grantland Rice, the ESPN of his day, wrote about Alabama. Auburn, meanwhile, became a study in mediocrity. From 1927 through 1947, the Tigers lost ten more games than they won. Grantland Rice didn't write about Auburn.

During the Iron Bowl's forty-one-year break, officials from both universities hesitated to renew the series because they feared that there would be too much emphasis on football. In 1923, the Auburn president, Dr. Spright Dowell, said that the game should not be played because "football would tend to become all the topic of both institutions." In 1944, Alabama's board of trustees said that the game would result in an "accelerated overemphasis of football in the state."

Like that would ever happen.

When Alabama president John Gallalee decided in the spring of 1948 to pursue a game with Auburn, he had no support in the athletic department. The late Jeff Coleman, the long-time athletic business manager, once told the *Huntsville Times*, "Our feeling was, we had nothing to gain from playing Auburn, whereas they had everything to gain." Coleman's counterpart at Auburn, the late Jeff Beard, agreed with him. "Frank Thomas, who had been a great coach at Alabama, was especially opposed to it," Beard said. "He knew eventually we'd beat them, and as it turned out, that's what we did the second year. It was a big, big boost for our program, and they saw it as a setback for theirs."

On December 4, 1948, in that first renewal of the rivalry, the Crimson Tide pummeled the Tigers 55–0. Auburn, after a 1–0–1 start, lost its eighth consecutive game. In that second year, 1949, Alabama came into Legion Field with a six-game winning streak. As in the year before, Auburn had won only one game. However, the Tigers won an upset 14–13 victory, spritzing a hot rivalry with gasoline. Auburn saw that it could be on equal footing with Alabama. And Alabama saw stars.

Nearly forty years later, the schools reached an impasse again over whether Auburn had the right to move its home games out of Legion Field and into Jordan–Hare Stadium. Well, of course, Auburn had that right, but woe be unto any Alabama man who admitted to it. Auburn athletic director and coach Pat Dye saw the revenue that could be gained from having Alabama play on his campus every other year. Bringing the Iron Bowl into Auburn allowed the university to enlarge Jordan–Hare to its current size of 85,214. Alabama fans took out their frustration on anyone who aided and abetted Auburn—even Alabama officials with unimpeachable credentials. Witness former Crimson Tide All-American quarterback and former coach Steve Sloan, the Alabama athletic director who signed off on the move. Sloan chose not to fight, recognizing that logic—not to mention fairness—dictated that Alabama not stand in Auburn's way. He paid for his decision with his job.

Not all the protests that rose against Auburn's intention to move the game grew out of partisanship. In those days, the schools split the tickets, save for a chunk that the city of Birmingham took for itself. That was one of the many aspects of playing in Birmingham that chapped the Auburn people. What purported to be a 50–50 stadium in reality tended to be 60–40 crimson and white. Birmingham was a Crimson Tide enclave.

There is something electric about a stadium that is even nearly equally filled with two groups of fans. In those days, the student sections, with first-come, first-served seating, filled up as soon as the gates were opened. Former Alabama assistant head coach Woody McCorvey, a native of Atmore, in the southwest section of the state, remembers his first Iron Bowl, in 1990. "The coaches would tell stories," he says of his fellow assistants. "You still didn't have an idea. My first big surprise was when my group went on the field for warm-ups. A lot of times, people trickle in. The stadium was full."

The fans spent the next couple of hours cheering themselves and jeering at their opponents. In 1976, for instance, when Alabama had accepted a Liberty Bowl bid to play UCLA and Auburn, at 4–6, wouldn't be going for a bowl, the Auburn students began yelling cheers for UCLA. The noise level only increased once the game began. "Somebody was always yelling and somebody was always excited," says University of Alabama trustee Joe Fine. "You couldn't afford to do it but I wish we could go fifty-fifty again." Fine feels so strongly about it that he refuses to attend an Iron Bowl at Jordan–Hare. While he represents the far end of the spectrum, it is undeniable that, even in the face of the gains Auburn realized in its heart and in its wallet, the rivalry lost something. Each school gets 10,000 tickets in the opponent's stadium, the same as they provide LSU or most any other opponent.

So now Auburn can claim equality. Bah, Alabama fans say. The whole of their response is contained in two phrases: twelve national championships, and twenty-one Southeastern Conference championships. Alabama fans believe in their heart of hearts that only one school has tradition comparable to their own. "We feel the same way about Notre Dame as we do Auburn," says Fine. "We just don't play them every year." There is one difference. The feeling toward the Fighting Irish is a competitive one. Not only has Notre Dame won eleven national championships, but Bryant never beat the Irish. He lost to them four times by margins of one, two, three, and seven points, respectively. The first two losses cost Alabama national championships, but all four were agonizing in the way that close losses are. The enmity toward the Irish has its roots in respect.

The enmity toward Auburn has its roots in disdain. Tide fans mock a team whose mascot is a tiger and whose "battle cry" is "War Eagle!" Take the Tigers' tradition of rolling Toomer's Corner when Auburn wins a big game. The fans throw rolls of toilet tissue into the trees and let them stream down. It is festive—a marriage of spirit and small-town nostalgia. Everyone goes to the town square as if it were election night and the local paper were going to write the returns on a chalkboard outside its office. What Auburn sees as a grand tradition, Alabama fans view as people throwing toilet paper into a tree. Thank you, Tide fans say with a smirk, we'll keep our national championships.

This haughty attitude drives Auburn folks crazy, which is surely another reason that Alabama clings to it. Tommy Bowden, one of five men who has coached at both schools, says that the Auburn coaches who hired him used that feeling of being looked down upon to spur their Tigers. "I remember when I was with [Pat] Dye and [Doug] Barfield," Bowden says. "They would say, 'They think they are better than us.' You play that card. 'Alabama didn't recruit you guys. You ain't over there because they didn't want you over there.'"

That sentiment carried more weight in Barfield's era (1976–1980), when Bryant dominated the rivalry. In his twenty-five years at Alabama, when he not only resurrected a dormant program but returned it to the level of greatness it had reached when he played for the Crimson Tide in the mid-1930s, Bryant went 19–6 against Auburn. Bryant loved to gig Auburn, mostly to play to his constituency. He referred to Auburn as "that little cow college across the state," and in his autobiography, Bryant pointed out that anything he did at Alabama, Auburn tried to copy. He understood the importance of beating his rival, especially given the state of the respective programs when he arrived in Tuscaloosa from Texas A&M. Auburn had won the 1957 national championship. Alabama had won four games in three years under J. B. "Ears" Whitworth. "Suddenly, you started seeing Auburn plates on the front of cars and bumper stickers," recalls Howell Raines. "We used to joke, 'Where have you been?'"

Bryant made it clear that he took the rivalry seriously. "The first time we ever met with him," recalls Bobby Jackson, a senior quarterback on Bryant's first Alabama team, in 1958, "Coach Bryant said, 'I promise you this: We're going to beat those War Buzzards' asses.'" Bryant took a team that had been 2–7–1 and went 5–4–1, but lost to unbeaten, once-tied, second-ranked Auburn, 14–8. "He apologized to us at the end of the year," Jackson says of Bryant. "Auburn had three good teams against one of ours. We had a chance to beat Auburn that day. He apologized to us and he didn't lose to them again for a while."

In fact, Auburn didn't score against Alabama again until 1963. The Crimson Tide beat the Tigers nine times from 1959 to 1968. Bryant wasn't just paying lip service to Auburn when he spoke of his love and respect for his rival, legendary Tigers coach Ralph "Shug" Jordan. But Bryant knew how to beat him. Ed Dyas, an All-American back in his senior year of 1960, recalls how much more physical Jordan's practices became after Bryant arrived in Alabama. It didn't make a difference. After the Punt Bama Punt game in 1972, Alabama beat Auburn nine consecutive games (1973–1981). Alabama dominated Auburn in the 1970s the way it dominated everyone. From 1971 to 1980, Alabama went 107–13 (.892), won three national championships, and eight SEC championships. Neil Callaway, another of the five coaches who has worked at both schools, lettered on Bryant's teams from 1975–77. "Re-

ally, when I played, it was never really that close," he says. "My freshman year (1973), the year after the 17–16 game, there was no question
we were going to win. It was just a question of how badly. The same
thing my senior year."

Before Jordan's retirement in 1975, and his death in 1980, Bryant's
respect for his rival increased. They had always been professionally
friendly, often working out disputes on the phone before they ever
reached the papers. When former Alabama quarterback Pat Trammell
succumbed to cancer in 1969, Jordan and several of his players attended the funeral. Bill Lumpkin, the retired *Birmingham Post-Herald*
sports editor, says that in Bryant's later years, the coach toned down
poking at Auburn because of his relationship with Jordan. Lumpkin
recalls being with Bryant in the old Parliament House, a Birmingham
hotel the coach and his friends used to frequent. Bryant looked out the
window and saw Jordan, fighting what would be a losing battle with
cancer, headed to see his doctor. "That guy has got more guts in his little finger than I've got in my whole body," Bryant said.

Bryant never managed to transmit his respect for Jordan to his
minions. But the Auburn folks, living in the shadow that Bryant cast
across the state, grew to recognize what he had achieved. Deryck Jackson of Mobile remembers the Iron Bowl from 1980, his freshman year.
"Both student sections were packed to capacity," Jackson says. "I remember the Bama players walking the field in their coats and ties before dressing for the game. Trailing behind was the man himself!
When he arrived at the Bama student section, we all stood to our feet
and cheered like mad. He then continued around the stadium unitl he
was right in front of the cow student section. He stopped and tipped
his ever-present houndstooth hat and took a bow. The cow students
stood and cheered wildly. I thought to myself, Hey, they love Coach
Bryant, too!"

Johnnie Aycock, the executive director of the West Alabama Chamber of Commerce, is an Auburn graduate. He lives among the people
who worship Bryant, and he understands it. Aycock came to Tuscaloosa shortly after Bryant's death in January 1983. "Alabama's tradition is so deep," Aycock says. "I get tickled at that. It's almost like you

can't let go of the past. He still walks the streets. His shadow is everywhere. What a thrill it would have been to meet him. It would have been just a tremendous experience."

Above all else, Bryant's career kick-started the rivalry with Auburn. "Those early Bryant–Jordan games in the first five, ten years, that was really the apex of the rivalry," Raines says. "You had equally matched teams and two coaches who reached something like folk-hero status. Jordan has been eclipsed over time. At that time, he was regarded as the man who brought Auburn out of the wilderness. Bryant was not yet the towering figure he would become. Those years had the blossoming of talent under two great chieftains."

Chieftains, yes. Great coaches, yes. But no one ever tried to draft Jordan for the state house. When Governor George Wallace could not succeed himself in 1966, the Democrats approached Bryant. At that time, the Republican Party barely existed within Alabama (although a decade later, Bryant made campaign appearances in the state for President Gerald Ford). Bryant declined to run, which is too bad, for it would have been interesting to see how many votes he would have gotten in Lee County, where Auburn is located.

The current governor, Democrat Don Siegelman, a former Alabama student government president, defeated the Republican incumbent, former Auburn fullback Fob James, in 1998. James, first elected as a Democrat in 1978, was only the second Auburn graduate ever to reach the governor's office. According to Fine, Bryant cut a commercial during the 1978 race for James's primary opponent, Jere Beasley, saying, "We can't afford to have an Auburn man in the governor's office. It hurts recruiting." Adds Dakin, the Montgomery lobbyist, "I have never known an Alabama man who admitted to voting for Fob James."

In his most recent term, James meddled with Auburn so sufficiently that the university community grew disenchanted with him. The rivalry "really doesn't impact politics," Siegelman points out. "I think I got more support from the university [Auburn] and the students and professors than he did." That said, Siegelman adroitly sidesteps the question of whether he favors his alma mater. "I didn't get elected by answering questions like that," he says with a grin.

Maybe not, but state government is no different than anything else in the state. The rivalry is part of life. While no one can point to a piece of legislation which had its fate determined by school allegiance, the belief exists that a politican's party sometimes matters less than his alma mater. Certainly, as Siegelman stated, no one gets on the stump and states an allegiance. "They don't want people to know," Dakin says. "It's a double-edged sword. Somebody from Auburn will vote for somebody from Jacksonville State ten times before he votes for somebody from Alabama." When Dakin hears the rivalry come up in the course of his business on Goat Hill, as the capitol is known, he cringes. "I've gotten to the point where I don't talk [to representatives] about the game anymore. It's such a divisive issue."

If the legislative process could be used to win points in the rivalry, so much the better. After the 1971 game, when the No. 3 Crimson Tide, 10–0, walloped the No. 5 Tigers, 10–0, 31–7, Representative Bert Bank, the longtime producer of the Alabama radio broadcasts, sponsored a resolution to buy Auburn University a football because the Crimson Tide, with its wishbone offense, wouldn't let the Tigers have one during the game. The resolution passed. A year later, thanks to two blocked punts, Auburn got the last laugh.

Bryant also had a hand in Auburn's reemergence as a national power in the 1980s. When Pat Dye took over from Barfield in 1981, he began to remake the Tigers the only way he knew. He had worked for Bryant for nine seasons before he became a head coach at East Carolina in 1974. "Whether it was when Coach Bryant went out and Coach Dye went to Auburn, things evened out a little bit," Callaway says. "They've done a great job."

Of the Tide's thirty-seven victories over the Tigers, there aren't more than a few that Alabama fans single out. As Ken Stabler described in the foreword, his 47-yard touchdown run through the slop to win the 1967 game, 7–3, is a milestone. Bryant's 315th victory, which put him in first place on the all-time coaching victory list, came against Auburn, 28–17, in 1981. The stakes have risen so high in recent years that the victories are by definition indelible. On the day before the 1996 Iron Bowl, coach Gene Stallings pulled aside assistant head coach McCorvey and DuBose, his defensive coordinator, and told them he had decided to resign at the end of the season. "He didn't want the players to know until the game was over," McCorvey says. "He had told Mike and I on Friday. He told the rest of the staff Saturday." McCorvey and DuBose would become the only two candidates to replace Stallings. "You really didn't know what would happen, who would get the job," McCorvey says. "You were trying to focus on the game."

Alabama leapt out to a 17–0 lead, but Auburn refused to fold. With time winding down, the Tigers scored a touchdown to go ahead 23–17. What happened next is the stuff of legend. After the return of the kickoff, the Tide began its final possession at its own 26 with no time-outs. The offense had stalled and the Alabama coaches wondered if Auburn defensive coordinator Bill "Brother" Oliver, who had worked with them for the previous six seasons, was stealing the Crimson Tide's offensive signals. "We did two things on that drive that were really odd for us," recalls running backs coach Ivy Williams. "We put Freddie [Kitchens] in the shotgun, which we had never done all year. Everybody was concerned that Brother had all our signals. We ran the plays in and used fake signals."

Kitchens ran the shotgun like he was Brett Favre, and threw a pass to tailback Dennis Riddle for the game-winning touchdown. A photograph of Riddle holding the ball over his head as he crossed the goal line hangs in the waiting area outside the office of Alabama athletic director Mal Moore. What the photograph, taken from the sideline, doesn't show is a man in a wheelchair in the end zone stands wearing his No. 74 Alabama jersey.

"We had just lost a good tackle, Kareem McNeal, that summer," Williams says. "He was in a car accident, got paralyzed. Kareem wasn't even driving.

"He was in the stands that last drive. We were 74 yards away. He wore No. 74 and they had just wheeled him into the end zone. First-and-10 . . . I leaned out over the sideline and looked. I said, 'That's 74.'"

The players on the field spotted McNeal, too. During a time-out, waiting for the TV commercials to run their course, the players talked about it in the huddle. After Riddle scored, recalls starting guard Will Friend, "Everybody ran down to Kareem. Everybody was waving at

him. Some guy jumps in front of him waving a sign. That man probably went home to his wife and said we were waving to him."

That victory, like all the others of the modern era, came at Legion
Field. The Crimson Tide didn't win at Jordan–Hare Stadium until
1999. Four visits had produced four losses, with the last two being par-
ticularly painful. In 1995, Auburn held on to win, 31–27, but not until
Alabama threw into the Tigers' end zone four times at the end of the
game. On first down, Curtis Brown caught a pass at the back line of
the end zone. The official ruled Brown out of bounds. A framed photograph hanging among the memorabilia in the restaurant at the
Tuscaloosa Four Points Sheraton appears to show otherwise. Then
came the painful, late-game fumble and last-second loss in 1997. By
1999, the inability to win at Jordan–Hare Stadium had become
mythic. The roles were reversed. Alabama came in with an 8–2 record.
Auburn, by virtue of an upset victory at Georgia, had climbed to 5–5.
In a stunning first half, the Tigers took a 14–6 lead. At halftime, Alabama's All-American offensive tackle Chris Samuels made an emotional speech demanding that his teammates play harder. "You could
feel the intensity," defensive line coach Lance Thompson. The game
turned on defensive end Cornelius Griffin's third-quarter sack of Tiger
quarterback Ben Leard for a safety. Thompson says the coaches had
noticed a tendency of Auburn's to try and throw when it was backed
up near its own end zone. "We would have a chance to make a big
play," Thompson says. "We did." After the safety pulled Alabama to
14–8, the Tide took the ensuing kickoff and scored a touchdown. In
fact, Alabama scored touchdowns on its next three possessions and
won, 28–17.

The three Iron Bowl games that Auburn fans cherish the most are the
Punt, Bama, Punt game, the Bo-over-the-Top game, and the 1989
game, which was played in Auburn for the first time ever. After so
much losing during the Bryant years, Pat Dye, and Bo Jackson ushered
in a new era at Auburn. In 1982, Auburn finally ended its nine-year
Iron Bowl losing streak with a 23–22 win. Jackson's one-yard leap over
a pile of bodies stacked high on the Alabama goal line secured the win.

However, the most significant game of all was the 1989 Iron Bowl, when Alabama came to Auburn for the first time. For years, Alabama said it would never lower itself to play at that cow college. On December 2, 1989, the Tide did. Before the game, ESPN-analyst Beano Cook explained why the Iron Bowl is the most intense rivalry in college football. "They hate each other every day of the year," said Cook. "Even Christmas."

The week before the game, Alabama coach Bill Curry called the FBI after death threats were made against Tide running back Siran Stacy and offensive tackle Charlie Dare. Auburn linebacker Quentin Riggins got a funeral wreath in the mail. Others received the usual hate mail.

The game was held exactly seventeen years after Newton's heroics in '72. Just like the '72 Iron Bowl, Bama entered the game with a 10–0 record and a No. 2 ranking, but Auburn ended the Tide's national-title hopes with a 30–20 win.

At Auburn, the success and failure of a season is viewed through the lens of one game. This year is no different. "I don't think that we'd be satisfied with our season if we don't win the game," linebacker Alex Lincoln says. "We don't want to end the season on a loss to Alabama. I think that it will spoil our season."

"We can go 0–10, but if we beat Alabama, it still will be a successful season," offensive tackle Hart McGarry says.

No one has ever accused Auburn of keeping football in perspective. In the spring of 2001, former Auburn president William Muse claimed that the school's board of trustees, specifically Montgomery banker Bobby Lowder, wielded too much power over athletic affairs. Of course, it does. What else matters?

In 1998, when the Tigers were struggling through a 1–5 start, Muse said that Lowder told coach Terry Bowden that he would be fired after the season. "Basically, Mr. Lowder told him he would not be around come the end of the season, and coach Bowden basically, in my opinion, panicked when he was told that and came and negotiated out of his contract," Muse told faculty representatives at a March meeting.

Muse said he was unable to reach Bowden until "the wee hours of the morning," then told him that Lowder didn't have the authority to fire him and "urged him to stay until the end of the season." But Bowden felt that his fate had been decided. Muse called the incident "the most celebrated case" of Lowder taking such a direct role in athletic decisions, but added, "There are many others."

And so the rivalry endures. It is forever. Auburn once had fierce rivalries with Georgia Tech and Tennessee. Those rivalries are dead. Once upon a time, Alabama, too, circled Georgia Tech on its schedule every year. The Southeastern Conference (SEC) has morphed from twelve schools to ten and back to twelve, in two six-team divisions. Alabama–Auburn endures. The state has transformed from an agricultural economy to a manufacturing economy to a service-based economy. The rivalry endures. "There's nothing like it," Governor Siegelman says in the smaller, less formal of his two offices in the state capitol. "The electricity and the energy that excites that game is unparalleled. People think about it 364 days a year. On the 365th day, they're watching it or listening to it."

When the schools resumed their rivalry in 1948, Birmingham was dominated by steel mills. The rivalry became the Iron Bowl because it was played in a city known as the Pittsburgh of the South. The economic engine in Birmingham is now health services. The game isn't even played in Birmingham. Yet the Iron Bowl is stronger than it has ever been, maybe even too strong.

"I've never seen people take a loss the way they take a loss in the Auburn–Alabama rivalry," Dakin, the lobbyist and native Louisianan, says. "When they walk down the street, they think people are looking at them and saying, 'There goes a loser.' They take off from work on the Monday after the game. When they get to work, they may as well have taken off. You can't rag them. If you call your friend and rag him, he ain't going to be your friend anymore. People in the Midwest now know who won. People in Idaho know. Here, they think, 'If I lose, I'm not only humiliated at home, I'm humiliated in Idaho.'

"What they don't realize is outside of the state, nobody gives a rat's ass."

That's not completely true. There are pockets of Alabama and Auburn fans around the world. Last year, during the week of the 2000 Iron Bowl, someone posted a message on TiderInsider.com. It concluded, "Though I, and others here in India who are Bama fans, have not had the privilege of seeing an Alabama game this season [and no matter the won/lost record, it is a privilege], we are encouraging all of you that remain in America to support these young men. Make Bryant–Denny a veritable living nightmare for the Village Idiots this Saturday. Roll Tide from New Delhi."

No matter where an Auburn fan is in this world, somewhere there's an Alabama fan thumbing his nose at him.

Prelude to the Iron Bowl

The Seasons

ALABAMA

On the morning of Thursday, July 27, 2000, Alabama football coach Mike DuBose entered the lobby outside the Birmingham Medical Forum auditorium with the air of a man comfortable in his celebrity. Which is to say, when DuBose was filmed by three news crews as he emerged from the men's room, he didn't flinch. He didn't react to the obvious intrusion (couldn't they wait until the man took a few steps?). DuBose would be the first speaker in the third and final session of Southeastern Conference Media Days, the unofficial kickoff of football season in the Deep South. As he strode toward the auditorium, DuBose signed a football for a fan. The coach had a little bit of John Wayne in his walk, a rolling rhythm. He is of average height, with a thinning blond combover that doesn't conceal his losing battle with baldness. His waistline ebbs and flows—at this point, it was flowing—and his arms did not fully extend, in the manner of well-muscled men. DuBose's upper body seemed tensed, ready to lash out, perhaps at an offensive lineman lined up opposite him. He had been a defensive lineman for coach Paul "Bear" Bryant from 1972 to 1974 and from 1983 to 1996. Either at Alabama or with the Tampa Bay Buccaneers, DuBose had been one of the best defensive line coaches in the nation.

DuBose's appearance on this morning was the highlight of the day. In part, that was an accident of geography. The Alabama and Auburn coaches always received a little more attention at the SEC Media Days, which are held across the street from the conference's headquarters. In addition, however, DuBose returned as coach of the defending league champion, as the 1999 SEC Coach of the Year and as the coach of a team that experts and Alabama fans alike thought would contend for the national championship. The Crimson Tide went 10–3 in 1999. Two of those losses had been by one point—one on a last-second pass by Louisiana Tech, one on a missed extra point in overtime of the Orange Bowl against Michigan.

Greatness had been predicted for the 2000 Alabama team almost from the moment that Ryan Pflugner missed that extra point, ending the Orange Bowl with the Crimson Tide on the wrong end of a 35–34 score. Most football coaches, upon being confronted by mountains of praise, take off in the other direction. That's how Bryant, the master of poor-mouthing, did it. DuBose, so obviously a disciple of Bryant, had never given any indication that he would stray from the lessons taught in the Bryant textbook. When he stepped before the microphone and looked up at the theater of writers awaiting his wisdom, however, he not only acknowledged the public expectations for his team; he embraced them.

"I like our football team an awful lot," DuBose said. "We live in a time when people don't believe I should say that. We live in a naysayer's society. I like the character of [our team]. I like the work ethic of it. I like the talent. And I like the staff. It's time now. A big part of my job is getting Alabama to be one of those seven or eight teams that contend for the national championship. We should be one of those teams, and there was a time when we were and we slipped away from that. There was a time in the conference when you talked of Florida and Tennessee. Now we're back where we should be. It's time to quit talking and see if we can do it."

DuBose then veered off into a discussion of the biggest question he had for this team: Who would lead it? In 1999, the Crimson Tide enjoyed the rare nexus of having its best players also being its best leaders. DuBose said that he leaned on them and learned from them, players such as Chris Samuels, Shaun Alexander, and Cornelius Griffin, as much as they learned from him.

"I do not have the words to express how grateful I am to this football team," DuBose said. He made a reference to a biblical verse from Ecclesiastes 4: "Two are better off than one, in that they have greater benefit from their earnings. For should they fall, one can raise the other; but woe betide him who is alone and falls with no companion to raise him!" Said DuBose, "I fell miserably this time last year. Our team and coaches picked me up and, because of that, we were SEC champions."

Few men experience the highs and lows in a lifetime that DuBose experienced in a matter of months in 1999. Then again, DuBose, after spending his entire career anonymously as an assistant coach, hadn't been able to escape the spotlight since the university hired him to replace Gene Stallings in December 1996. He had not been the first choice of new athletic director Bob Bockrath, who had hoped to interview Frank Beamer of Virginia Tech. But the alumni coalesced behind DuBose. Finding someone who had played for Bryant remained important to the Alabama football community. The truth was that there weren't many candidates who qualified. Although quite a number of players from the early and middle years of Bryant's career went into coaching—men such as Charlie McClendon, Jerry Claiborne, Charley Pell, Mickey Andrews, Bill Battle, Jackie Sherrill, Ray Perkins, and Danny Ford—few players from his latest, most successful years did so.

DuBose, nearly forty-four years old when hired, appeared to be the perfect candidate. He loved Alabama. He knew Alabama. He had been a graduate assistant coach under Bryant. In 1982, DuBose, then an assistant coach at UT-Chattanooga, accepted an offer to coach at Southern Mississippi. When he returned to Chattanooga from Hattiesburg, his phone was ringing. "Coach Bryant wanted to offer me a job," DuBose says. "He said, 'I don't know what I can pay you.' I wanted it. I didn't care about the money." When he explained his dilemma to Bryant, however, Bryant told DuBose what he already knew. Says DuBose, "He said, 'Mike, your word ought to be your bond. You think about it. You call me back in the morning.' " DuBose stuck with his word and went to Southern Mississippi. "Coach Bryant said, 'It will probably be just for a year. We'll get back to you.' " Within the year, Bryant retired, then died. DuBose never got the chance to rekindle his relationship with Bryant.

When he was his defensive lineman, he had been the kind of player that Bryant loved the most—one who didn't have talent and didn't know it. DuBose, a native of Opp, in southeast Alabama, had a career best remembered by two incidents. In 1972, his sophomore season, third-ranked Alabama trailed Tennessee 10–3 and scored with less than three minutes to play. Bryant started to go for two points only to be talked out of it by defensive coordinator Pat Dye, who promised Bryant the defense would get the ball back. Sure enough, DuBose sacked Volunteer quarterback Condredge Holloway and forced him to fumble. The Crimson Tide recovered and scored a touchdown to win, 17–10.

Later that season, DuBose got stepped on in a pileup and was hurt so severely that he lost a testicle. "The doctors told him he couldn't play again," says Dye, who had recruited DuBose to Alabama. "I went into the hospital to see him. He said, 'I ain't quittin' football. I'm going to Troy State [to play]. I went to see Coach Bryant and said, 'Coach, he's fixing to transfer to Troy. If he's gon' play, he needs to play here.' Coach Bryant called Mike's mama and daddy." DuBose returned and made second-team All-SEC as a defensive lineman in both his junior and senior season.

Shortly after Bryant's death, his successor, Ray Perkins, hired DuBose as his defensive line coach. DuBose worked for Perkins for the next four seasons at Alabama and for three years after that with Tampa Bay. He returned to Tuscaloosa under coach Gene Stallings in 1990. In 1992, when the Crimson Tide won the national championship, defensive ends Eric Curry and John Copeland, both tutored by DuBose, led a defense that allowed only five rushing touchdowns. Both players made All-American. When defensive coordinator Bill Oliver left Stallings's staff after the 1995 season, DuBose took over those duties. A year later, on December 9, 1996, he became head coach.

From the beginning, DuBose had trouble making the adjustment from position coach to head coach. The nasty secret of college football is that head coaches don't coach; they organize, referee disputes among their assistants, set the tone for the team, and deal wirh the media. In the days before DuBose's first game, starting defensive tackle Eric Kerley said of his former position coach, "He wants to coach so bad. It drives him crazy to stand there for two and a half hours."

Dye, who resigned as head coach at Auburn after the 1992 season, showed up in Tuscaloosa to watch his protégé's team practice the week before DuBose's debut as a head coach against Houston. "He can't miss. He can't miss," Dye said. "I'll be shocked if he doesn't do a great job."

The 1997 season became a nightmare. The Tide, burdened by scholarship cuts imposed by the NCAA for rules violations under Stallings, finished, 4–7, with a bullet—the late-game collapse at Auburn. DuBose fired four assistant coaches in the days after the game, including the other finalist for the job when DuBose was hired—running backs coach Woody McCorvey. A year later, Alabama improved to 7–5, although again with an embarrassing finish—a 31–7 rout at the hands of Virginia Tech in the inaugural Music City Bowl in Nashville.

With an 11–12 record through two seasons, DuBose had endured some criticism, although most of the fans remained supportive. That is, until the revelation in August 1999 that he had had an affair with his secretary Debbie Gibson. The crisis nearly cost DuBose his job. Three months earlier, as rumors about the affair began to circulate on the Internet, DuBose chose to confront them. Appearing at a charity golf tournament in the southeast Alabama town of Dothan, DuBose released a statement that said, in part, "There is absolutely no truth or factual basis to any of these rumors that you have heard involving me or other university employees. They are unfounded and hurting innocent people."

The rumors died until August 5, when DuBose and the university revealed, at another hastily called press conference, that this time the university would pay $350,000 to "an employee" (reportedly Gibson) to settle a potential sexual harassment and sexual discrimination complaint against DuBose. The coach agreed to reimburse that sum to the university through a reduction in pay over a three-year period. He also lost two years off of his five-year contract. "My statement [in May] . . . misled all of you, and I am truly sorry," DuBose said. "I made a mistake and made the situation worse with my response."

The settlement floored everyone, from the university trustees to DuBose's assistants to the players. "It definitely affected us," center Paul Hogan says. "I believe he's a good man. I make mistakes like he does. It's not my place to judge him. If we've got 140 guys on this team, he's given everybody a second chance at least once." When athletic director Bob Bockrath didn't fire DuBose, the trustees didn't want to overrule him so close to the season. However, the trustees expresssed their displeasure by forcing Bockrath out. DuBose remained unusually calm during the ordeal, perhaps because he had turned to religion. His wife, Polly, is deeply religious and in his time of crisis, DuBose rediscovered his faith. He began to quote scripture at press conferences as well as to his team. One of his favorite lines: "We are on God's team or we are on Satan's team."

As he tried to save his job and repair his marriage, DuBose also had to coach a football team. When the Crimson Tide lost the third game of the 1999 season—29–28, to Louisiana Tech, which scored on a desperation, 28-yard, fourth-down pass with :02 to play—it appeared as if DuBose wouldn't last the week, much less the season.

In a Monday meeting, however, DuBose asked the team to come together, and not to split into factions. DuBose also promised quarterback coach Charlie Stubbs that he would no longer have any interference from the head coach. DuBose let Stubbs call the offensive plays. The players responded by winning eight of their next nine games, including the 28–17 victory at Auburn.

The offense, in particular, began to thrive. The running of Shaun Alexander, balanced by the throwing of quarterbacks Andrew Zow and Tyler Watts and the multiple talents of receiver–kick returner Freddie Milons, peaked in the SEC Championship Game against Florida. Alabama won, 34–7, in a virtuoso performance on both sides of the ball.

The loss to Michigan in the Orange Bowl did nothing to hold back the expectations of the Alabama fans. The university couldn't fill all the requests it received for season tickets. In many ways, the 2000 season appeared as if it would be a magical one. The first game, at UCLA, would be Alabama's first appearance on the Rose Bowl field since the Crimson Tide won the 1946 Rose Bowl, 34–14, over USC. Some 25,000 Alabama fans bought tickets for the game—more than two thousand miles away.

With that drumbeat of excitement in the background, DuBose felt confident that his fifth Alabama team would be his best. During workouts in August, the Tide didn't appear to be sharp. Over the course of the summer, in fact, some of the players began to believe they would be in top five just because everyone said so. At a July staff meeting, DuBose asked strength coach Terry Jones, "How's Lannis Baxley look?" Baxley, who won the most improved lineman award in spring practice, had been penciled in as the right tackle, the one new starter on the offensive line. "I don't know," Jones said. "I haven't seen him in three weeks." That's not the kind of discipline that winners display—either players who must perform the work or coaches who demand it. Baxley started the opener against UCLA and didn't start again the rest of the season.

In August, however, no one expressed any emotion resembling panic. On Thursday, August 24, the Tide went over to Bryant–Denny Stadium for its last preseason scrimmage. On that day came the first foreboding that the 2000 season would not be what Alabama fans hoped it would be. When the defensive starters concluded their work in the scrimmage, DuBose called for them to go one more series. During that series, junior defensive end Kindal Moorehead, an All-SEC player in 1999, tore his Achilles tendon. Moorehead didn't suffer the injury in a collision; he suffered it as he got up and watched one of his teammates return an interception for a touchdown.

"That was a sad day around here, when I had to call his coach and his mom," said running backs coach Ivy Williams, who recruited Moorehead out of Memphis. "They asked, 'Who hit him? Who blocked him?' He came off the line of scrimmage. Nobody was around him." He would be lost for the season, which set in motion a catastrophic series of events regarding the defensive line.

The offense, meanwhile, looked raggedy. On the day before the scrimmage, DuBose hoped that Andrew Zow would be the starter, as he had been in the 1999 season before he suffered a high ankle sprain against Tennessee. In the scrimmage, Zow played terribly and the offense was sluggish. Afterward, DuBose said, "If we were playing today, we would have gotten beat by four or five touchdowns. We got very little accomplished today. Leadership comes when things are not going as good. Anybody can lead when things are going good."

Yet again, no one panicked. A week later, the team flew to Los Angeles. On Friday, the Tournament of Roses—as the organization that stages the Rose Bowl is known—held a luncheon for the Alabama party. Among the guests were Vaughn Mancha, Harry Gilmer, and Clem Gryska, all of whom had played on Alabama's last Rose Bowl team more than a half-century before. Senior associate athletic director Finus Gaston, speaking at the luncheon, cracked a joke that if the Tournament would be willing to offer an invitation to the 2002 Rose Bowl at that moment, the Crimson Tide would accept. It will be the Rose Bowl's turn to serve as host of the national championship game after the 2001 season.

Only the coaches sounded a note of wariness about the game ahead. UCLA, after consecutive Pac-10 championships, had gone 4–7 in an injury-filled 1999 season. After the Alabama team worked out in a beautiful, temperate Southern California Friday afternoon in the Rose Bowl, defensive coordinator Ellis Johnson bumped into a couple of writers outside the Alabama locker room. "This will be one of the most talented teams we play," Johnson said. "If they can get over the problems mentally from last year, they are going to be a really good team."

Alabama forced UCLA to punt on its first possession. Freddie Milons fielded the punt and returned it 71 yards for a touchdown. With a 7–0 lead, the Tide promptly fell apart. UCLA won, 35–24, by running tailback DeShaun Foster right through the Alabama defense. Foster rushed for 187 yards, 105 of them after contact. Yards after contact strike directly at a defense's machismo. Alabama simply didn't tackle well. It was the first sign, but certainly not the last, of the toll that Moorehead's loss would take on the team.

After the game, there was grumbling about scheduling an opening game so far away from home. How could no one understand the effect it would have on the team?

The fact is, it wasn't until the season had nearly ended that anyone fully understood the consequences of the loss to the Bruins. "I don't think playing UCLA hurt this football team. I think how we handled the loss hurt this football team," DuBose said. "Even after the loss was over, UCLA was a better football team than we thought. That shouldn't have happened but it did. We underestimated them a little bit. I didn't, but as a football team, we underestimated them a little bit. . . . I think I also put a little too much pressure on this team by talking about [national championships] and agreeing with everything. It also sent the message to a lot of people that we would go through this season, and when it's over with we'll be 11–0 and going to Atlanta. All of a sudden, you lose the first game and people don't know how to handle it. I did a poor job with it."

It wasn't a question of DuBose not reacting quickly enough to stem the fallout of the UCLA loss. He reacted too quickly, demoting Zow and installing Tyler Watts as starting quarterback. DuBose also junked the spread offense that the team had practiced since the spring, deciding in an instant that the offense had to become run-dominant.

Ivy Williams, the running backs coach, had criticized the performance of the offense after the UCLA game. "We were supposed to throw the ball all around the field, and we didn't," Williams said. "And guys were open and we were missing them. And for the last three weeks, that's all we did [in practice]. . . . Everybody talked about how predictable we were [last year], because everyone knew who was going to get the ball. All I know is when the guy [Shaun Alexander] got it, he produced. We would have loved to be predictable Saturday. I know that."

Williams could see what the UCLA defense saw. Not only were tailbacks Ahmaad Galloway and Brandon Miree no substitute for the departed Alexander, but the offensive line, which figured to be a strength with four returning starters, never jelled. In fact, once sophomore tackle Dante Ellington moved from right tackle to replace Chris Samuels at left tackle, the Tide effectively had only three returning starters. The veterans—Paul Hogan, Griff Redmill, and Will Cuthbert—spent so much time worrying about their colleagues that they didn't perform their own jobs as well. The self-proclaimed "Pancake Posse" didn't flatten its opponents. It just came out flat.

Although Alabama won its second game, 28–10, against Vanderbilt, the Crimson Tide sank in humiliation against Southern Mississippi. The Golden Eagles are perenially shortchanged by the football public. This team, as has been the norm under coach Jeff Bower, played a physical brand of defense. Southern Mississippi returned an interception of Watts for a touchdown in the first quarter, then returned a fumbled kickoff for a touchdown in the second quarter. The Eagles led, 21–0, in a driving rainstorm and Bower took the air out of his offense from there. It's no exaggeration to say he was charitable in letting the game end with the score still 21–0. For the first time in memory, Alabama played as if it were beaten. "Obviously, the Southern Miss was a very disappointing loss," DuBose said. "That was probably the point where we started to have some people who didn't believe. After the second loss, they say, 'Well it's over with from a national standpoint.' We still had a lot to play for but I don't think we handled that part of it as well as we should."

Ten days after the game, Steve Kirk of the *Birmingham News* revealed that in the locker room after the loss, DuBose offered his resignation to athletic director Mal Moore. Mal did not accept it, understanding the emotion from which it came. "After Mike told me what he wanted to say [on the record]," Kirk says, "that it was the heat of the moment, he really, truly broke down. He shed tears. That was the first time I ever saw him cry. He said, 'Steve, I just don't know what I'm doing wrong. I'm doing everything exactly the same I did it last year.' I felt horrible. He was close to a breakdown. He was already under such fire. I expected him to react angrily. Mike's an old-school Southern boy. I expected anger instead of tears. I thought he would throw a chair. He started crying."

Alabama fell to 1–3, with a tough 28–21 loss at Arkansas, then rebounded to defeat South Carolina, 27–17, in Tuscaloosa. The victory over the Gamecocks lessened the pressure somewhat on DuBose, who appeared hopeful after the game. The team had two weeks to prepare for Ole Miss and archrival Tennessee. What he liked the most about his team's performance was that the players had come together, an act he attributed in part to the team's viewing of the Denzel Washington film *Remember the Titans* on the night before the game. The movie depicts the struggles of Washington, a high school football coach in Virginia a generation ago, to bring together a newly integrated team. "There's an awful lot of similarities between this team and the movie," DuBose said. "Football is about changing lives and changing momentum." He spoke of his own struggles and mistakes during the first half of the season, as he tried to balance the demands of his job with his religion. "The thing that has made it so hard for me is trying to be submissive and surrender, [coach] the way God wanted me to do it." DuBose came to terms with that problem by deciding that God had given him the talent to coach, so he would coach his way. He would not quit. "I've prayed and considered the question," he said. "There are two ways that I would walk away: if God ever spoke to me and told me He wants me to do something different, or if I felt like I was not doing the job for these players, if I wasn't helping him become a better player, a better student, a better young man. I know in my heart that God has not told me that."

Certainly a 2–3 record was better than a 1–4 record. And the half-full fans could draw a parallel to the 1999 season, when the Crimson Tide rebounded from its loss to Louisiana Tech to finish 10–3. As in the 1999 season, the air around the program was sulfurous. Paul Finebaum, the *Birmingham Post-Herald* columnist and the most influential sports journalist in the state, told a sportswriter who came into the state that week to do a story on the Tide, "As you drive into Alabama, you'll probably hear a fat lady singing."

And as in the 1999 season, the Crimson Tide initially rebounded strongly. After two weeks of work, Alabama steamrolled Ole Miss, 45–7, with both sides of the ball performing, well, the way everyone expected them to perform when the season began. Alabama had an answer for everything, even bad news. When Watts tore a knee ligament, bringing his disappointing season to an abrupt close, Andrew Zow responded with a record-setting performance.

The timing couldn't have been better, for Tennessee loomed ahead. The Volunteers may have been the only rival to approach Auburn in its ability to rile the Alabama-faithful. It is an intense week around the football building. The hours are longer, the tempers shorter. Bryant knew beating Auburn was important because he couldn't go anywhere in the state without someone bringing it up. Tennessee, however, was personal. Shoot, Bryant hadn't even suited up against Auburn. Not only was Tennessee his biggest rival as an Alabama player but in Bryant's eight seasons at Kentucky, he went 1–5–2 against them. The victory came in 1953, the year after legendary Vols coach General

Robert Neyland retired. It galled Bryant that he never beat Neyland. In Bryant's twenty-five years at Alabama, he went 16–7–2 (.680) against Tennessee, including eleven consecutive wins from 1971 to 1981.

Now, however, Tennessee had won five consecutive games from Alabama. After the Tide's victory over Ole Miss, the Alabama players thought that they had recovered their old persona. Add to it the fact that the Vols would give freshman Casey Clausen his first start at quarterback against Alabama, and it appeared as if the Tide had an excellent opportunity to turn the corner from a mediocre first half of the season.

The Tide turned, all right—a U-turn. Alabama trailed from the outset and lost, 20–10. "A game like Tennessee," says senior guard Griff Redmill, "which Alabama hadn't won in a long time, had the players thinking, 'Can we do this?' Everybody on the field knows we had the players and the physical ability to beat them."

Tennessee exploited Alabama's obvious weaknesses. The Crimson Tide offense struggled to run the ball. Milons, who tweaked his knee during the off week before the Ole Miss game, had all but disappeared as an offensive weapon. The defense, though game, could not make up for Moorehead's absence and was neither big enough nor talented enough. Sophomore end Kenny King, hampered by a nerve injury in his shoulder, was a shell of the player he had been as a freshman. Freshmen Albert Means and Antwan Odom, who had been expected to step into the lineup, played like freshmen. Alabama had been so desperate for healthy bodies that tackle David Daniel, a walk-on, played a lot despite his lack of size. Opposing offenses took advantage of the Tide's lack of ability up front.

Not only had the rout of Ole Miss been the fluke—it also was the last victory of the season. One week later, Alabama lost its Homecoming game, 40–38, to a mediocre team from Central Florida. The fans in Bryant–Denny Stadium actually booed their team. While this is accepted behavior at many schools, no one in Tuscaloosa could recall it ever happening before. The Tide came back from a 13-point deficit to take a 38–37 lead with 2:24 to play. However, the defense couldn't prevent Central Florida from driving 59 yards in twelve plays to put Javier Beorlegui in position to kick a 37-yard field goal with :03 to play.

The fans quickly dispersed from the stadium. When DuBose left the locker room, about ninety minutes after the game, he saw a friend who had stayed behind to commiserate. DuBose's comment was plaintive and succinct: "I can't get through to them," he said.

Three days later, at about 11 A.M., Moore called DuBose down to his office. Moore told his friend and former fellow assistant coach under Stallings that the DuBose era was over, with three games remaining in the season. "I'm pretty straightforward," Moore said in his office the following day. "Mike has told me, whatever situation comes up, he would do what I felt best. He understands the profession, what is demanded and what is expected. I simply told him that I had made my decision that I wanted to make a change. He said that he understood. He said, 'I'll do whatever you ask and as best as I could do it.' "

The decision leaked that night, and once the lawyers got everything squared away, Moore held a brief news conference late Wednesday afternoon to formally announce that DuBose had "resigned."

"I felt that it was difficult for me to face Coach DuBose, our coaches, and our players, knowing in my heart what I had decided," Moore said at the press conference, "So I felt that it was best to go ahead and do this and say that to them, also. I think it will take a burden off of them, and I hope and feel that we can win the remainder of our games. I hope this will have a good, positive effect as far as approaching these last games."

Moore then met briefly with the players. He told them he planned to hire a "great coach and a great staff." The current staff, asked to remain for the rest of the season, considered that statement one more public humiliation. "The kids came right into the meetings and told us [what Moore said]," one staff member said. "How are we supposed to control them?"

DuBose didn't speak to the media until after practice Thursday, two days before the Tide traveled to Baton Rouge to play a much improved LSU team. To minimize the distractions, DuBose moved the practice to the indoor facility. When he emerged to find an larger pack of writers and minicams awaiting him, he smiled grimly and said, "I feel like a lamb being led to the slaughter." The pack soon enveloped him.

"I am extremely grateful for the opportunity that was given to me, and I'm grateful for the opportunity I still have," he said. "They've given us a tremendous opportunity. We didn't get the job done." He related some wisdom a friend had shared with him: "If you're saved, you're living in your hell right now, because this is as bad as it's ever going to get, because you got heaven to look forward to. If you're not saved, you're living in your heaven right now."

By that definition, DuBose was saved. The funny thing was, though Alabama was 3–5, it was 3–2 in the SEC. It was still possible for the Tide to win the SEC West. Moreover, Alabama hadn't lost at LSU since 1969. The players, fueled by emotion after a wrenching week, led 21–14 but couldn't hold the lead. After the 30–28 loss, Redmill was more mystified than ever. "If you had told me before the season we would be 6–3, I would have laughed," he said, "and here we are 3–6."

A week later, reality crashed down upon the Tide. Mississippi State, 6–2, played physical football. The Bulldogs' offensive line averaged 6–4, 323. Scott Field may be the smallest stadium (43,656) in the SEC, but it is also one of the loudest. The fans ring cowbells at the slightest provocation, such as when the opposing quarterback walks to the line to call signals. Mississippi State had won fifteen straight games at home. The Bulldogs humiliated the Tide, 29–7, gaining 538 yards of total offense. Scatter-armed quarterback Wayne Madkin threw for a career-best 262 yards. In the final seconds of the game, Alabama moved inside the Mississippi State five-yard line and could not punch the ball into the end zone. The lack of success spoke volumes about the season.

When Iron Bowl week began, Alabama had nowhere to go but up.

AUBURN

On the night before the Georgia game, the second-to-last game of the regular season, several of Auburn's seniors gathered in the dining room of the team hotel, the Ramada Inn in LaGrange, Georgia, a few minutes from the Auburn campus. The players munched on chips, donuts, and beef jerky and talked for an hour and a half about the valleys of their college careers. They could have stayed there all night and talked about those trying times. When they signed with Auburn, the Tigers were a Top 25 team and a SEC contender. As freshmen in 1997, some went to the SEC championship, then the Peach Bowl, and finished the year ranked No. 11.

"I was naïve enough to think that it would be like that every year," says Rob Pate, a senior linebacker.

In 1998, everything unraveled when head coach Terry Bowden resigned under pressure in the middle of a 3–8 season. Defensive coordinator Bill "Brother" Oliver took over for the rest of the year, but Oliver was not hired as the head coach, to the dismay of many players.

"I don't think there's a fifth-year senior class that has gone through what we've gone through, you know, with coaching changes, with having to learn two different offenses," senior offensive tackle Colin Sears says. "You know, a lot of the guys that we came in with didn't even make it past our sophomore year. A lot of them flunked out, a lot of them got kicked out, a lot of them transferred, and some of them left last year. I mean, we signed like twenty-six guys coming in here and there's only six of us left. Plus, I think everybody who's still here from that 'ninety-six class has had a major surgery since we've been here."

After the disaster of 1998, Tommy Tuberville was hired from Mississippi. His first task was to rerecruit the current players on the team. In his first season in 1999, the Tigers went 5–6. Slowly, both sides learned to trust each other.

Tuberville says: "You can imagine, the enthusiasm wasn't very high entering that first year, and I changed everything. Trainers. Managers. Weight room. Just everything that I could change just to get their mind looking in another direction. We went to six A.M. workouts. Study halls, curfews. It was pretty much a shock. It's tough for those seniors who have habits built, judgments formed. Now they are freshmen again. That's basically how I got to treat them. But they hung with us and I saw a lot of them grow up. Saw a lot of them accept change. Some of them resented it for a while and then started gradually accepting what was happening. You go 5–6 the first year and it's pretty tough to convince somebody that you are doing the right thing. But we were successful later in the year. We beat a very good Georgia team. I think that that was probably the major point of year. I think probably the lowest point was when we lost to Mississippi State. We got a 13-point lead with a few minutes to go and we lose. There were some big ups and some big downs, but they hung with us. And this group of seniors had to endure more of my wrath, because I expected them to be leaders and accept change when they didn't have the opportunity like the other guys to gradually accept it.

"The thing I try to do is to let them know that we are not an offense and a defense. I think sometimes when your head coach has been your offensive coordinator, like Terry Bowden was, you run the offense and your defense coordinator is the other coach and you have a separation of your team. So when I came in, I said we're not an offense, we're not a defense, we're not a kicking team, we're all gonna play together. We're gonna meet together as much as we can. We're gonna stretch together. We're gonna laugh together, we're gonna cry together. The only way that you can survive in football to me is to combine units as much as possible. You have to separate them enough as it is, because it's two separate practices and two separate game plans. A big mistake that people make in the head-coaching chair is you don't see the big picture. You have to believe in each other, even though they are playing on different sides of the football. You have to understand what everybody's going through. And so your offensive guys have to be able to lead your defensive players. Your defensive players need to be able to lead the offensive players. I think that this is what has happened here."

Not much was expected of the Tigers heading into this season, as they were picked to finish near the bottom of the SEC West for several reasons. They hadn't won a SEC game at home in two seasons. No one on the defensive line had ever started a game. Quarterback Ben Leard was coming off an injury-plagued season. The running game ranked among the worst in the country the previous year and no one quite knew if running back Rudi Johnson, a junior college transfer, would succeed at this level. The team's best defensive player, linebacker Rob Pate, was riddled with a mysterious illness. Tight end Lorenzo Diamond was accidentally shot in the stomach by his wife. Wide receiver Deandre Green was suspended after firing a gun into the air at a campus party. The kicking game was a mess, as Auburn had the SEC's worst field-goal percentage last year with Damon Duval. Though the team signed Phillip Yost, a *USA Today* All-American, the Tigers were stuck with Duval after Yost was injured.

Still, the players themselves had a good feeling about this season. Through adversity, they had grown especially close. The senior class was also full of leaders like Leard, Pate, linebacker Alex Lincoln, center Cole Cubelic, and corner Rodney Crayton.

"Even before it started, we were all talking about how successful the season would be," Pate says. "The difference was we were a team. I didn't know how much I was going to play this year because of my illness. I didn't know if I was going to play at all. I didn't know if I was gonna have to take a redshirt. But I told everybody I wanted to play because I know this team has a shot to play in Atlanta in the SEC Championship game. And I want to play in that game. This year, there wasn't anybody here saying, 'I'm gonna go out there and do what's best for me. I'm gonna get mine. Screw what the coach says. I'm doing it my way.' That's what we had a lot of last year. Not all the way around the board. Just some individuals. That's why we lost. We didn't do things together."

The team started to attend prayer meetings together and simply got to know each other better, off the field. Says linebacker Alex Lincoln, "There are positions where we are outmanned. There'll be a lot of times where I have to cover a back who is a lot faster than me and who's got a lot of athletic ability. But I won't give up, because I'm not gonna let him beat me, because I'm close to the guys on my defense and I don't want to let them down. That's where the chemistry becomes involved. That's where in times past we just came over here and played football together and went home and led our separate lives. I think that's why we didn't have any chemistry. But now we genuinely like each other. We genuinely care for each other. You got guys who hang out away from football that you wouldn't normally see together. If we were home in Mobile, you won't see someone like me with corner Larry Casher or left tackle De-Marco McNeil. [Lincoln is white and Casher and McNeil are black.] But us coming here and coming together, they're two of my closest friends on the team. I was in [defensive tackle] Roderick Chambers's wedding and would never had been in his wedding if it wasn't for us coming to-gether as a team. When you experience things like that and you get to share in people's lives, when you experience a wedding, or if they have troubles and you can help them out, that's when they learn to trust in you and you in them. That's what you need out on the field, because when it is fourth and one and I know Roderick is in the game, I know that he is gonna give me everything that he's got. But if I don't really know him, maybe I have some doubts about him."

The coaches had plenty of motivational material to use throughout the season. Says offensive coordinator Noel Mazzone, "At the start of the year, I told the players to go rent *Spartacus* with Kirk Douglas because that's us. We were ranked fifty-fifth in the country by *Sports Illustrated*. We're supposed to finish in the bottom of the West. We've got no one re-ally marquee playing for us. No running game. Offensive line, average. No tight ends. Guy always injured playing quarterback. That's what our deal is. I'm Spartacus. Hey, no I'm Spartacus. No, I'm Spartacus. Hey, we all got to be Spartacus. We all have to be in this together."

So did any of the players rent the movie? "I don't know," Mazzone says. "Half the time that coaches give those Rocky talks, it's mostly for us. But I thought it was kinda neat."

Mostly, the Tigers were inspired by the example set by players like Rudi Johnson. "What's really made that whole premise go is Rudi's unselfishness," Mazzone says. "He could have said, 'I'm the fifth leading rusher in the country, give me the ball,' but I may go a couple series and not hand him the football. I've been around some guys and they're pissed and they're pouting, saying what the hell's going on. Hell, it doesn't matter to him. If we went the whole game and didn't hand him the ball once and we won the game, I promise you he'd be just as happy. Because of his attitude the other kids have bought into it. It wasn't like that when we got here. It was every man for himself."

At the start of the year, the defensive line was ranked as the worst in the SEC. Says defensive ends coach Terry Price, "I think they remember that every time we go out there and play a game. They're the guy that nobody wanted, nobody liked. Get no respect. The worst unit. Buy a preseason football magazine, and they see they're named as the worst defensive line in the conference. And the guys got pride now. And, shoot, if you don't have pride, you shouldn't be playing this game. They all took pride in that and worked hard every day to make sure that point was not proven true. And I don't know if there's a game we went into where we were the most talented defensive line, but I promise you we've outworked quite a few of them. But, sometimes you make up lack of technique and lack of know-how with effort. That's what kind of saved us. We're not very good, but we're able to hold up. If it was all about talent, we wouldn't be able to stop anybody."

And so, Auburn started winning. Rudi Johnson opened the season, rushing for 174 yards in a win against Wyoming. Then, the Tigers defeated Tuberville's former team, Ole Miss, behind Rudi's 165 yards and two touchdowns. They ended their home SEC-losing streak with a win over LSU, followed by victories over Northern Illinois and Vanderbilt. Throughout, Johnson established himself as one of the best running backs in the country. Ranked 15th in the country, at 5–0, Auburn lost its next game to Mississippi State, then lost to No. 10 Florida. After wins over Louisiana Tech and Arkansas, No. 22 Auburn entered its game against No. 14 Georgia with confidence. The defensive line had gained maturity, as had Duval, whose kicking was more consistent. Leard was healthy, and had adjusted his game to the new run-oriented scheme. Johnson was the favorite for SEC Player of the Year.

Down 13–3 at halftime, a Tigers comeback forced the game into overtime. Georgia settled for a field goal on its overtime possession. Trailing 26–23, Johnson took over and led the Tigers to Georgia's one-yard line. At that point, Auburn called a timeout. What happened next has come to define Auburn's entire season.

Mazzone planned to give Johnson the ball again, but when the offense came over to the sideline, the strategy changed. Johnson insisted that the Tigers run a quarterback sneak. The Tigers did just that, as Ben Leard, a Georgia native, fell forward. Auburn won, 29–26, and finished 7–0 at home.

Afterward, players and coaches ascribed plenty of meaning to the play.

Pate: "For Ben to be able to score against Georgia right in front of all those Georgia fans, for him to say, 'The last play of my college career at home, I beat ya.' That's just a testament to the kind of guys on this team. I swear to God, I would rather have Ben score the way he scored than for me to have an intercepted pass and run it back in overtime. It showed the closeness, the unity, and the unselfishness of Rudi because ninety-nine percent of the tailbacks in this nation would say, 'I've got us there. Give me the ball.' Around here, the big thing is to go over top. Let Rudi go over the top. Let me do it. Let me score that touchdown. But he was so animated about a quarterback sneak."

Mazzone: "When Rudi comes over to the sideline and he's jumping around like that, I'm expecting him to say 'Give me the ball. I'll score for you, Coach.' Here's a kid who ran for 152 yards. Without him we're not even in the thing. Here it is, the game is on the line. So he looks right at me and says 'Run quarterback sneak.' I looked at him and he looked at his offensive line and says to them, 'We're gonna run quarterback sneak.' And Ben scored. That was pretty neat."

Running backs coach Eddie Gran: "It was one of the greatest moments I've ever been in, in coaching. Most guys, ninety-nine percent of the people in this world, would say, 'Give ME the ball, I WILL score.' And Rudi was jumping up and down and hollering, 'Run the quarterback sneak. Ben will score.' He's looking at all those offensive linemen and don't you think they believe in that kid? Shoot! That was like the good Lord talking, you know? And really, it's unbelievable. There we are in the biggest game of this football program in a while, you know, in our two years as a staff, and you know, you gotta love it. You gotta love it."

Rudi: "I looked at them all in the eyes and told them, one play and the game is over. We've worked so hard and if we can't do one play, then we don't deserve to win. Ben fell forward. It worked."

Athletic director David Housel sees poetry in most aspects of life, even in blocking and tackling. To him, the 2000 team is one for the ages. "I think this is the team that bridged the gap between Auburn's glory days of the past and Auburn's glory days of the future," Housel says. " I think this is the team that found the port. We've been sailing some rough seas. And this team, the seniors on this team in particular, have done a good job of guiding the ship, manning the ship, and they have found the port, whether we beat Alabama or not.

"I don't want to get deep on this, but I think most people tend to think of a human being—I am getting into the question of faith here when I say this—as a physical creation with a spiritual dimension. As I've grown older and wiser, I've come to think of the human being as a spiritual creation with a human dimension. The race doesn't always go to the swift or strong. Sooner or later, the race goes to the person who thinks he can. And I think in any human endeavor there's an element of the spirit, there's an element of the will. And I think what you see in this team in particular, in this senior class, is a triumph of the human spirit. A triumph, if you will, of what we call the Auburn spirit. I think the Auburn spirit—at its very best—is a human spirit at its very, very best. I think this team has been able to persevere because they've got some tough people on it. Competitive people. I think they are compassionate people and I think they are caring people. Not in a sissy, weak way, but in a strong way. I think this team, especially the senior class, are there for each other because they've *had* to be there for each other. I think that's the reason they've been able to have the success that they've had that you wouldn't expect them to have just based on talent alone.

"I got an e-mail here today that I think may sum it up pretty well.

It's from a fellow named Greg Sommerman, a fan. He writes, 'I'd like to suggest we devise a way to permanently honor the 2000 Auburn football team. We will not win a national championship, nor are we likely to get a chance to win the SEC Championship, yet I believe this team is one of the greatest in Auburn history. These Tigers were picked to have an average season, but they proved everybody wrong. However, the wins and the lack of losses did not inspire me to write you. I think this is one of the best Auburn teams in our history because of their actions off the field. This team came together under difficult circumstances, each player supporting the other, and each player has a tremendous story to tell. Think about it. [Wide receivers] Ronney Daniels mentoring Deandre Green. Rob Pate overcoming his illness. Rudi Johnson giving his first game ball to a kid he doesn't know, and countless others. I've never known a team to have more determination and loyalty and heart as this year's team. I think we should find a way to memorialize this team so that future teams will know what it takes to be an Auburn Tiger.' "

Though all of that poetry may be true, the seniors see the Alabama game in more pragmatic terms. A win, and their legend is secure. A loss, and the season's success is rendered meaningless.

Sunday

Iron Bowl Week Begins

ALABAMA

Patrick McDonald, a student assistant at Alabama, pulls into the Hardee's Restaurant in Childersburg, Alabama, roughly two hours east of the Tuscaloosa campus. Ten minutes later, a student assistant at Auburn pulls into the parking lot. They swap coaching videos of their games Saturday, shake hands, get back in their respective cars, and go home. In the old days, before FedEx, a lot of schools exchanged game films this way. Even in this era of overnight deliveries, it would be difficult to arrange a faster transaction between two schools a three-hour drive apart. By mid-afternoon, the videos will have been taken apart and put back together by the opposing coaching staffs. And so the week begins. . . . The Iron Bowl promotion machine is already humming. The *Tuscaloosa News* focuses on the PURE DOMINANCE, as the headline reads, of Mississippi State's 29–7 victory over Alabama. The *News* also includes a twenty-page special section devoted to the Auburn game, the highlight of which is a photo montage on the cover. Of the twenty-one photos, only three depict anything earlier than 1984. Sports editor Cecil Hurt sheepishly says that the *News* has either lost or has had stolen nearly all of its photos of the Bryant years.

The Fox affiliate in Birmingham begins shilling its Iron Bowl coverage during the noon telecast of the New Orleans–Charlotte game. On the 10:00 P.M. newscast Wednesday, the station promises THE LEADERSHIP SECRETS OF COACH PAUL BEAR BRYANT. The ad runs familiar clips of Bryant. Then, the man himself speaks: "I ain't nothing but a winner."

Now there's a secret.

Armed with credibility, the announcer concludes the promo. Another commercial runs, then the five-second "bumper" before the telecast resumes. TANGLE IN T-TOWN, FOX 6 SATURDAY AT 1:30.

The fans are primed. In Mountain Brook, a wealthy suburb of Birmingham, real estate appraiser Walt Pittman says that a neighbor sees him and says, "We're going to kick y'all's ass." Pittman says the neighbor drives a blue Suburban with a tiger tail hanging out the back and Auburn window flags on each side. The neighbor named her dog "Bowden" in 1993, when first-year Tigers coach Terry Bowden led Auburn to an 11–0 record. The rumors earlier this month that Clemson coach Tommy Bowden, Terry's older brother, was a candidate to replace Mike DuBose presented quite a dilemma for Pittman's neighbor, he reported. When Tommy Bowden said he had no plans to leave Clemson, he reduced the homeless dog population by one.

There may be no one who has a better understanding of the emotions roiling in the week ahead than Auburn alumnus Johnnie Aycock, the executive director of the West Alabama chamber of commerce located in Tuscaloosa. The chamber played a critical role in the movement to expand Bryant–Denny Stadium, getting the local governments to put $47 million in the pot to get the expansion under way. The chamber also helped make the Birmingham power brokers understand why the Auburn game needed to be moved from Legion Field to campus.

"Because this is the first year Auburn will be at Bryant–Denny, we need to make this special," Aycock says. "Auburn did a super job when Alabama played there for the first time. We're trying to have a whole week of activities. There's a street party Friday and a pep rally. Thursday, there's a parade. Wednesday, there's a basketball game. Tuesday, there will be cultural activities."

The chamber even helped sponsor a delegation of leaders from the Auburn campus and community to come to Tuscaloosa. Dr. Andrew Sorensen, the University of Alabama president, held a reception for the delegation at his home. Timing is everything. As they traveled around the city on the long-scheduled date of November 1, they passed the herd of satellite trucks on campus to televise the announcement that DuBose had been forced to resign. The Auburn visitors also got a tour of Bryant–Denny Stadium. That would be the last time the chamber, or anyone else in Tuscaloosa, would formally help them enter Bryant–Denny. "There are no tickets to be given," Aycock says with a smile. "There are no tickets. They'll have to use their Auburn sources."

It is a week that Aycock has been looking forward to since he took the job nearly eighteen years earlier: seeing his alma mater at his adopted home. He says it's obvious who he will root for. In fact, it's not obvious at all. "I will pull for Alabama that day. I really don't have any problem with that. It's even easy for an Auburn graduate to support and be enthusiastic about a winning program. It's not all that difficult to do."

Aren't you worried about being struck by lightning?

"I might be struck," he agrees, before finding refuge in one of Tuscaloosa's fondest legends. "Coach Bryant is in charge. I may be okay." He flashes a devilish grin, then gets serious again. "You'll always show a sentimental attachment to your alma mater," Aycock says. "That's a great time in your life. But here, these are friends. It's my community. When Alabama loses, the economy suffers around here. People get in the doldrums. When they win, there's a spirit of buying."

The city has been so far down in the doldrums this fall that only one thing could lift it up. That's another reason Aycock is pulling for Alabama. Alma mater is one thing. Bidness, as it is pronounced in this state, is something else.

The bidness at hand for the Alabama coaches involves no parades, receptions, or street parties. They already are hunkered down in the Alabama Football Complex, the crimson-bricked rectangular building adjacent to Coleman Memorial Coliseum on the southern edge of campus. After the disaster that took place at Mississippi State, the routine of game week couldn't begin soon enough. In the seven-day cycle of a college football week, Sunday has more than its share of work. Coaches wrap up the previous week by watching and grading the video of Saturday's game, and then immerse themselves in assembling the game plan for the following Saturday. The players are off, although the injured are expected to report to the training room. However, there's no treatment for the epidemic of bruised egos that has swept through this locker room. The mighty Crimson Tide is 3–7.

One floor above, the Crimson Tide defensive coaches have joined DuBose in his darkened office to review a video of the Auburn offense. The office looks like it might belong to the CEO of a multimillion-dollar enterprise, which it does, given the amount of money that Alabama football generates. The room is warm, with dark wood paneling and a thick, mostly crimson oriental rug on the wood floor. DuBose's desk is at a diagonal in the northwest corner. Behind his chair is a brick-faced wall adorned with large framed photos of his family. To his right, a crimson leather couch sprawls along the west windows. On the wall opposite the couch are several framed tributes to Bryant. There are ink drawings and sheets of Bryant postage stamps. Each of the four successors to Bryant has granted him a degree of presence in the room. Even Bill Curry, who didn't play for Bryant, displayed a framed photo of him on a coffee table.

DuBose is leaning back in his chair, feet on his desk and a computer mouse in his hand, clicking through the plays that show on the screen on the east wall of his office. Alabama, like most major schools, uses a digital video system that allows coaches to quickly categorize plays any way they like—by formation, down and distance, hash mark, etc. As is the case with most Auburn plays from the 2000 season, tailback Rudi Johnson comes around the end.

"Rudi—what kind of speed has he got?" DuBose asks.

"About 4.7," defensive coordinator Ellis Johnson answers, referring to the Auburn tailback's time in the 40-yard dash. For a tailback, that's not very fast, but someone forgot to tell the defensive players he eludes.

The coaches watch Auburn attempt a pass near the opponent's end zone. Two tight ends crisscross to confuse the defenders.

DuBose: "Do they just do it in the red zone?"

Johnson: "I've seen them do it other times."

Auburn's victory over Georgia the previous night comes on the screen. The Tigers hustle quickly to the line of scrimmage and start a play quickly and efficiently.

"They must be going at a pretty good tempo," defensive line coach Lance Thompson says.

"Last year, they got out pretty quick against us, didn't they?" DuBose asks.

"No huddle," Johnson replies.

"*Lots* of no huddle," Thompson adds.

Shortly before 3:00 P.M., Cecil Hurt, the *Tuscaloosa News* sports editor, slips into the office. That's a sign for the meeting to break up. DuBose has a weekly teleconference with the half dozen or so beat writers every Sunday at this hour. Someone turns up the lights. Alongside the west wall of DuBose's office lie cardboard boxes. The coach has made it clear that when he leaves the office Friday night before the game, he isn't coming back. Perhaps part of him has already left. He can't remember the number he must dial to be connected to the teleconference. He looks across the desk at Hurt.

"You don't have that number, do you?" DuBose asks.

Hurt rattles it off.

"My secretary didn't leave it," DuBose says, "and I've thrown everything else away."

DuBose understands he will get four kinds of questions this week about: the rivalry, his team's slide, Auburn's rise, and his reflections on the final week for him and his staff. What he says to the writers Sunday, he will repeat in various forms throughout the week. To wit: "This is a special football game. If we're the right kind of people, we'll be excited to play. If you can't get excited, either at the University of Alabama or Auburn University, about this game, you got no business playing this game."

It is a sign of the problems that have plagued Alabama that DuBose even has to bring up getting excited about playing Auburn. Having watched his team play at Mississippi State with all the aggressiveness of a whipped puppy, DuBose is concerned. While worrying about his team's lack of emotion, he must also focus on his own work with only one week left.

"It will be an emotional day for us," he says. "This is the last week. This is the last Sunday. Monday will be the last Monday. Tuesday the last Tuesday, and on and on and on...."

He praises the Auburn offense. Of course, no coach will ever speak disparagingly of an opponent, much less an archrival. However, DuBose's comments are genuine. "They have a powerful running back. I've just been watching some tape. Tommy does a good job. The offense gives you a lot of different looks. If you put too many people in the box, they throw it. If you take them out of the box, they run it. They're doing what we've been trying to do all year. Rudi has been the difference in their football team. Tommy may tell you different. We can scheme to slow it down," DuBose says, meaning devise a formation to stop Johnson. "But we can't get enough people to slow it down without giving up something else. . . . He's a very physical running back. He has a low center of gravity. He's got good feet, got great balance. We've got to get two, three, four people coming to the football and gang-tackle. You can't expect a safety or a defensive back to tackle him."

Finally, DuBose acknowledges what it must kill him to say: "We're at a real low point right now. I don't think this game will take that away. . . . Hopefully, this game will bring out that something extra that we haven't caught on all year. It can take away a bit of the pain. It's a one-game season for us."

The call ends. DuBose and Hurt chat for a few minutes. Athletic director Mal Moore slips in through one of the three doors to DuBose's office. The coach looks up and greets him by saying, "I was about to ask you if you could suit up and play defensive tackle."

Nowhere has the Tide's lack of physical play been more evident than in the middle of the defensive front. The Bulldogs' offensive linemen, who averaged six-four, 323 pounds, spent the day knocking the young Tide defenders backward.

"I'd love to go see what Mississippi State does in their offseason program," DuBose says. "They weren't that big when they recruited them, or else everybody would have been recruiting them. Antwan is just not ready for that kind of competition," DuBose says, referring to freshman defensive lineman Antwan Odom. "Antwan can't bench 250. He's going against a guy who can bench 450. Antwan will be a heck of a player someday. He wants to be. He'll be in a matchup that's a little better Saturday."

The small talk continues, largely complimentary of Tuberville and the Tigers. "DeMarco McNeil is a good nose player," DuBose says, referring to the Auburn freshman named Mr. Football as a senior at Blount High in Prichard, near Mobile, in 1998. "He'll play well. He's still mad at me for not taking him."

Moore slips out as quietly as he came. Hurt follows. The offensive coaches spill into the office. Neil Callaway, the offensive coordinator, plants himself next to the desk at DuBose's right. Quarterback coach Charlie Stubbs and receivers coach Dabo Swinney are in front. Tight end coach Ronnie Cottrell sits to the side of them. Graduate assistant Will Friend is directly under the screen. Running backs coach Ivy Williams takes the couch, farther away than anyone.

For nearly three hours, the coaches stare at the screen, watching the Auburn defense against Arkansas, Florida, Georgia, and against the Alabama offense a year ago. DuBose initially asks who certain Tigers are. The fan in the projector installed overhead whirs constantly, as plays are run forward, backward, and over again. Then the coaches begin to issue judgments of the Auburn players.

SWINNEY: "Number 8 [free safety Stanford Simmons] is not much physical. He played last year. He just didn't hit."
DUBOSE: "How big is 96 [left end Javor Mills]?"
CALLAWAY: "Six-four, 253."
DUBOSE: "How big is 82 [right end Reggie Torbor]?"
CALLAWAY: "Six-three, 238. That's where Alton Moore plays."
DUBOSE: "How big is he?"
CALLAWAY: "He's not very physical."
DUBOSE: "What are the two tackles doing at the snap?"
CALLAWAY: "Coming inside. They been doing that a lot. Everybody pinches down [crowds toward the middle] for them. Even the ends."

A Florida receiver catches a pass in front of Alex Lincoln, Auburn's senior middle linebacker. Lincoln is known as a "smart" player. In other words, a guy his size (six feet, 238) with no speed has no business playing major-college football. "A mismatch would be one back on 43," Swinney says. "I don't think he's a coverage guy."

Adds Stubbs, "From what I've seen, the pitch would be great against these guys."

Florida lines up with three wide receivers. "What's Casher doing?" Swinney asks, referring to Auburn's best cornerback, Larry Casher. "He should be playing the field. He's playing zone. That puts the safety in a real bind."

A vertical beam of sunlight knifes through the blinds like a bull-rushing lineman and sits on the right side of the screen. The coaches ignore it. Occasionally, one of them gets up for a bathroom break, or to grab a soft drink out of the kitchenette adjacent to DuBose's office. No one stops the projector. A number of running plays from Alabama's victory at Auburn in 1999 arrive on screen.

"Last year," Stubbs says, "they had the simplest defensive plan we faced. We prepared for a lot."

The coaches watch as the 1999 offense matter-of-factly creates a seven-yard gain for All-American tailback Shaun Alexander. Left tackle Chris Samuels, the 1999 Outland Trophy winner, comes outside to be Alexander's lead blocker. Fullback Dustin McClintock blocks the strong side linebacker. Tight end Terry Jones Jr. seals off the defensive end. Jones, the son of the Alabama strength coach, tore up his knee at mid-season. McClintock is the only one of the four who will play against Auburn. After the Tide rushed for 31 yards on 28 carries a day earlier, the coaches may as well be watching the New Orleans Saints blocking for Ricky Williams.

"Got a lot of push on that end," Callaway says softly.

"That's the key to the play right there: getting that edge," Williams says.

Jones's replacement, Shawn Draper, is a blocker, not a receiver. A few plays later, DuBose asks, "Could Draper get open?"

"He can get open," Callaway says. "He can't stay open."

Finally, DuBose rattles off a number of tailback rushes that he wants to look at, each out of several formations. At 6:25 P.M., the lights come on. "Y'all look at it," DuBose says, "and let's get after it in the morning."

The coaches rise and leave, only they don't look at anything tonight. They are early risers. The coaches will meet again at 7:00 A.M., Monday. They're out the door, in their trucks, and gone.

The players won't start their formal preparation for Auburn until Monday. The lure of redemption that a victory over their cross-state rival holds is a welcome salve for their bruised pride. "It's such a fine line between winning and losing," senior offensive captain Paul Hogan says, reflecting on the Mississippi State game, a loss that left coaches and players alike embarrassed at the lack of effort. "That game, at one point, it could have been really close. The first drive we had, we drove down to the 20 and missed a field goal." Senior guard Griff Redmill, one of Hogan's closest friends, backs him up. "What people don't understand," Redmill says, "is how plays like that [missed field goals] impact a game. All of those times last year, we'd be in the same situation, we always made a play. It swung the momentum our way."

Hogan, a native of Valdosta, Georgia, arrived at Alabama in 1996 as the result of an intense recruiting battle—not between schools but between the coaches on the Alabama staff. Jeff Rouzie, the coach who recruits south Georgia, wanted him. Coach Gene Stallings wanted him. No one else on the staff saw anything more than a skinny (six-three, 240) center. Callaway says that when he decided to join DuBose after the 1996 season, he called friends at Georgia and Georgia Tech and asked about Hogan. Neither school had even recruited him.

"When you're wrong, you have to admit you're wrong," DuBose says. "When we recruited him, I thought Paul Hogan would be a really good backup player. We needed to find a bigger, stronger, quicker, faster center than Paul Hogan. Jeff Rouzie looked at me and said, 'You're wrong. He's going to be a special player.' "

Rouzie liked Hogan for a few reasons. One, he had played for a legendary high school coach, the late Nick Hyder at Valdosta High. "I had known Coach Hyder for years," Rouzie says. "If Coach Hyder recommended one, that says a lot. Some people rate you by size and weight. The kid had all the intangibles. I saw a kid that would do anything he had to. He played defensive end his junior year and they didn't move him to center until his senior year. If you went to see him play, went to his house and talked to his family, no way do you turn down that kid."

The coach had a secret weapon in recruiting Hogan. Rouzie's daughter Jennifer was a recruiting hostess, known on campus as a Bama Belle, when Hogan arrived on his official visit. "Paul got hooked up with Jennifer," Rouzie says. A conspiratorial smile spreads across his face. "You know how women are. They scheme. Jennifer told my wife, 'I'm going to go after him.' Women," Rouzie concludes, still smiling, "are awful."

And Hogan, the player he championed, will be his son-in-law. Rouzie, as a linebacker coach, didn't coach Hogan. Rouzie considers that "a blessing. I keep a distance. That's between my daughter and Paul. As far as I'm concerned, he's a good kid."

Redmill, who grew up in Jasper, a mid-sized town north of Birmingham, always wanted to go to Alabama. His favorite players as he grew up were Eric Curry and John Copeland, the bookend defensive ends on the 1992 national championship team. Redmill once stood in line five hours just to get Copeland's autograph. Redmill went on to make all-state as a defensive end at Walker High. "I didn't want to be an offensive lineman. Defensive end is way cooler," Redmill says. "You get to sack the quarterback. When I was recruited, I thought, dreams come true. I'm going to play defensive line for Alabama. Eric Curry and John Copeland. Five years later, I'm a guard. Still, it's the school I've always loved and been a fan of, and I've been able to contribute a whole lot, too."

Both players redshirted in 1996, Stallings's final year. In 1997, Hogan started in the opener. Two games later, Callaway, trying to shake up his offensive line, started fellow redshirt freshmen Redmill and Will Cuthbert on either side of Hogan against Arkansas. The Razorbacks won, 17–16, on a late touchdown, a tough loss in a tough 4–7 season. Hogan and Redmill played about like you would expect freshmen to play. "I was still pretty green as far as offensive line goes," Redmill says. "I had never played the position before. I never considered myself ready for big-time playing time, especially against a powerful SEC school; I was just [trying] to understand the terminology. Coach Callaway tried to tell me it's just like playing tackle. That's easy for a guy who's been coaching twenty-five years. Game day came around and I'm shaking in my boots. I'm more worried about how bad I'm going to look on TV. Rightfully so. Every mistake I made, they showed a hundred times. I watched the tape of the first half, maybe. I turned it off." Hogan's memory of the videotape is more definitive. "I got caught for holding," he says. "The announcer on TV said, 'Hogan must have been a wrestler in high school. That was the best takedown I've ever seen!'"

Hogan kept starting. Redmill didn't start again the rest of the year. By 1998, however, Redmill settled in at left guard between Hogan and Chris Samuels. In three seasons, Redmill has started thirty-five consecutive games. Hogan, in his four years, has started forty-four games, missing three starts because of injuries. He has been nagged by an ankle sprain this season but has continued to play.

Hogan's offensive teammates elected him their captain before the season. Alabama's struggles have eaten away at him. Throughout the fall, DuBose has talked about a lack of leadership on the Crimson Tide. He hasn't singled out Hogan or, for that matter, the other captains—defensive lineman Kenny Smith and deep snapper Bradley Ledbetter. Yet Hogan feels responsible.

"I think some guys thought it was going to be easy," Hogan says of the season.

"Old hat," Redmill chimes in.

"People are going to play their best game against us," Hogan continues. "Last year, we played with so much more emotion. Opening kickoff, going down and knocking hell out of people, getting up and celebrating."

"This year," Redmill says, "somebody makes a play, gets up, and walks back to the huddle. I don't feel like we were ready to be No. 3. I didn't feel like we were ready for that burden. It's November. I just hope that things are going to come together."

"We do have a lot of talent," Hogan insists. "Our confidence just got so hurt early in the season. I don't think we realized how good Southern Mississippi is. Coach Callaway told us they probably have the best front seven we'll see all year. That was one of the better defenses I've ever played against."

"There's nothing that's going to happen Saturday that would make all the other stuff go away," Redmill says of the Auburn game. "I hope the younger guys understand the rivalry. The old guys do. It's about a lot more than the last game and the SEC championship. It's like the state championship."

Both players continue to insist that Alabama is better than its record indicates. "Man," Hogan says, "we deserve something good to happen. The better team doesn't always win."

AUBURN

The Auburn Tigers, still tired from the improbable win over Georgia the night before, walk into a meeting room in the athletic complex and settle into their seats. It is Sunday, nearly two in the afternoon. Caps cover mussed hair and players swallow their yawns as Tuberville, wearing an orange button-down shirt and blue tie, calls the room to attention.

"Well, we're 8–2, we've got an opportunity to be 9–2 and either share the conference championship or win it outright," says Tuberville, launching into a speech that will set the tone for the entire week. "You can win a ring no matter what happens. We win this game, we can get either a co-championship ring or a championship ring. That's one thing that you go to college and you play football for—to get a ring to put on your finger stating that you were champion, and to be a champion in this conference is a chore. We're playing to move up in the bowl championship and playing for a chance to go to Atlanta for the SEC title game. We're playing for a lot of things. The pressure's on us.

"We're going to play Alabama. And that's the reason for coming here. I don't care what the records are. We're the team playing for the conference title. I've seen a lot of good rivalries before, but there ain't nothing like Auburn and Alabama. Auburn–Alabama means somethin' to everybody in this state. We're 8–2, they're 3–7; that don't make a hill of beans. The roles are reversed from last year. They were playing us for a conference championship, they were playing us here at our place. Now we're going over there to play for a chance to be in the conference game. We played good last year, for three quarters, then we ran out of gas. That's not gonna happen this year.

"This is the first time in one hundred years that Auburn has played in Tuscaloosa. First time. You don't think there's gonna be some people ready to see us lose? National TV on CBS. They will play their best game of the year. This is their bowl game. This is their conference championship game. If you don't believe that and don't understand that, you'll find out what will happen. We're not going to let that happen.

"This week we got to get a lot of people healthy. Gotta get everybody back in the game. Come Tuesday, live in the training room. You go in there and get in the hot tub and don't get out until you're well. Because we're going to need everybody. Everybody. Because this is the one we want, right here. They're ready to fall. They're sitting over there ready to fall."

For Tuberville, the day started at 5 A.M. First, there's the taping of his TV show in Montgomery. Then there's church with wife Suzanne, sons Tucker, five, and Troy, three. And lunch, as usual, at the catfish joint close to campus. "I love catfish, I'm a big catfish freak," he says.

Truth is, Tuberville might still be frying catfish in Tullahoma, Tennessee today at age forty-six, if not for a conversation with Miami coach Jimmy Johnson. After coaching defensive ends and linebackers at Arkansas State, a Division I-AA program, for four years in the early '80s, Tuberville struggled to find an assistant job in Division I-A. So he quit coaching in 1985 and opened up Tubby's Catfish Inn in Tullahoma, where his sister Vicki lives. The house speciality: Tubby's Pond Platter—two catfish steaks, two catfish filets, two frog legs, hush puppies, and Tubby's Pond Water, which was a fruit punch concoction.

"It did good. We were making money. But after doing that for about five or six months, I thought there had to be something better than cooking catfish on Friday and Saturday nights," Tuberville says. "But I learned a lot from that experience, about how to meet people, about how 'the customer's always right' type of deal, kind of like you have to do in this business, and I learned that having your own business is a lot more work than what people would ever imagine.

"Then again, it kind of gave me a break away from athletics, playing, coaching, learning my way up. Getting away from it for a little bit made me all of sudden go, 'Hey, I miss this. This is what I always wanted to do, so let's get back in it and go full steam ahead.' "

In January 1986, Tuberville went to the national coaches' convention in New Orleans with a résumé in hand. He hung around the hotel lobby with the rest of the coaches, looking for work. "I just happened to be sittin' down in the right place and Jimmy Johnson needed a graduate assistant," Tuberville says.

GA's (graduate assistants), as they're called, occupy the lowest rung of the coaching food chain. Even though Tuberville was much older than the average GA, even though he had already been a full-time assistant, he was thrilled to be underpaid and overworked. Miami meant big-time college football.

Ironically, Tuberville was raised in Bear Bryant country, in Camden, Arkansas, a town of 15,000. "There is a big sign going into town saying, 'Home of Bear Bryant,' Tuberville says, with a chuckle.

There, his father, Charles, who passed away before Tuberville became a head coach, worked at a company which made soft drink syrup. Charles, a longtime referee in town, also helped start the Camden football program when Tommy was in seventh grade. His mother, Olive, worked for a weapons manufacturer, and still lives in Camden except during the season, when she comes to Auburn. Olive hasn't missed one of her son's games yet.

"Oh, when there's nothing on TV, I'll just pop in a game tape," Olive says. "I've watched the Arkansas game two or three times. But I have a good collection of some oldies. I watched an old Michigan–Miami game the other day."

For years now, Olive has been after Tommy to call a play that the Hurricanes ran against Notre Dame a while ago. "It was third down on the five-yard line," Olive explains. "Two guys were on the line, one crossed over and . . . oh, I'll have to show him that tape."

Tuberville didn't plan on playing college football, but he knew he wanted to be a coach. At Southern Arkansas University, he walked on the football team and became a free safety. "I knew that if I wanted to be a coach, that I should be part of the football program, so I walked on," he says.

All the coaches there were tough bastards, especially an offensive line coach named Eldon Hawley. "I'll never forget one day I'm on the punt block team in practice and we're blocking punts at half speed and this guy puts his helmet right below my neck, raises up, and slits my chin. I still got a scar there. Blood goes everywhere. My hands are trying to stop the bleeding. I go over to Coach Eldon, who's running punts, and say, 'Coach, I'm cut pretty bad. I'm bleeding. I can't stop the bleeding.' And he said, 'Get your ass back in there and make it quit bleeding—you're not coming out.' That was one of my fondest memories of Coach Eldon. Every once in a while I pay him back and make him do something that I don't want to do." Coach Eldon is now Tuberville's director of football operations.

Coach Eldon is also the man who helped get Tuberville into college coaching. After Southern Arkansas, Hawley joined head coach Larry Lacewell at Arkansas State. There, Hawley opened a door for Tuberville, who became a volunteer coach. At Arkansas State, Tuberville absorbed everything Lacewell knew about defense. (Years later, it would seem ironic that Lacewell was from Fordyce, which was Bear Bryant's hometown. Lacewell also coached for Bryant at Alabama.) Lacewell, now the director of college and pro scouting for the Dallas Cowboys, helped Tuberville land at Miami when he put in a good word with his close friend Jimmy Johnson.

Tuberville's career flourished with the Hurricanes. In his eight seasons as a defensive coach, the Hurricanes won three national titles. Jimmy Johnson's laissez-faire coaching style and emphasis on special teams influenced Tuberville greatly. "I also learned how to handle the staff, how to handle players when you have problems, learned about discipline, and how to handle success and failure." After Johnson left for the Dallas Cowboys, Tuberville picked up more about offense from Johnson's replacement, Dennis Erickson.

After a year as defensive coordinator at Texas A&M, Tuberville spent four seasons as head coach at Mississippi, where he inherited a losing program on probation and turned the Rebels into a bowl team in three years—all amid a bitter controversy over the Confederate flag, which some Rebels fans saw as a symbol of school pride and others saw as a symbol of hatred.

When Auburn hired Tuberville in late 1998 as its twenty-fifth head coach, the school, too, needed Tuberville to rebuild a program in turmoil. Tuberville did just that in this, his second season.

Though this is the biggest game of his brief Auburn career, Tuberville is downright relaxed. DuBose says that he doesn't sleep during the season, but that's not the case with Tuberville. "I sleep great. I try to never stay up past eleven. It's a long season. And if you start staying up to one, two o'clock in the morning, it doesn't work because I get up at about five-thirty. I go out and get the newspaper, kinda glance through it. Get [my son] Tucker up. Make him take a shower. Clean up and get his clothes on and I get him to school about seven. There is only so much you can do as a coach. The thing that I tell these coaches here is unless you are up here making calls to recruits or something like that, go home. There's no reason. If you're not here doing something with the players, you're not making any progress."

Tuberville is so at ease, it's not unusual to find him in the sports information office passing time with a few students. Wander in the back area where student minions clip newspaper stories and stuff envelopes and there is Tuberville talking about his Arkansas expressions which slip out occasionally. " 'Crazier than a nine-pound robin' is one of them," he says. "Then if someone asks me about a running back, I could say, 'He looks like a rolling ball of butcher knives.' " The students laugh. "He's so cool," a grad assistant says later.

This afternoon, ten beat writers crowd sports information director Meredith Jenkins's office waiting for Tuberville to arrive for the day's press conference. Tuberville leans back in Jenkins's swivel chair and jokes with the scribes. As usual, the scene is as casual as the jeans and sneakers everyone has on.

A reporter asks Tuberville if he's surprised the Tigers are 8–2 and ranked No. 14. "I'm shocked, to be honest with you," Tuberville says. "But it shows what you can do when you have determination and no quit in you."

Reporters then inquire about the meaning of the rivalry, Rudi Johnson, and the kicking game which faltered last year against Alabama.

Alabama beat Auburn 28–17 at Jordan–Hare Stadium in 1999. Kicker Damon Duval missed a critical 22-yard field goal attempt that could have put the Tigers up 17–6 in third quarter. Earlier in the season, Duval missed a field goal that would have given Auburn a win over Ole Miss. Against Tennessee, he botched a fake punt and then had a heated exchange with Tuberville on the sideline before he was sent to the locker room. Tuberville had run out of patience. After the Alabama loss, he said, "We will have a kicker next year. We're going to remedy the problem. I think it cost us three games. I've never been around this inconsistent kind of kicking." Two months later, Tuberville signed *USA Today*'s All-American kicker Phillip Yost. Yost, however, would get injured before the season began, forcing Tuberville to stick with Duval.

Near the end of Tuberville's press conference, a reporter wonders if quarterback Ben Leard can win the big one.

"Ben's struggled, but he's 13–3 as a starter and he's overcome a lot. People will have a lot to say about Ben after this game."

For all the seniors, this is the defining game of their career. And for Leard, especially so. After serving as quarterback Dameyune Craig's understudy in 1996 and 1997, Leard got his chance to start in 1998. But turmoil soon followed when coach Terry Bowden quit amid a 3–8 season. Leard lost his starting position and ended up as third string when interim coach Bill Oliver took over. In 1999, he began the season as a back-up, won the job, suffered a severe shoulder injury and a concussion, but finished the year as the team's starter.

Even when Leard was healthy and playing well, there was plenty of criticism. He was labeled as a guy who didn't like to get hit, a guy who couldn't throw the deep ball. All the while, he just ignored it. "You know, I don't really know any quarterback who likes to get hit," Leard says. "I'll be damned if I'm not gonna try to get out of it. They're not going to knock me out of the game unless I'm seriously hurt. I've really taken pride in how tough I am. And how many licks I've taken. That's just the way I've always been. I've always known that I got to stay in the pocket and take shots and make throws, and I've been successful doing so. When people say things like that, they are not only an insult to me; they are a motivating thing. If somebody tells me I can't do something, I'm going to show you I can. And probably rub it in your face.

"As far as throwing the ball deep, a lot of people just say I don't have a strong arm, and this and that. That's not our offense. We don't have to throw the ball seventy yards downfield. Our offense is based upon quick, short routes. Getting the ball to the playmakers and letting them make plays. That's just people, though. They are skeptical of your abilities and they don't realize that you must be doing something right to have the success that you've had. I've been dealing with them for so long. It's one thing that's kinda bulletin-board material for me. Fortunately, I've been able to deal with it and grow from it and have it make me a better quarterback."

Though Leard shugs off most criticism, the memory of the 1999 Alabama game lingers. Leard played well against the Tide, throwing two touchdowns, but was criticized in the aftermath for a safety. He had led the Tigers back from a 6–0 deficit to take a 14–6 lead, which stood late in the third quarter. However, he was sacked in the end zone, a play seen as a momentum-killer.

Leard's boyish face seemingly grows older when he talks about the Alabama loss. "It was very tough, mentally. I thought after going through what I went through in 1998—you know losing my job and all that kind of riffraff—I thought I had been to the bottom. But after going through the Alabama game in 1999 and having that safety which probably turned the game around, having fingers pointed at me, armchair quarterbacks thinking I could have done something different, it made me start thinking about mistakes I made and I really started harping on things. You know, hindsight is always twenty-twenty. It was real hard for me to deal with. Plus, I was involved in that play when time ran out in the game, an interception. I was the guy that got the safety and I was the guy that threw the interception. There was a lot of me this, and me this, and me this, and it was something I always, even to this day, have been looking for, something that I could have done better."

Leard, from Hartwell, Georgia, wasn't born into this rivalry, but after his five seasons, its essence is now a part of him. "People back home can't understand it," he says. " Even my parents. My parents thought something was wrong with me—just the fact that I was so motivated and so closed when trying to prepare for this game, they thought I was sick. They thought something was wrong with me. People at home don't realize the importance of this ball game and I don't think they ever will."

For Leard, a win against Alabama would be a just reward for a trying career. "For what he's gone through since he's been here, for him to beat Georgia and Alabama in the same year and take this team to 9–2, would be awesome," offensive coordinator Noel Mazzone says. "He ain't the most talented kid, you know. He's just a great example of a little perseverance."

In a players-only meeting this afternoon, center Cole Cubelic gets everyone's attention when he tosses a stool across the front of the room. For Cubelic, this game means everything. "Auburn is always the underdog-type team, the kid that nobody else would take a chance on," Cubelic says later. "Hell, I'm an example of that. Here and UAB were my only Division I scholarship offers. Every other SEC school recruited me until I got my knee hurt my senior year. Alabama recruited me hard until the injury. Then it was over. It's always been like that. Rodney Crayton didn't get an offer at Alabama. Alex Lincoln walked on here and got a scholarship. Alabama didn't talk to Ben. To me it's always been about that. It's always been about kids coming down here and getting a chance. I think that says a lot about us. It says a lot about heart and desire. Something about coming to play here. You know people are gonna give you a fair shot. That's a good thing. I know that I would want to have my kids play in a program where everybody is gonna get a fair chance, not just who was the highest recruited guy."

Cole Cubelic looks exactly like his name. His full face forms the letter O and his body is shaped like a cube—squat and wide. Even his position matches the alliteration of his name—center Cole Cubelic.

Cubelic was the team's starting center entering the season until he injured his right foot, which he had broken in 1998. Before the first game of the season against Wyoming, Cubelic was demoted to second string.

After the Tigers trounced Wyoming, the emotions Cubelic had locked inside came flowing out. He walked to the fence where his mother was waiting. Standing in the darkness, with a towel over his head, he sobbed. "I just lost it, completely lost it. I mean, I bawled my eyes out. My mom rode home with me in my truck and I think it took us about forty-five minutes to get home and I was still crying. It was tough to deal with. I felt like I had let my family down, let myself down, and didn't know what lay ahead. I think I was real scared about what my future would hold in terms of the rest of the season, and it just hurt not being out there.

"Being the starter for two years, then coming out and having that kind of taken away from you somewhat just kind of hit me. I think after that Wyoming game, when I just let it out, it just was a lot of frustration that had been built up. It was not easy, but I'm definitely glad that I stuck with it. I've got some good friends on the team that have made it a lot easier on me. Guys like Alex and Ben and Rob [Pate]. Those guys have been there for me and helped me and talked to me. Thankfully, I have teammates like that, that want to be my friend before they want to be my teammate. If I didn't, I don't know if I would have made it."

Cubelic missed two games with a sore knee and played the rest of the season behind sophomore Ben Nowland. But this afternoon, Cubelic receives encouraging news. The coaches tell him that he has a shot at starting against Alabama if he has a good week of practice. For a boy who grew up in Birmingham, nothing means more.

"I've started the Alabama game the last two years," Cubelic says. "I'd like there to be a third time."

For linebacker Alex Lincoln, it was always Auburn. Tiger posters filled his boyhood bedroom in Mobile—one featured swarming tacklers and read "Defense, Auburn style." In the backyard, he pretended he was Bo Jackson. But those boyhood dreams remained just that. Coming out of high school, neither Auburn nor Alabama recruited the undersized linebacker. He landed at a Division III outpost instead, Mississippi College in Clinton, Mississippi.

After two seasons at Mississippi College, Lincoln longed to play big-time football. He longed to play at Auburn. And so he transferred and walked on the team. "I didn't want to be forty years old and say, 'Well, I never had an opportunity and nobody gave me a chance,' and so I went ahead and transferred. It was a childhood dream I wanted to chase," Lincoln says.

Though the coaches didn't expect much out of Lincoln, they were impressed by his hard work. During a team meeting before the '99 season, Tuberville announced that Lincoln would receive a scholarship. The entire room stood and clapped. "I think, to this day, that will be one of my most memorable and emotional moments that I think I've ever seen or ever will see," Leard says. "There was just a big sigh of relief to know that it finally paid off. He followed his dream and it paid off." Lincoln started every game and led the team in tackles.

This season, Lincoln is also the leading tackler. Today, after the team meeting, he spent two hours at East Alabama Medical Center getting X rays on his right shoulder, which he injured against Georgia. Plus, he suffered a concussion. "I finally found out there wasn't anything broken," he says. "I didn't want to miss this game for anything in the world."

Even though Lincoln grew up watching this rivalry, he says, "I didn't really understand the extreme nature of the game until I played in it. Last year, I felt what it was all about when I was standing in the end zone and the Alabama fans were cheering 'We just beat the hell outta you.' And you start to feel that urgency that you never want that to happen again. You never want to be in that situation again. That's when I truly began to understand what it is to play Alabama. What it is to want to beat Alabama and game plan for an entire year. And to go in the off-season and work to beat Alabama and have them on your mind. You don't do that with other teams.

"We're having a pretty good season this year, and if Alabama beats us, it's all for naught. I don't think that we'd be satisfied with our season if we don't win the game. And that goes to show how big this game is. Of course, we don't want to lose any game. But having the success we've had and being on a roll as of late, we don't want to end the season on a loss to Alabama. I think that it will spoil our season."

Heading into the season, defensive coordinator John Lovett felt that linebacker Rob Pate was his best player on defense. Then in June, Pate's world was upended. He started to have severe stomach pains and muscle twitches. Doctors were baffled. "They put me on so many different types of medication. I had an MRI, I had a blood test done, I had a muscle-nerve conduction test done, a muscle biopsy taken," Pate says. "At first, doctors thought maybe it would be multiple sclerosis or McArdle's disease. Obviously, I got scared for my wife and for me, my family. Luckily, all those tests ruled the major stuff out." Still, doctors were unable to diagnose Pate's illness. He spent most of the summer shuttling between doctors' offices.

Pate had been a three-year starter for the Tigers, but entering fall practice, he was clearly not himself. He carried his pills in a large sandwich bag. There were pills for diarrhea, for muscle spasm, for anxiety, and for inflammation.

The worst of it all was the uncertainty. "Basically, they said to him, 'Okay, there's something wrong with you but we don't know what to do to fix it and we don't know what to tell you to do to make it better,'" Cubelic says. "Every problem I've ever had and most people have had, they say, 'Well, you'll need two or three weeks of rehab, ice, take this medicine and you'll be okay.' Well, this guy is coming to practice, cramping up almost every day, and nobody knows what to tell him to do."

Much was expected of Pate but the illness put his season, as well as his pro future, in doubt. "You know, I tell all these scouts when they come in here, I say, 'Here's a guy now, if he could just get himself right physically like he was, he's faster and quicker than you think he is and he's a big kid and he's got it all upstairs, he's real sharp. But you know how they think,'" Lovett says.

At the start of the season, Pate considered redshirting, but then he reconsidered. After all, he's married. His wife, Dana, is an elementary school teacher and today, Pate told his coaches that Dana is five weeks pregnant. The couple, both from Birmingham, have been together since eighth grade when they went on their first date after the last football game of the season. They were engaged the final weekend of high school and were married in July 1999.

And so, Pate thought it was best to get his career started. So he tried his best on the field, and applied to optometry school.

In the third game of the season, against LSU, Pate started to feel better. A cold front had moved in and suddenly the cramping eased a bit. Doctors still don't know what Pate's illness is, nor do they understand why his condition improves in cooler weather. But now that it's November, Pate is feeling and playing better. He's taking only two medications, for muscle spasms and diarrhea. When Pate learns that the forecast is 40 degrees at kickoff, he smiles. "That looks good for me," he says.

It's been a day of meetings. After the team meeting in which the Tigers go over special teams' tapes from the Georgia game, after the players-only meeting in which Cubelic throws the chair, there are position meetings in which each group reviews film of the Georgia game. In each of the small classrooms there is a sign on the front wall. "Beat Bama," they read. They have been on the walls all season.

A year ago, Joe Whitt Jr. was sitting in the wide receivers meeting room as a player. Now the senior is a volunteer receivers coach. Joe Jr.'s career ended after he had his second surgery on his left shoulder in April. "That was the hardest time of my life. I was sitting in the doctor's office and he went and got my dad. And when my dad walked in, I just about bust out crying. That's when he told my dad, you know. I had never seen my dad cry before. I was like a little baby. It was just . . . football's the only thing that I really just love. And just to know that I wouldn't be able to play anymore. It just tore me up. It took me . . . I'm just getting where I'll be like, it's okay, well, you know, it's decent, but the first couple of games, I was just like, I don't know."

Joe Jr.'s father, Joe Whitt, has been Auburn's linebackers coach since 1981, through the tenures of Dye, Bowden, and now Tuberville. For Joe Jr., this rivalry runs as deep and is as personal as a family feud. "I hate Alabama. I mean, I really, really deep inside, I hate Alabama. And that's all. I hate Alabama. I really couldn't care less that they're 3 and whatever, what, 3–7. I wish they were 0–10.

"I guess that was the way I was raised. My dad hates Alabama. When he says it, you will see in his eyes that he really hates Alabama with a passion. He didn't even like me being friends with Joni."

Joni Crenshaw is a senior on Alabama's basketball team and the two met on a Southeastern Conference student advisory committee. "When we met she didn't know where I was from. She found out I was from Auburn and then we didn't speak to each other. She hates Auburn and I hate Alabama. Then, after the next meeting, we spoke a little bit. We started to talk whatever, but it took six months before we would even speak to each other. We started talking and then we had a great relationship but there would be trouble when we talked about our schools, so we had to make a bet because we would always dog each other's school. She gave me an Alabama sweater and I gave her an Auburn sweater. So the first one that would say something about the other one's school had to wear the sweater on campus. That pretty much put an end to us talking about each other's school."

After the position meetings, the team gets ready for practice, and Joe Jr. becomes Coach Whitt. "It's sort of funny. Like, during the week, to the older guys, I'm Joe. And most of the younger guys call me Coach. But when we get in the game—they're just so focused and everything, they call me Coach. Surprisingly, they listen to everything I say. They listen more than I thought they would. Sometimes I think this might have been the best thing that ever happened to me, in the long run, because it gives me a head start to what I want to do—coach. My dream is to come here and be the first black head coach because my dad was the first black assistant coach here. Maybe fifteen, twenty years down the road they will be ready for it."

For now, though, father and son pace the sidelines at practice as assistant coaches. It's perfect football weather, for Rob Pate, for everyone. Above, the streaks of clouds look like a painter's brushstrokes. The field is a lush green. The air is crisp. Grunts, whoops, and whistles rise above the field. Alabama week has begun.

Monday

ALABAMA

Coaches are fond of saying that "on time" means being five minutes early. At 7:00 A.M., the announced time for the Alabama offensive staff to begin its work, the projector is already warm, and the coffee is beginning to cool.

Neil Callaway, a pair of half-glasses on his nose, sits at the head of a long table. He's wearing a golf shirt, jeans, and deck shoes without socks. With his husky rasp of a drawl, he could be a Southern stockbroker, except that most brokers don't have a well-muscled upper body from years of weight work. Dabo Swinney, clean-cut and preppily attired, sits to his left. Ivy Williams, who is fond of sweater vests, sits left of him. Charlie Stubbs and Ronnie Cottrell sit at Callaway's right. At the other end of the table is Will Friend, in a sweatshirt and the pants of a jogging outfit. As with most graduate assistants, who are paid next to nothing, he wears whatever is free.

Monday is the biggest planning day of the week. The plans must be in place before practice Tuesday, when the most physical work of the week begins. The coaches are discussing blocking on the strong side— that is, the side of the tight end, out of the "I" formation. Callaway points out that the fullback will have to come up and block alongside the tight end.

"I don't mind that if it's Dustin," Williams says, referring to senior Dustin McClintock. "The other fullbacks aren't going to make him right. They are going to block their guys only." Translation: Making someone right means helping him carry out his assignment. McClintock, who would take on blocking a Mack truck, can make the tight end right.

"They're not going to let us run off tackle," Callaway says, referring to Auburn. "They're going to pack in just like this." On the screen, Tiger defensive tackle DeMarco McNeil is swallowing up a Georgia tailback. "They wouldn't let us run off tackle last year. This is the same thing."

The coaches meet for forty-five minutes, then break up for to prepare for the 8:00 A.M. staff meeting. Stubbs lingers in the room to make notes. "Today is a look-and-see day," he says. "I look and see what looks good, what doesn't look good. We got way too much stuff. We can't even practice this. . . . Sometimes, in the running game, we just have too much. It all looks good but it's also what you can execute. We fight that."

Each Alabama coach can tell his own nightmarish version of a season that began with a quest for a national championship and ended with a quest for a job. For Stubbs, the forty-five-year-old quarterbacks' coach, the firing may not have been quite as painful. He had already told DuBose he would be leaving the staff. In so many ways, Stubbs never fit in Tuscaloosa.

On the field, Stubbs believes in the spread passing offense as espoused by his mentor, Brigham Young Coach LaVell Edwards. DuBose brought Stubbs to Tuscaloosa from UNLV after the 1997 season to install just such an offense. However, DuBose never quite let Stubbs do what he was hired to do. It's not that Stubbs has been a fish out of water; he's been more like a piece of fish on a meat-and-potatoes menu. DuBose has never been able to divorce himself from the belief that running the ball is paramount. In 1999, after Alabama lost to Louisiana Tech, 29–28, DuBose gave Stubbs the offense and got out of his way. With an adroit use of the spread offense, the Tide ran well, passed well, and won eight of its next nine games. Stubbs emerged as the play-calling hero. In 1999, however, Alabama had tailback Shaun Alexander running behind left tackle Chris Samuels. With those two, Alabama could have run the single-wing and won ten games. This season, with mere mortals at tailback and left tackle, the Alabama running game has never been good. When it looked bad early, DuBose decided to concentrate more time and effort on it. As a result, the passing game got rusty, so the Tide ended up doing neither well. Once DuBose decided to retrench, Stubbs decided he had had enough.

"I've gone to him and told him, 'I'm the wrong guy,'" Stubbs says of DuBose. "I'm more comfortable, not just passing, but with the spread-type attack Auburn is going to do to us. I try to get what he wants, what Neil wants, and get some kind of flow to it on game day."

Stubbs knew when he came to Alabama that it would be a gamble in a number of ways. He is a member of the LDS church in Southern Baptist territory. He is not a member of the Southern coaching fraternity—one that demands of its members a drawl and a swagger. Stubbs is a slight man with wispy hair, a reedy voice, and a certain naivete about the media. He couldn't help but talk about his job when it was good and when it wasn't. In September, after DuBose shelved much of the passing game in response to the UCLA loss, Stubbs privately told DuBose he would resign at the end of the season and publicly continued to complain about the direction of the offense. DuBose responded by banning the assistant coaches from speaking to the media. He later relented and allowed the assistants to speak to the beat reporters on Mondays. Without much prodding, Stubbs began to defend his philosophy again.

The offensive staff meeting in DuBose's office Sunday, Stubbs says, is a perfect example of the dilemma that DuBose has created for his offense. All the emphasis on the running game makes it impossible to effect the precision needed in Stubbs's passing game. "What I try to do after all this is done [on the practice field]," Stubbs says, "is I try to find that extra five minutes to work on what I like. It's hard. We don't practice some of these things that take a whole lot of timing and precision. . . . he wants to have so many different ways of running everything. How do you rep the things enough to execute at a high level? That's the challenge—scripting practice, how to make sure we're scripting what will be called in a game.

"He may give me ten different ways to run one running play. I need to have some kind of ranking. He wants the corner to make tackles. He wants to [gain] four yards or more per carry, which would keep down and distance in our favor. That would make first downs for us and keep our defense off the field. It almost gets overwhelming just how much we have. These kids don't have as much time for football as we do. You have to coach to your weakest link. If one guy messes up, you don't have a football team. You got to do what you have time to do and what you're capable of doing. It gets to be cumbersome. You end up choking out the whole system. I grab ten minutes and go practice. You run out of time.

"It's just his [DuBose's] style," Stubbs continues. "I've learned not to mess it up inside his office, not be unprofessional. I just tell him that all my career has been devoted to a wide-open style of attack. I just want to get back to that. . . . He can decide what he wants. I am more wide-open and aggressive than he is. That's just the way it is. It's not like he is wrong. It's just two different philosophies."

Stubbs gathers his things and heads down to the staff meeting room. The coaches talk quietly until DuBose steps through the short, private hallway from his office. It is defensive coordinator Ellis Johnson's turn to begin the meeting with the devotional, a religious thought for the day. When Ronnie Cottrell came to this staff from Florida State in the winter of 1998, he brought the devotional with him. Seminoles coach Bobby Bowden refers to the daily devotional as his secret weapon. The coaches take turns, based on where they sit, in coming up with the devotional and reading it aloud. Not all base their remarks on Scripture. Jeff Rouzie, for instance, once read some of his favorite wisdom from Coach Bryant.

Religion, however, is not a personal issue on this team. Thanks to DuBose's newfound discovery of his savior, Christianity has an overt presence on the squad. Take, for instance, the "Unity Rally" scheduled for Thursday night at Stillman College, a historically black institution in Tuscaloosa. DuBose planned to speak at it. He invited the coaches and players to attend. He even asked the team video coordinator, Don Rawson, to set up his cameras and tape the testimony given by DuBose and the other speakers. If that's not against university policy, it's inappropriate. Though it is a public university in a religiously conservative state, where one's faith seems to be everyone's business, it's still a public institution. Officials should not be promulgating their beliefs to the people who work for them, much less to the students in their charge.

Yet DuBose is the head coach. Who is to tell him no? He wears his religion on his sleeve as sure as the script Crimson A appears on the breast of the white shirt he wears to practice. The idea that religion is private, or that it should have no prominent role on a publicly funded team at a public university, is not considered.

After Johnson finishes his devotional, DuBose wastes little time and fewer words. His team demonstrated Saturday that it had been defeated mentally. He wanted to make sure that his assistants didn't allow that to happen again. He didn't want their attention to stray toward their own uncertain futures for at least one more week. "If we had a son on this football team, with one week to play, how would we want him coached?" DuBose asked. "Let's go coach him that way. If it was our son or daughter, we'd expect the coach's best effort. They deserve it. The university deserves it and we as coaches deserve it. If we're enthusiastic, then they will respond."

DuBose doesn't ask for comments. No one volunteers any. DuBose moves on. He looks at Bill McDonald, whose title is director of sports medicine. Actually, McDonald also puts out a lot fires for DuBose.

"In the past," DuBose says, "we've added extra security this week."

McDonald confirms that a guard will be on duty from 4:00 P.M. to 8:00 A.M. every night for the rest of the week. He will sit in the hallway where the coaches' offices are, just inside the top of the stairs that lead to the locker room and practice fields. Spies, or, as the Alabama assistants refer to them, "skunks," are an expected risk. No one can remember a specific instance where an Auburn skunk infiltrated Tuscaloosa and stole plans. But Rouzie, who played and coached under Bryant, remembers how Bryant made sure that none of the apartments that had windows overlooking the practice field ever got leased to anyone who might pass along what he saw. Callaway says that after defensive coordinator Bill "Brother" Oliver switched from Alabama to Auburn in 1996, the Tide coaches took greater care during Auburn week because Oliver had so many friends in Tuscaloosa. However, it's difficult to imagine that anyone in Tuscaloosa would be more loyal to a person, especially one who went over to the enemy, than to the university itself.

DuBose gives his staff an example of how a poor record can be overcome against Auburn. "Our second year with Ray," DuBose says, referring to 1984, when he was a young assistant coach on Ray Perkins's staff, "we were 4–6 going into the Auburn game, and we were the worst staff in the country. We won the game and the next day we were the best staff in the country. That's how quickly things change."

DuBose scans the room, then asks questions that are painful to hear and must be devastating to ask. "What have they got the staff doing next week?" he asks. "Have they got you recruiting?"

Cottrell, the recruiting coordinator, shakes his head no.

"You can't go out until December, can you?" DuBose asks, referring to the NCAA recruiting schedule. He is concerned about what will happen to these men whom he had hired. "I can check for you or you can do it individually. You need to check with Mal in the next week or so. Let me know whether you want to go see him individually or you want me to check."

DuBose presses his lips together. He looks down the table as if he is looking for something. He checks over his notes.

"Let's get them ready to play, okay?"

The half-hour meeting concludes. The offensive coaches leave to go down the hall for their meeting. The defensive coaches follow DuBose to his office. Since the topic is the Auburn offense, the focus is on Rudi Johnson—not only how he runs but how offensive coordinator Noel Mazzone uses him.

"Can the safety make the play on the cutback?" DuBose asks.

"I don't see the guy [Rudi] being a cutback runner," defensive coordinator Ellis Johnson says. "I see him breaking tackles. I spent some time on the phone with [Ole Miss defensive coordinator] Art Kaufman. Noel doesn't want to put 44 [fullback Heath Evans] on the field, and he doesn't want to run the ball wide. You used to make Noel throw the ball on every play. Now they're looking inside to run even with seven and eight in the box because of that back."

Ellis Johnson didn't just pluck Kaufman off of his Rolodex; Kaufman is the only assistant coach Tuberville didn't take with him to Auburn when he left Oxford. Kaufman's loyalty to Tuberville evidently stopped at that point. Embodying the old Arab saying that "the enemy of my enemy is my friend," coaches within the league freely share information with whomever their friends may be that week. DuBose mentioned Sunday that he had spoken to Arkansas coach Houston Nutt about Auburn.

"He'll bank on the run somewhere in the game," Johnson says of Mazzone. "Then he [Rudi] gets all his yards in the last fifteen minutes."

Lance Thompson chimes in. "He had 24 yards at halftime against Georgia. He had 55 yards on the first play of the second half. He finished with 106."

Johnson continues, "Art says he would blitz in pass situations early. If you blitz a lot, Noel will try to pick you"—that is, two receivers will line up next to each other and one receiver will "pick," or get in the way of, the defensive back of the other. It is illegal. So is jaywalking in New York. "If they spread," Johnson continues, "they're more vertical [throwing down the field]. Art doesn't think the boy throws the ball real well outside of twelve, fifteen yards."

The last reference is to Auburn quarterback Ben Leard. "In the fourth quarter," Johnson sums up, "thirty-two will take the game over. They're not making the pass plays that they did, but they don't have to. The running back is the difference."

"We've got to stop it and not give up the big throw," DuBose says. "We're going to get somebody to the ball carrier. We're either going to end up tackling him or on our backs. If we try something new, we're going to get lined up wrong."

"If we tackle like we did Saturday," Johnson says, "they'll have 170 yards early and we'll have a tough time winning the game. If we tackle like we did other times, we'll be okay."

"We've got to find some creative ways to find inside pressure," says DuBose, referring to his beleaguered defensive tackles. "When Leard steps up, somebody has to be there."

"I think the kid is very overrated," Johnson says. "He does a good job with his mind. He's very average. He's taken a beating."

"What kind of blocker is Rudi Johnson?" DuBose asks.

"He never blocks," Rouzie says.

"He just stands there," Thompson adds.

"We can make him have to try to block," DuBose says.

"The other one is pretty good," Ellis Johnson says, referring to No. 44, fullback Heath Evans. "Forty-four is a good player but I don't think that's what Noel wants to do." Johnson draws some Xs and Os on the greaseboard and they discuss defensive options. DuBose returns to what his defensive coordinator said a few minutes before. He says, "If we play like we did Saturday, it won't matter what you call."

Johnson agrees. "It's been slipping a little bit, but they've been fighting it. On Saturday, they didn't fight it."

After the ninety-minute meeting, Ellis Johnson tries to describe the difference one running back can mean to an offense. Before Rudi Johnson arrived at Auburn, Ellis says, "You could defend them one-handed. You can't do that anymore. You could make them throw the ball by giving them a certain look. . . . All the good one-back teams, the back is a very physical guy. When they put 44 [Evans] and 32 [Johnson] together, that's a good tandem. They do it when they're backed up. They do it when they want to eat up time." If Alabama can back Auburn up, Ellis Johnson will take his chances.

After the defensive coaches leave, DuBose summons the offensive coaches to his office to watch video of Auburn's run defenses for ninety minutes. They see the Tigers in a four-man line with two linebackers. Rashaud Walker, the rover who wears No. 37, is lined up wider than usual.

"You think the guard can get to 37?" DuBose asks.

"Griff could get to him," Callaway says, referring to senior Griff Redmill. "Dennis [Alexander, the left tackle who's actually closer to Walker] would struggle."

"Dustin could get him," running backs coach Ivy Williams says of his fullback. After ninety minutes on the running game, at 11:40 A.M., DuBose looks at Stubbs. "Tell me what we got in throws," he says.

Stubbs rattles off five different sets of passes.

"I just think it's too much," DuBose says.

"I like it, Coach," Callaway says. "It's just a question of whether we have time to get to it [in practice]."

The meeting breaks shortly after noon. Callaway returns to his office, which, befitting his status as offensive coordinator, is two doors down from DuBose. He explains in detail what Stubbs referred to that morning. The Alabama offense has too much to do in order to do any of it well.

"We'll run our four or five basic plays," he says. "You just don't know how many times to rep it in practice. There's where you got to be careful. Too many plays, by the time you do it with all the different looks [formations]. You got seven different looks and you got to match it up against three different looks on defense. . . . That's where you get into problems. Six plays times seven looks times three defenses is 124. You're only going to call seventy plays and you're going to throw it on thirty of them."

Callaway reaches into his desk as he talks and takes out a white envelope of game tickets. He has more friends during the week of the Auburn game than he does the other fifty-one weeks of the year. "My wife's people are from here," says Callaway. "I get four comps. I'm allowed to buy six. I can buy four more through the A Club [the former football lettermen]. Like anything, it's never enough. It's about telling people, 'No.'" He glances at the tickets on his desk. "I had three calls thus far for those four tickets and I ain't calling them back."

In any week, the Monday 1:00 P.M. press conference is the bread and butter to the beat reporters who cover Alabama football. DuBose, who changed from a sports shirt to a shirt and tie in order to go before the cameras, holds court for twenty minutes or so, then cedes the floor to several players. During Auburn week, the beat reporters are joined by columnists, feature writers, and nearly every television station in the state. The dominant theme among the exactly two dozen questions asked is how to motivate a team that played so heartlessly two days before. It doesn't escape the journalists' attention that asking about motivation during Auburn week is remarkable, in and of itself.

"It does bother you," DuBose says. "It bothers you as a man, as a football coach. I've always believed this: irregardless of the record, irregardless of the situation, irregardless of the circumstances, when you're competing—when you're competing to win—the competitiveness should make you want to do the very best that you can do. And I didn't see that competitiveness in us as coaches and as players last Saturday, and that concerns me."

DuBose goes on to say, however, that if there is any fire left in his team, the Auburn rivalry will stoke it. "Whether we won or we lost, whether as a player or an assistant coach or a head coach, I've never been in [this] game and not, once the game's over, looked at it and said I wish we could get our players to play with that type of intensity in the other ten football games. There is just something special about the game that allows the players just to reach a little bit deeper. There's that something down there that their moms and their dads or their grandmothers or granddads have given them. I would hope this football team and this coaching staff understands that and they can reach a little deeper and know when they walked off that field that they gave everything they had. If they do that, everything will be okay. I can never remember coaching a football team in this game or playing that when we walked off that we didn't feel like we gave everything."

That is exactly the opposite of how the Crimson Tide played at Mississippi State. To a man, the players who come into the interview room understand what is at stake. Many of them, of course, grew up in the state. "I was six years old," says Griff Redmill, a native of Jasper, "before I realized Alabama played anybody else but Auburn." Free safety Tony Dixon grew up in Reform, a dot on the map about a half hour outside of Tuscaloosa, as a Tide fan. "If my father had liked Auburn, I would like Auburn," he says. "I still have some uncles and cousins who are diehard Auburn fans."

Will they cheer for you?

"They'll definitely pull for me," he says, laughing. Someone asks Dixon about his teammates who didn't grow up in the state of Alabama. "When they step on the field, they are going to learn," he says. "When the ball is kicked off, there will be no doubt that this is the biggest game of the season. Players who may not have a good game all year are going to give it their all."

Reserve offensive lineman Alonzo Ephraim describes a Birmingham childhood in which school ties transcended blood ties. Ephraim grew up an Alabama fan. His cousins, who lived across the street from him, cheered for Auburn. "When we were growing up, we'd call each other after every score," Ephraim says. "And they knew who was calling, so they wouldn't answer the phone. My little brother and I would run barefooted across the street, but they wouldn't come to the door. They'd get up and leave probably about three minutes before the end of the game because they knew we were coming over. They wouldn't have to hear us talking."

After the press conference peters out, the team congregates for its 2:30 meeting. It is the first gathering of the players during the week, the players' official start of preparation. The team meeting room is a large rectangular room smack in the middle of the second floor of the football building. It has a screen and computer console at one end of the room, and then a vast number of chairs in almost-neat rows going all the way to the back wall. Out in the hallway, a couple of managers check off the players as they arrive in varying stages of prepractice dress—some in tights, preparing for the chilly weather, some still in T-shirts, shorts, and socks. They wedge themselves into the tight formation of chairs. The assistant coaches take their customary seats in the back row, close to one of the room's two doors.

DuBose begins to speak, pacing a few steps back and forth.

"I've got to ask you some tough questions," he says. "I've got to go over some tough issues. Down to a one-game season. It's a special one-game season. If you understand what the crimson jersey is all about, you understand the significance and specialness of the Alabama–Auburn game.

"I've been very disappointed in what I saw on tape this past Saturday. I've had a number of players come by and talk about how disappointed they were. We talked about what we had to do to win. I know Coach Rouzie did a great job giving you a scouting report and telling you *exactly* what you had to do. Nothing complicated about it. It was to the letter. We had to play the game how?"

A few players respond: "Physical."

"I asked the coaches yesterday: Did we even have five guys who played the game physical? And we knew we had to play the game physical to win. Can you, in your own mind, justify not playing physical?"

He paused and scanned the room, which had become church-quiet. "Can you do that? Can anybody do that? Can you justify, in your own mind, why you would not play the game physical? Coach Rouzie stood up here—guys, he cares about you. Two guys jump on you in the middle of the street out there, Coach Rouzie would be out there. He'll get in a foxhole with you. And he told you honest.

"All of you understood.

"All of you said you would.

"And then you didn't.

"Ask yourself why: Why did you not play physical?" He paused again. "Can you justify it? Can you?" DuBose's voice remains relatively flat. The force of his words is sufficient to carry his sentiment. "When you don't say anything, does that mean no or does that mean yes?" DuBose looks at tight end Shawn Draper, then to center Paul Hogan, one of three team captains. "Can you, Drape? Can you, Paul? I'm only asking them because they're seniors. I know they'll say something.

"We can hang it up. We can go out there the rest of this week. We can roll the ball out there, not put on a pad, not do anything. We can get through this week, get your game over with, and some of you get ready to go next year, some of you go on to the National Football League, some of you just get on with your life.

"Or we can be men.

"We can answer some questions. We can move forward. We can play this one game the way this year should have been played. Should have been coached. Again, I've asked you this question many, many times, because I think it's appropriate: Are you honest people? I didn't say, are you perfect people? I said, are . . . you . . . honest . . . people? Are you?"

The players nod affirmatively, mumble yes.

"So how many want to play the game Saturday the way the game is supposed to be played? Raise your hand."

Everyone raises a hand.

"Okay. How is the game of football supposed to be played?" DuBose is facing them, his hands on his hips. "What's it start with, guys? Most of you know. Most of you know the problem. I've been asked this fifty times by the media. This was the last time I'll do a press conference with them. My office will be cleaned out the end of this week. They keep wanting to know, 'What's the problem?'

"You want to know what the problem is? The problem is, this is not a football *team*. This is a group of guys. This is a group of coaches. And this is a group of players. This is not a football *team*. Ray Perkins, who I was an assistant coach with back in the mid-eighties, said, 'You earn the right to be called a football team.' I didn't understand that. I thought as soon as you come together, you were a team." Here DuBose indulges his anger and dips his voice into a coat of sarcasm. "We can go out there, we can go get a bus, we can ride through the neighborhood [and] put together a group of guys to play the game, can't we? They're not a team.

"Everybody's got individual agendas. Everybody's got their own ideas. Staff, players, all of us. We can come together. As a football team, we can put our differences aside, as coaches and as players, and play a one-game season. If we come together as one, and play and coach as one, we'll win. If we don't, we'll get our butt beat again.

"The first meeting we had, did I not tell you that? Coaches and players, did I not tell you that? That's the key. *Coaches* and *players* coming together as one. With a singleness of purpose. If we do that, if we go out and practice that way, we coach that way and we play that way, guys, I'll guarantee you, you'll win. And if you don't, I'll guarantee you, you won't win.

"It's not complicated. We didn't do it Saturday, although we knew exactly what we had to do. As coaches—it starts with coaches first. Coaches, we've got to come together as one staff. Players, you've got to come together as one group. Collectively, together, we've got to come together as one team. Now, again, if we're willing to do that, you'll do something that's special.

"I was here, going into this game back in 'eighty-four. We were 4–6 going into the Auburn game. And we were the worst team in America. We won the game. And overnight, we were one of the best teams in America. That's what this game is all about. It is special. It is special because it is played between two special schools, between special people.

"Your mothers, your fathers, your grandmothers, your grandfathers, all those people that have sacrificed for you all the years, who have given you something that's deep down inside of you, this is one of those games that if you come together, you'll reach down and you'll draw from it. I have never, as a player or as an assistant coach or as a head coach, come away from this game not thinking, 'Wow! Why couldn't we just play that way all the time?' You can't. You can't play that hard. You can't reach that deep all the time. It is just not humanly possible. There is something significant, here is something special about this game that allows you to reach down there and get that little something extra.

"That's what you have right now. You have that opportunity. But I'm not going to stand up in front of you and b.s. you. If we want to do that, if we want to come together, as coaches, the guys on the back wall, starting with me, and you, willing to come together as one, refusing to find a reason why not to.

"Because you can find a reason why not to. We can grab a knee, we can grab a hamstring, we can grab a shoulder, we can go look for a job. We can go find all kind of distractions.

"Or we can say, 'Hey. I don't care what goes on. We're going to find a way to win, because it's important to the team.'

"What do you want to do?

"You want to win?"

There is a low chorus of, "Yeah, Coach."

"There ain't but one way then. Coaches, you want to win back there?"

"Yes, sir."

"Players, you want to win?"

"Yeah. Yes, sir."

"There ain't but one way. There ain't but one way. That's team. Come together as a team, as one. If you do that, I promise you, you'll win the game. If you don't do that, I promise you, you'll lose the game. It's not complicated. I promise you this: There ain't a group out there, if you'll do it, that deserves something good to happen to them more than you do. Good things don't just happen to you. They don't just happen to you in life. You got to go out and make them happen.

"You add to your advantage with oneness, with singleness of purpose. . . . You need to listen to it one more time. Ecclesiastes 4:9: Two can accomplish more. Two can accomplish more than twice as much as one. The results will be much greater when one falls if the other picks him up. If we come together as a group, as one, when somebody falls, we're gon' pick him up. If we're not together and somebody falls? That's just somebody else on the ground. That's just another hole to be filled. When pieces start to fall, and you don't come together, what happens? Collapse.

"We can come together, we can dedicate ourselves to one cause, and that's winning the football game. Everything we do should reflect that. That's what we said we're gon' do as coaches, starting with me. I've got to do a much better job. I've got to be unselfish. We've got to be unselfish. You've got to be unselfish. You've got to come together. Sixty minutes of oneness.

"Willing to do it?"

Responses come from throughout the room.

"Let's everybody practice."

Don Rawson looks like a golf coach, which is to say, he is built nothing like a football coach. Rawson is the video coordinator. He is in charge of recording every practice and every game, as well as making the tapes the coaches and players use to study during the week. When the football staff meets every morning, Rawson sits away from the conference table, in a back corner of the room. He speaks when spoken to, and takes his turn giving the morning devotional as well. Last week, Rawson realized it will be his turn to give the devotional Thursday morning. He says this and pauses for it to sink in. "The last meeting," he says. The last thing Rawson wants to do is to give the devotional the last time that this staff will be together. He is worried. "I went to Coach and pointed that out and offered to let him do it," Rawson says. "He said, 'No, you go ahead.'" Rawson has a book of spiritual readings, *Day to Day*, on his desk. He has already bookmarked a few passages.

Practice begins at 4:10 P.M. It is bitterly cold. Practice lasts for a shade more than two hours and in that time, it does not get any warmer. When it ends, the players hustle quickly to the locker room. The coaches linger outside. According to DuBose's early-season edict, this is their one time to speak to the media.

Ellis Johnson, forty-eight, wearing a windbreaker and black gloves, is finishing his second tour at Alabama. He coached linebackers from 1990 to 1993, Gene Stallings's first four years as coach, then left to coach for three years at Clemson before returning as DuBose's defensive coordinator in 1997. Like Callaway, he has a husky, smoky drawl that one only hears among men in the Deep South. Johnson is a South Carolina native. He graduated from The Citadel, the I-AA military college in Charleston, and has coached twenty-four of his twenty-six years in the game, either in the Carolinas or in Tuscaloosa. He met his wife, Caroline, during his years at Clemson, where she worked in the athletic ticket office. They have an infant daughter.

Any coach who has been in the business for more than a quarter-century has earned the right to be called a survivor. In 1993, during his first stint in Alabama, Johnson discovered he had Hodgkin's disease. He caught it early and beat it without missing much in the way of coaching. The disease left its mark on him, however. When he starts talking about what the future holds for him, he says, "I don't know what's going to happen. When I came back here, I asked for a two-year rollover contract. I had cancer in 'ninety-three. I didn't want to be stuck without insurance and have something happen." Johnson, Stubbs, and Cottrell, the recruiting coordinator, have two-year rollover contracts, which means they will be on Alabama's payroll through June 2002. The rest of the assistants will be paid only through June 2001. Johnson wanted the security of a two-year deal because of his health, not the possibility that he would be fired. He appreciates it just the same.

"If I am not a head coach or a coordinator somewhere or an assistant head coach," he says, " I may just sit out for a year and see what happens."

The comments DuBose made both in the staff meeting that morning and to the players themselves have resonated within Johnson all day. When he is asked about them, it's clear he has been thinking about his players and the effort they gave at Mississippi State. While he has every right to rip them, he does the exact opposite.

"To be honest," Ellis Johnson says, "I don't know how this could not have been expected. During LSU week, when we were let go, the players didn't know what happened. Last week, it just caved in on them. . . . I was hoping something good would happen early in the game. It was the first time I'd seen it in their eyes, the frustration. They were just kind of expecting something bad to happen. A couple of bad things happened early. They didn't realize, 'Hey, there's forty-eight minutes left to play.' We never regrouped and got our confidence back. They didn't quit but they gave in, if that makes any sense. They just kind of gave in to it. That was the first week we made mistakes that made me realize we were distracted. Saturday, we were not ready to play. Our hearts weren't there. Our minds weren't there. The players have basically had their hearts ripped out the last two weeks."

Now comes a rival that, in emotional terms, makes Mississippi State look like Tuscaloosa Central High School. Johnson knows the depths from which Alabama must begin in order to climb over Auburn. He wouldn't allow himself to think it a hopeless task.

"If I understand it, the story line is not Rudi, or what Auburn is going to run," Johnson says. "The story is if we can regroup and put an effort on the field. Mike made a comment this morning; 'Coach them as if your son is out there.' They deserve it. They don't deserve all the crap that's fallen on them. We need to make sure we spend the next five days on them."

While the assistants speak to the media, DuBose usually drives over to Wings Sports Grille, the restaurant owned by his former teammate and All-American defensive lineman, Bob Baumhower, to join Alabama play-by-play radio announcer Eli Gold for *Hey Coach!*, the weekly statewide radio show. DuBose fields questions from fans around the state. Gold says that the fans, while always respectful of DuBose, asked increasingly tough questions of him as the season went on. "These are knowledgeable football fans," Gold says a few days before the final show. "One of them asked Mike, 'If we're sitting in the stands and we notice that every time Arvin Richard comes into the game, he gets the ball, don't you think the defense has figured that out?' "

On this, his final show, DuBose doesn't drive over to the restaurant. He walks upstairs to his office and takes calls from the sanctity, and the safety, of his chair. He takes a handful of calls, and Gold deftly and quickly switches his attention to men's basketball coach Mark Gottfried.

Paul Hogan and Griff Redmill arrived in Tuscaloosa together. They had started thirty-five games cheek to cheek, Hogan at center and Redmill at left guard. They continue to enjoy the lineman's anonymity.

Once they squeeze into a booth at Chili's, a few miles off campus, none of the other patrons say a word to them, even though Hogan is cocaptain and Redmill is one of the team's most popular players.

Among the many rumors and other sniping comments that go along with being 3–7 has been the issue of race. The two quarterbacks who have competed to lead this team are Tyler Watts, a white sophomore from the Birmingham suburb of Pelham, and Andrew Zow, a black junior from Lake Butler, Florida. The sports talk shows throughout the state have openly discussed whether the offense and the team has been riven by their battle. The issue first appeared in 1999, when the team was successful, so no one paid much attention. Winning, of course, is as effective a racial healer as Dr. Martin Luther King Jr. When you're losing, nobody's happy, which leads you to believe that the 3–7 record, and not the race of the quarterbacks, is the source of the problem. DuBose's comments in the meeting today, when he spoke of the Crimson Tide as being players but not a team, resonate. The players, black and white, say race is not an issue.

"I just think that's something somebody made up," Hogan says. "We're all friends. We all get along good."

Adds Redmill, "When things aren't going good, they look for something. That all started from some radio show last year. This year, you got the quarterback situation again and things aren't going good. They bring it back up."

Zow says the whole issue left him "sort of surprised and disappointed. Even if you're for me in that discussion, I don't need that around me."

Junior wide receiver Freddie Milons, who is black, says there are no racial problems in the locker room. "If it had been the offensive line or receiver, it wouldn't have been that big," Milons says. "The quarterback is the center of the team." The mere discussion of it, however, means people are conscious of it. Once that happens, like the New York Yankees' second baseman Chuck Knoblauch, who battled throwing erratically to first base for several years before moving to left field, it can become difficult to ignore. "Whoever started that, started the thing, that's when people start looking for it," Milons says. "The racial part will always come up. It breaks friendships. Black fans and white fans will always have their favorites. But you end up trying to make sure you're not saying something in the locker room like, 'White boy can't jump.' We're playing around. You try not to have fun. You don't want the wrong ears to hear. You become self-conscious of how you talk to teammates. You entrap yourself."

Milons, like the team as a whole, began the season with dreams of being the best in the country, only to have those dreams fall hard. So much of what doomed Alabama this season could be measured more by what DuBose said to the team today than by any statistics. "I think what coach DuBose said touched some hearts," Milons says. "I felt like that all year. For one game, put all your feelings aside for whoever. There's no doubt. I'll put our guys against anybody in the country. From top to bottom, you can't find better talent. It's so frustrating. You think all you need is talent. You got to have that chemistry. But not only between players, but between players and coaches. We didn't get that and it came back on us."

With five days left in the season, Milons says, it's time for the team to face the task before it. "Reality is setting in. Some guys, Saturday will be their last day ever. Some guys may not be back next year if the new coach doesn't want them. Some guys, it's a big game for the NFL. You don't have a bowl game for people to watch. This is one of the biggest games of the year. A lot of people will be watching us. A lot of us are getting our minds right. You win the game on Monday and Tuesday. You don't win it on Saturday. You put your time in. You want to get your benefits. I put my time in. I talked the whole day. I don't know who's listening. I just make sure everyone knows what's at stake here."

AUBURN

At 7:00 A.M., the phone rings in Ben Leard's room.

"Ben, what are ya' doing?" asks offensive coordinator Noel Mazzone.

"Sleeping."

"Get your butt over here, you're wasting time. You have Alabama this week."

By 7:45, Leard is in the trainer's room getting treatment on a deep thigh bruise. Afterward, he watches about an hour and a half of Alabama's games against South Carolina and Central Florida. Every day he watches about five hours of film on his own.

"You want to see a situation like in their Central Florida game, when Central Florida was driving down at the end of the game. You want to see what they do, put yourself in their shoes, just in case you get into the same situation. Watching film I can see so many situations. Everything that you can imagine is broken down, from formation to motions to blitzes to whatever. It's divided up and put on individual tapes. And that's what I watch throughout the week. I watch game film, situational film.

"It's all just in one big program in the computer. So I'll go and click on 'offense coordinator' and it will pull up stunts, blitzes, motions, formations, no back offenses, situations by distance, or first and ten, second and long, third and sixth, third and long."

• • •

While Leard studies, the coaches congregate. Before the start of the 9:00 A.M. staff meeting, a man in a weathered baseball hat, muddy work boots, and Wranglers ambles into the meeting room.

"Get it over with. Tell us about 'eighty-nine," Tuberville says to the visiting Pat Dye, with an exaggerated sigh.

Dye, a former coach, could talk about 'eighty-nine, the greatest game in Auburn's history, the day undefeated Alabama came to Auburn for the first time and lost. But he is here to talk about the present.

"This game is not going to make or break your season," Dye says as he stands at the head of the table, hands in his back pockets, hips swaying as he leans forward on his toes, then backward on his heels. "You've already had a tremendous season. But let them know Auburn is not afraid to go to Tuscaloosa. They want you to have an inferiority complex because they certainly have a superiority complex. When you go there, you'll drive down Bryant Avenue, pass the Bryant Museum, they'll bring out everything they can to intimidate you. They were picked to win this conference. They got all the talent and ability. But to me, this game comes down to who can face the other team's weakness. If the pressure's on, who will weaken? Preparation is key. Be prepared, mentally and physically. This is a man's game. We don't want no children."

"We got some of them starting for us," Tuberville says, smiling.

"Hell, coach," Dye says. "If they've been playing all year, they should be grown by now."

Dye continues: "If you have any fear in your eyes, the first people to see it is the players. If you're winning, plan how you're going to handle it. If you're losing, it's not the end of the world, either. I've been there both times. I know what it's like. But it is fun to whip their ass. Wait until you whip their ass. You ain't seen nothing yet. It will be a different world."

Dye usually comes by the athletic complex to visit with the coaches at least once a week. On Thursdays, he joins Tuberville and a few other regulars for lunch at Byron's, the best barbecue joint in town. Before the Georgia win, they ate sliced barbecued beef sandwiches and pecan pie. All highly superstitious, they will eat the same meal again this week.

On Saturday, Dye will fly into Tuscaloosa in a helicopter three hours before the game and do a radio show. Then, he will be flown home and be back in his living room an hour before game time. He doesn't like to watch games in those fancy boxes—too many women yapping and babies crying. At home, he can fret in private. "I just feel helpless watching a game," he says in a private moment. "There's nothing I can do about what's goin' on. I'm helpless watching."

From the start, Dye welcomed Tuberville into the Auburn family. "When I took the job it was a Saturday and Coach Dye called me on Sunday morning in the hotel and said, 'Let's have breakfast,' " Tuberville says. "So I go down and he gives me his two cents worth. What he did right and wrong when he was here. So he's been like a father figure to me. Tellin' me how he thinks the head coach should act in certain situations. How he should handle alumni, the media. Over this two-year period, he has given me this crash course. He never suggests plays. He'll give a story about what happened to him in situations that might have happened to us in a game. He was actually more supportive last year when we were 5–6, which we needed him to be last year. He's more a friend of the coaches than anything. He hunts with them, fishes with them."

These days, Dye keeps plenty busy on his six-hundred-acre farm just outside of town. "I work on it every day," Dye says. "I no longer drive a Cadillac. I drive a pickup." Dye also hosts a hunting and fishing radio show and can tell you everything there is to know about either topic. "We've got more water than any state east of the Mississippi. The Mobile River is the fourth largest ecosystem on the North American continent," he says. As for hunting: "You can start in November and kill one buck a day until the end of hunting season, if you wanted to."

Dye is a legend in Auburn, not simply because he won four SEC championships in twelve years—a run which ended in 1992 amid an NCAA investigation. (An assistant coach and booster had made cash payments to a player.) Dye is revered because he brought the Alabama game to campus on December 2, 1989.

"He's the guy who has really put this place together over the last twenty years," Tuberville says. "When he was hired, Coach Bryant said to him, 'Now that you're here, you think you're going to get this game in Auburn.' He said, 'That's right.' Coach Bryant said, 'That'll never happen when I'm here.' Probably the biggest single thing that has happened to this university is getting that game moved to this campus. He could have never won a game, but just getting that game moved to this campus means everything."

Ironically, Bryant gave Dye, who had been an All-American guard at Georgia, his first big break when he hired him as Alabama's linebackers coach in 1965. Dye then went on to build programs at East Carolina and Wyoming before coming to Auburn in 1981.

"The 'eighty-one game was big because Bear Bryant beat us to become the winningest coach in college football. Of course, 'eighty-two was a bigger game to me personally than the 'eighty-one game because it was the first time we won in nine years but there will never be another one like the 'eighty-nine game," Dye says.

Before the forty-one-year break in the series, Auburn and Alabama met in Birmingham, Montgomery, and Tuscaloosa, but never in Auburn. After the series resumed in 1948, every game was played at Birmingham's Legion Field.

In the '70s, Auburn coach Ralph "Shug" Jordan suggested that Auburn might want to play the Alabama game at Auburn one day. Never, Alabama said, arguing that Auburn wasn't big enough to handle the game. For years, games against rivals such as Georgia, Tennessee, and Georgia Tech were played in Montgomery, Mobile, Columbus, and Birmingham, but as Auburn began to grow, these games were moved to campus, thanks in part, to Auburn's engineering graduates, who built highways leading to town.

The late Bill Beckwith watched all of this through his five decades at Auburn, as a student assistant in the publicity office, then as the publicity director, and finally as ticket manager. "As the road engineers in the highway department started building the interstate exchange, Atlanta went from being three and a half hours away to less than two hours. Montgomery used to be two and a half hours. Now it's forty-five minutes," Beckwith explained in 1993. "We were an engineering school. Who runs the highway department? Engineers run the highway department.

Engineers can decide if they want to take the highway this way. We got it run through here. We got 280 four-laned from Birmingham to here. That killed the University of Alabama. They hated it over there. The Alabama legislature ain't going to pass anything that helps us. The success started in the highways area. Winning brings the highways. Every time we got a highway, we'd add more seats. We never sold out before we started adding seats. We could see the future coming."

The future came when Jordan–Hare Stadium—which is named after Cliff Hare, a member of the school's first football team, and Ralph "Shug" Jordan, who won the school's only national championship in 1957—was enlarged to 85,000 in 1987. Contract negotiations to bring the Alabama game to campus ensued. "It won't happen," Alabama coach Ray Perkins said at the time. Though Alabama threatened to drop Auburn from its schedule when the proposal was made, a compromise was finally reached.

In the December 2, 1989, game program, David Housel, the sports information director at the time, wrote: "As long as our cross-state rivals could dictate where we play our home games, the rival held the upper hand, the high ground. There was no equality. Today, for the first time, there is equality."

Heading into the game, Alabama was undefeated and ranked No. 2 in the country. Auburn was No. 11. "Your ass on your grass," became the mantra of Alabama fans.

The day began with the Tiger Walk, a tradition dating back to the 1960s. Two hours before the game, players walk from Sewell Hall, where most of the underclassmen live, to the football stadium. On this day, more than 20,000 fans lined Donahue Drive, the largest crowd anyone can remember. "Well, you know I never liked the Tiger Walk," Dye says. "It was something that was a tradition before I got to Auburn, and the kids liked it and we just did it. You know, I didn't want to come in and take away all of the things that they have been doing. Parading down the street in front of a bunch of fans before a football game is not my idea of preparation. But I will honestly say the only Tiger Walk that I would not want to trade for anything was the one in 'eighty-nine. When we left the dorm, it is not but a two-hundred- to three-hundred-yard walk, it was single file. From the time we left the dorm until the time we got to the stadium—I mean, it was students, young folks, grandmas and grandpas, mamas and daddies, former players, former coaches—and the look in their eyes was like, 'Free at last.' "

Athletic director David Housel gets emotional when he speaks about the day, too. "I'll remember it for as long as I live, the blue haze of 75,000 shakers, orange-and-blue paper shakers. When the team came on that field, you could see a blue haze over the whole stadium. I believe in the spiritual world. You have a veil between the spiritual world and this world. I think, for whatever reason, the veil was slightly lifted. Because Auburn people had longed, and dreamed, and pushed, and fought so hard for that day. Something happened that was bigger than those guys on the field. It was bigger than any of us that were here because Auburn people were making a trip they never thought they would make. Alabama came here. You can enter the promised land only one time for the first time."

The game itself made Auburn's moment of history that much more poetic. The little guy won, 30–20.

Watching from the press box that day was a young Miami assistant named Tommy Tuberville, who was scouting Alabama, Miami's next opponent in the Sugar Bowl. "One of the reasons I took this job at Auburn was because of that game," Tuberville says. "Because this is a football state. This state is football 365 days a year, whether there is a golf tournament going on or whether there is basketball going on, or a NASCAR race, football is always mentioned, and it is normally about the Auburn–Alabama game."

Monday morning is still young. As Dye leaves the staff meeting, his words linger: "To hear him speak, he still sends chill bumps up me," says outside linebackers coach Philip Lolley, a former high school coach who attended Dye's practices over the years.

"I don't know how to follow that," an academic adviser says as Dye shuts the door behind him.

The first order of business is a report from the academic adviser who reads a list of all the players who have exams and papers due this week. Star running back Rudi Johnson, who has a paper due on Friday, is a particular concern.

"We've got a bunch of guys with tests today which is kinda bad for us," the adviser says. "A lot of professors are trying to give assignments this week before the break. They will get hit hard this week. I'm gonna talk to Rudi today and do a preemptive strike on that teacher. Let that teacher know what's happening. What they are doing. One thing teachers don't like is a surprise. They don't want to find out on Friday that Rudi doesn't have it done. I'll talk to them today about that."

"Get them up here at five in the morning," Tuberville says. "We'll make them write."

"I don't want it hanging around them Thursday night," the adviser says. "They'll be worn out Friday. The professors don't know who we're playing this weekend."

"They don't care," Tuberville says. "Just let us know tomorrow morning how much of the paper he got done."

After the academic report, the trainer gives an injury update. Linebacker Alex Lincoln suffered a concussion and injured both shoulders against Georgia. "He had a little headache this morning," the trainer says. "The game plan is to not have any contact all week. His right shoulder is pretty sore, his left has improved." Rudi's ankle injury is being monitored closely, as well.

"Hammer them tomorrow," Tuberville tells the trainer. "Get them better. The game is in your hands."

Tuberville then talks about the team's bowl possibilities, mentioning the Citrus, the Peach, and the Outback. He reminds his assistants to send out letters to their recruits congratulating them on their state playoff games. He reviews the travel list and the coaches decide what walk-ons should make the trip and then reads the early weather report for game day. "The high fifties," he says.

Finally, he announces the news of the day which should hit the papers tomorrow. "I got us a new contract, 1.25 million dollars for five years," he says. "They can't afford to fire me now. You'll all get raises. Christmas comes early this year."

At 1:00 P.M., several coaches and players drive to nearby Wrights Mill Road Elementary School for a "Beat Alabama" pep rally. Two of the coaches' wives and linebacker Rob Pate's wife teach at the school, and several of the coaches' children, including Tuberville's son Tucker, are students. Even former coach Terry Bowden, who remained in town, has kids in school.

At the school's entrance, a sign reads: CANNED FOOD DRIVE ENDS TODAY. BEAT BAMA! The schools are sponsoring competing food drives, which goes to show that even cans of creamed corn aren't immune from this rivalry.

Outside the school's entrance, the children sit on the pavement with their legs crossed, as the cheerleaders and the tiger mascot, Aubie, lead a few rounds of "Waaaar Eagle!" the school's battle cry.

Boys are wearing orange Auburn jerseys and a few girls have cheerleader uniforms on. When the players gather in front of the group, the kids chant, "Rudi! Rudi! Rudi!" But alas, Rudi is not here. He is back on campus working on his paper, at least his coaches hope so. The kids aren't sure which black player in the group is Rudi, since they chant "Rudi" for each one.

When Rob Pate, who is very white, turns to introduce himself, he leans into the microphone and says, "Hi, I'm No. 32, Rudi Johnson."

The kids sit in stunned silence as everyone else laughs.

"No, No. My name is Rob Pate, No. 31. I want to say a special hello to Miss Pate's third grade class."

When running back coach Eddie Gran tells the kids that Rudi sprained his ankle, there is a collective groan, "Ooooh."

"But he'll be okay," Gran adds.

Tuberville takes center stage, as his son Tucker watches and Tuberville's mother, Olive, snaps pictures of her son and grandson.

"There's six days left until we play the elephants on the other side of the state!" Tuberville says. "The first thing we're gonna do when we wake up for breakfast that day is eat some elephant sausage, then ten thousand of our fans and Aubie are going to Tuscaloosa. Then the whuppin' will commence on those Crimson Tide Elephants!"

Back in their offices after lunch, the coaches settle in for their longest day of the week. There is no practice today, leaving all day and night for the coaches to put together the game plan.

Monday through Wednesday, the day begins at 5:30 A.M. and doesn't end until 10:00 P.M. This morning, defensive coordinator John Lovett drew up Bama's pass plays and tracked the Tide's tendencies on down and distance. Lovett knows that the Tide will come out with two backs, run the football, then spread the field with four wide receiver sets and throw screens and quick passes.

Offensive coordinator Noel Mazzone watches several complete games to get a feel of how Bama calls their defense during the course of the game. Then he starts looking at down and distances and breaking down the film, all with the aid of the computer.

"We get every game that they played for the whole year," Mazzone says, as he points and clicks. "We have ten games on it. We can go back and get last year's, too. Usually, I'll get four or five games they played in which the offense is similar to ours, like Southern Miss, LSU, UCLA, Central Florida. Then the GA's will break that down in terms of downs, distance and formation, play, field zones. They'll put it into this program. And then the program will break it out. You look at John Lovett's and he's got twice as many as me, because defensive guys are more paranoid than offensive guys. Defensive guys always think that someone is always out to get them.

"If I want to watch all the third-and-six and watch to see what they are doing on that, I know there's twenty-five plays in those games and they are all right there. I look to see what they are doing and then say here are the plays I want to run this against this. It's not brain surgery.

"When I started coaching, everything was on sixteen millimeter. What you had to do is come in, break down the film, as you watched through you'd write down what it was. You'd have to write it on a little piece of tape, rip the film right there, put the tape on it, and put the film on the wall. Those twenty-five plays would be hanging on the wall like third-and-six. Then the GA's or me would splice the tape together all on one reel. And they'd sit there and watch the one reel. You'd be here all night. You wouldn't go home. So, this makes it a lot easier.

"That said, it's just as long a night. It's a little more convenient. It helps you a little bit. But it still comes down to blocking and tackling. That has never changed. You have to block and tackle. You have to throw and catch. Calling plays—every once in a while you get lucky and you call a good call. If your kids execute what you call. It's not like you design plays that don't work. You put in plays and say, 'Hey, it should work against every one of these defenses.' "

In addition to the computer program, each week, 450 tapes are circulated among the coaches and players. There are about 170 different tapes, about 80 offensive and defensive cut-ups combined, thanks to the computer technology. Prior to 'ninety-four, before digital film, coaches received 4 cut-ups for the offense and 5 for the defense.

This week, security is tighter than usual. The tapes are all numbered, collected when the coaches are done, and then erased. When the players are finished studying the game's scouting report, the reports are handed back in. Pro scouts are barred this week, but are welcomed every other week of the season.

One time, during Alabama week in the early 'nineties, a plane circled over practice three times, raising suspicion. An assistant coach told the video guys to stop filming practice and zoom in on the plane's call letter instead. It turned out to be a student from Auburn's aviation management program out on a joy ride.

During Alabama week under Terry Bowden a few years later, a student climbed a tower across the street at the school's television station, to check on a line. When he pulled out a disposable camera and took a picture of practice, the coaching staff took action. When the student climbed down the tower, several GA's and team managers were waiting for him. "Who are you? Let us see your ID," they asked. The guy turned out to be just a big fan.

"Alabama week, everyone's ears perk up. Their eyesight gets a little sharper. They look just a little more paranoid, watching out, what's being said and who's saying what, and reading the papers," team videographer Brian Williams says. "Yeah, we definitely kind of lock down."

By 8:00 P.M., the defensive meeting room is buzzing. The words "Swarm" and "Turnovers" hang on one wall. Defensive coordinator John Lovett stands next to the dry erase board with a blue marker in hand. A tin of Copenhagen and a few cell phones rest on the table.

Defensive ends coach Terry Price is twirling a coffee stirrer in his mouth. He smoothes down his unruly hair. Since he stopped getting his haircut, the Tigers have won every game, which means he can't jinx things now. Throughout the night, GA's scurry about like squirrels and report what's on the Internet. The announcement of Tuberville's new contract is the lead item. Through most of this activity, Lovett stares at the board.

He scratches some X's and O's on the board. He stares at the formation for several minutes as if it is some complex math problem. "If they do this, we should have an answer with this," he says and then scribbles some more. It is the ultimate game of cat-and-mouse.

Administrative assistant Andy Lutz stops by and helps himself to a wad of chew.

"I don't know how you guys do it," Price says pointing at the Copenhagen tin.

"You should try it," Lutz says.

"I did," Price says. "I got sick for six days and threw up in three languages."

Tuesday

Legendary head coaches:
Auburn's Ralph "Shug" Jordan and
Alabama's Paul "Bear" Bryant

Ken Stabler's touchdown run, 1967

"PUNT, BAMA, PUNT!"
Auburn returned two blocked punts for
touchdowns to upset Alabama in 1972.

One of Alabama's most memorable plays:
Van Tiffin's 52-yard field goal against Auburn in 1985
as time ran out.

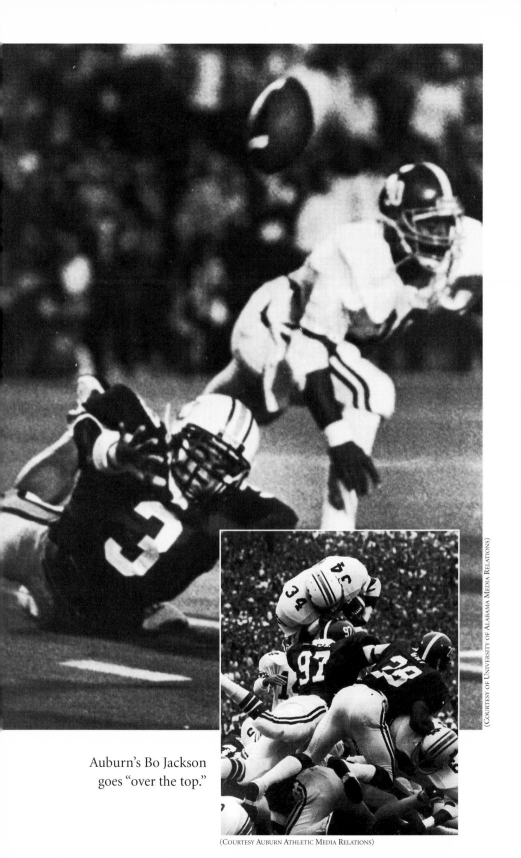

Auburn's Bo Jackson
goes "over the top."

Mike DuBose led Alabama through a
disappointing 2000 season.

Tommy Tuberville, Auburn's head coach

Ben Leard and Cole Cubelic

Paul Hogan

Rudi Johnson

Andrew Zow

(Courtesy Auburn Athletic Media Relations)

Alex Lincoln

Griff Redmill

DeMarco McNeil

Shaun Alexander

Toomer's Corner

ALABAMA

The 7:00 A.M. meeting is in full swing. The coaches are viewing Monday evening's practice, looking at 7-on-7 passing drills known as "skels." On the television program *NYPD Blue*, skels are bad guys. From the comments made about Monday's practice, so are these players, although in this case skels is short for skeleton drills. Coffee cups are on the table but no food, although Callaway grumbles teasingly about not being brought breakfast. Friend, the graduate assistant, has already popped the top on a cold Dr. Pepper. They meet for an hour, then break up.

"Tomorrow is my birthday," Callaway says.

"Mine is Monday," Swinney replies.

"Saturday is my sister's," Friend chimes in.

With a perfect deadpan, Callaway says, "I don't care about Dabo's or your sister's."

Swinney ignores the jibe. "My birthday wish is the same every year," he says. "Beat Auburn."

Down the hall, where graduate assistants Mike Bloomgren and Kevin Sherrer share a small office, they talk about the week ahead. Bloomgren, a Florida State graduate, says, "I was part of the Florida State–Florida rivalry for three years. I thought that was as good as it gets. I was wrong." His colleague, Sherrer, wistfully says, "I can't imagine what the town would be like Saturday if we were what we should be. We ought to be 8–2."

The staffers congregate in the staff meeting room. As they await DuBose, the coaches are discussing a morbid feature on ESPN the night before. "Thirty years ago was the Marshall plane crash," director of football operations Scott Skene says.

Rawson, the video guy, shudders. "Y'all don't need to be talking about that stuff."

"Wichita State," Ivy Williams says, bringing up another school whose team suffered a plane crash. "I coached with a guy named Ted Coleman. He was on the plane at Wichita State and survived the crash."

"I'm not scared to fly," Ronnie Cottrell says. "I'm scared of crashing. What I want to know is, they ought to make these airplanes out of the stuff they make that black box out of."

Rawson is visibly uncomfortable. "Definitely not a good attitude around here. Everybody talking about death and disaster."

DuBose arrives in the room and asks Rodney Brown, the trainer, about injuries. The bad news: defensive end Kenny King's shoulder rebelled again in practice Monday. The defensive line could use a healthy King, who made fifty tackles as a freshman in 1999. The six-four, 270-pound King came from Daphne, Alabama, near Mobile, as a can't-miss prospect. Unlike the freshmen defensive linemen this season, King didn't miss. Not only did he play extensively as a freshman, he won Lifter of the Year among the football players in the weight room. The coaching staff awarded him the No. 55 jersey worn by the late Derrick Thomas, the Alabama All-American who died in February 2000, following his paralysis in an automobile accident. King won the number because he "exemplifies the qualities that propelled Thomas to an All-American career at the Capstone."

This season, with his shoulder weakening day by day, King has survived on guts. It is clear that he hasn't been the same player physically. Brown says King is out for the season and surgery is in King's future. Without him, tackle Jarrett Johnson will have to move to end. Going inside will be either junior Aries Monroe, who's really a linebacker, or freshman Albert Means. Heralded as one of the best high school players in the nation the year before, the Memphis native was listed in the media guide as six-six, 310. He reported to preseason workouts in August weighing 377. The NCAA limits what demands may be made on a signee before he arrives on campus. Since the coaches couldn't teach the freshmen over the summer, they sent Means and his classmates detailed workouts and diets to follow so that they would arrive on campus ready to go. According to defensive line coach Lance Thompson, Means read that he should eat chicken every night and he did—his mama's fried chicken.

With so much weight, Means sprained an ankle in August practice and has been, like the rest of the team, a disappointment. "Lance," DuBose asks Thompson, "how did Albert do?"

"He didn't push good," Thompson says. "He wasn't moving his feet real well. I thought David [Daniels] and Kelvis [White] did play well." Later in the morning, when the defensive staff is in DuBose's office, they freeze the video of Monday's practice on Means in his stance with his left leg stuck at an angle instead of beneath his bulk. It's a high school habit.

"What can we do about it?" DuBose asks.

"For that kid to move the way you want him to," Thompson says, "they're going to have to break his leg and reset it, Coach."

DuBose asks the other position coaches about a player here, a player there, then gets to his point.

"I want to know who it is important to and who it is not," he says. "If it is not important to them, they will not step on that field. I will play with one guy. It has to be important to them. I think it's extremely important that we have more enthusiasm than we did yesterday. If we get excited, they will feed off that. That's not easy to do. But it is important to do."

After the meeting, the offensive coaches follow DuBose into his office to look again at the Auburn defense. What the head coach sees excites him. He is convinced that Alabama will be able to find running room for its tailbacks. "They don't have enough people [up front]," DuBose says. "They're not sound in what they do." He repeats that last sentence as if to appeal to the football gods. If the defense isn't sound, then the offense must succeed, right? Never mind that Alabama just got through rushing for 31 yards on 28 carries at Mississippi State. "If we get the ball deep enough to the back and he gets vision, they can't stop [him]."

A year ago, Alabama had a running game and Auburn didn't. The roles have reversed. For the Alabama defense, it will be no small task to tackle Rudi Johnson. Crimson Tide defensive line coach Lance Thompson liked it better a year ago, when Auburn didn't have Johnson and Alabama had Cornelius Griffin and Reggie Grimes at defensive tackle. Both of them are in the NFL.

"Rudi is going to get four or five [yards] when you put a body on him," Thompson says. "When you have a gap or your tackler don't get off a guy, once Rudi's in the secondary, he's dangerous. You got to make sure you have two guys in the same gap. Last year, if you gave them a certain number of guys in the box, they would change their play. This year, that ain't the case. He'll still get yards for them. He adds so much to their team. Auburn isn't a perfect team. A player like that gives you a chance to build leaders and play hard. His style of play has permeated that team. You don't have a back in this league gain nine 100-yard games and not be good. Noel's done a good job of calling his number and shortening the game. Football is the ultimate team game. When your offense is on the field, you got a good defense. In the seventies, the Alabama defense was never on the field. Look at a defense that has good numbers. You never have a good defense with a bad offense." It's a typical Thompson conversation. He flows freely from one subject to another, taking a microscopic pause for breath. Thompson, thirty-five, is a big, strutting man who wears his ambition openly.

"In ten, fifteen years, I do want to come back and run this place," he says. "If you run this place right, if you run this place like Bobby Ross, like George O'Leary, you can build a dynasty." Thompson spent eleven seasons at Georgia Tech, nearly all of them working for Ross and O'Leary. Like O'Leary, Thompson says what's on his mind. He likes people. He combines machismo with a common touch and a salesman's appreciation for a good line. In other words, he is a good recruiter and a good motivator. How good a recruiter? Thompson, who grew up near Atlanta, played at The Citadel in the mid-1980s. Back then, The Citadel was an all-male military school. One summer, Thompson got a job in Charleston and arranged to live in a house otherwise occupied by women.

On the defensive line, where emotion plays a bigger role than it does with the technicians of the offensive line, Thompson is a good coach. Even a good coach can only do so much. Vince Lombardi couldn't have turned Thompson's defensive line around. No one, Thompson says, really understood how much the Tide lost on the defensive line from last season's team. "Reggie, Cornelius, Jamie [Carter] and Canary [Knight] were four big-time players. In this league, you got to stop the run. Good teams are physical. I got a saying: You don't see donkeys win the Kentucky Derby. It takes players to win." When fall camp began, Thompson had to replace Griffin and Grimes, seniors who were good leaders. Three months later, two starters he expected to have—sophomores Kindal Moorehead and Kenny King—were injured and unavailable. Five days before the game against Alabama's biggest rival, Thompson is a lame-duck coach plugging linebackers, freshmen, and anyone else he can find into the breach. Senior Kelvis White, who started the first two games of this season, then returned to his customary seat on the bench, is likely to start against Auburn. "Kelvis and Todd [Whitmore] are good kids. They are not SEC players," Thompson says. White, the son of a high school coach, has already been offered a job as an assistant coach at Greensboro High, near his hometown of Courtland, Alabama. He knows what to do, but bad knees have limited his ability throughout his career. That's who Thompson has: linebackers, freshmen, and cripples.

What's worse, he has no leaders. The leadership vacuum on this team is most noticeable on defense. Senior end Kenny Smith is a solid player and the defensive captain. Though his teammates elected him, Smith is ill-suited for the job. For one thing, he injured his knee late in the 1999 season, and only at the end of this season did he begin to approach his previous standard of play. For another, Smith is a quiet guy. No one follows him. The coaches, speaking outside of earshot of one another, say almost exactly the same thing. "Our attitude was good today. I don't know how tough we are," defensive coordinator Ellis Johnson said after practice Monday. "I don't know how much leadership we have. I don't know how physically mature we are. We just don't have a lot of guys who have been out there in a war in a position of leadership." On Tuesday, Thompson adds, "We got to have some leadership emerging from within the team. I don't know if we ever had that. Good teams are no different than good businesses. They got guys who make those around them better. This year, I don't know if we've got one, if you're honest with yourself."

Leadership might have prevented this team from getting caught up in the preseason talk of a national championship. Once Alabama lost the opener to UCLA, Thompson says, a leader would have refocused the team. "The expectations were really high," he says. "Don't tell anybody you're going to do something. Show them. Bryant and [Georgia coach Vince] Dooley did it that way. So did Coach [Lou] Holtz. Don't kid yourself."

"This is a very special place," Thompson says. Look at the number of national championships Alabama has won in the past thirty-five years—my life." Alabama won national championships in 1965, 1973, 1978, 1979, and 1992. "Then I looked at Georgia Tech. I said, 'I just got to try this.'"

Thompson accepted DuBose's offer to come to Alabama for the 1999 season. What Thompson thought was a step up the coaching ladder turned into an emotional maelstrom. First, DuBose's near-firing in 1999 over his involvement with his secretary. From there, the rise to the top of the SEC. And now, this. "I don't know if frustrating is the word," he says. "Disillusioning. When all the stuff last year happened, I thought, 'What in the heck have I done?'

"Something like this season should have never happened. There's no excuse for it. A lot of times, when something like this happens, people want to point fingers. Everybody here had a hand in it. Coach DuBose is such a good guy. I came over here and watched him in 'ninety-one. He's a damn good defensive line coach. As a head coach, he lets you coach. He lets you play. I told him Saturday, 'I just appreciate the opportunity you have given me.' He said, 'Hey, you've done a good job. Something good will come of this.' Hopefully, it will all work out. I'm hoping I get a chance to stay here."

When Thompson walks into his 2:30 P.M. position meeting, he finds most of the defensive linemen waiting for him. He sneers at White, a senior. Thompson isn't mad at him but it's a way to break the ice and get the meeting going.

"What did I do?" White asks in self-defense.

"You didn't do much of anything," Thompson says.

The freshmen on the defensive line have been a particular source of disappointment. For that, DuBose has only himself to blame. The players have played, well, like freshmen. More was expected. In the weeks leading up to signing day in February 2000, the talk of recruiting gurus across the country was that Alabama had signed a class of defensive linemen unprecedented in talent. DuBose did nothing to discourage the talk. He embraced it just as he embraced the national championship talk at the SEC Media Days press conference in July. In September, DuBose acknowledged he had made a mistake in handling the recruiting talk. He said he let it go wild in order to stroke the ego of Ronnie Cottrell, his assistant head coach and recruiting coordinator.

"The mistake we made is making recruiting the 14th game [of the 1999 season]," defensive coordinator Ellis Johnson says. "What we signed and what showed up here on the grass were two different things. I think that hurt Mike. There is some good talent here but it's not what people think. We don't have anyone in the secondary who will play on Sunday except maybe Tony Dixon. We don't have a linebacker who will play on Sunday. [Albert] Means was overrated. He's an average player."

The best players among the freshmen group of defensive linemen, Anthony Bryant of Newbern, Alabama, and Mac Tyler of Bessemer, Alabama, didn't qualify academically to play as freshmen. Means has started twice. Antwan Odom, the six-six, 255-pound freshman who struggles in the weight room, started once. Nautyn McKay-Loescher, the Canadian, is a talented athlete who has to learn to play against competition of a higher caliber than he had ever seen.

"I think it's very unrealistic to count on a true freshman to carry your team in the SEC," Thompson says. "Good teams have juniors and seniors. Bobby Ross used to tell us you're only as good as your senior class. Last year we had a damn good senior class. Four damn good football players. You're only as good as your senior class. You got to have a little luck. Marvin Constant [injured in November 1999 and still not the same] was our most physical player at linebacker and we've missed him there.

"Look at what we've done with what we've had. They need to be redshirted on the scout field. Look at the top ten programs in the country.

How many freshmen have they got on the defensive line? I looked at Oklahoma, Miami, Florida State, Florida. George O'Leary always said, 'It's easy for freshmen to play the further away from the ball they are.' That's where your athletic ability takes over. Up front, if you're not a fighter or a scrapper, you're in trouble." Fighting and scrapping in college football can be tough for a freshman. A lot of baby fat can disappear between the time a player arrives on campus and his twenty-first birthday.

"Confidence is a big thing," Thompson says. "Confidence comes from experience. It's hard for youth to have confidence. The hardest thing is getting them to understand the speed of the game and the calls. If you don't like contact, the brutal nature of the sport, you can't play. You've got to enjoy the contact. You've got to like to hit people."

Thompson has one other issue with his defensive linemen: they are not very bright. Here again, offensive linemen, the technicians on the field, must be smart to handle the complicated blocking schemes. Defensive linemen deal in emotion and strength and reflexes. There's the ball. Go get it. Thompson doesn't speak vindictively or with any ill will. He accepts that his players are who they are. He just says, in any number of ways, some more inventive than others, that his players' sidewalks don't reach the curb. "When I was a kid, I'd read things about Vince Lombardi, about John Madden, that inspired me," Thompson says. "I don't think they read anymore. They listen to Tupac. They play video games. Nobody ever made them think before. I ask them, 'What are you supposed to do?' They tell me. I say, 'Why aren't you doing it?' I make them tell me. I'm not looking to place blame. All I want to do is get it right. If they can't tell you what they're supposed to do, that's your fault. You can do too much. In our staff room, there's almost one hundred years of coaching experience, teaching kids who been playing six years. They're not very intelligent and they don't sit over here all day studying it. The worst thing you can do is do more than they can do."

If Thompson is right, and the Alabama defenders can't handle a sophisticated defensive scheme, then the Auburn offense is a good match. "Auburn tells you what they are going to do," Thompson tells his linemen. "By the formation, by the splits [the space between the offensive linemen]. You guys are smart. I don't believe your SAT scores." As they giggle, he pretends to scold them. "Don't be laughing."

Aries Monroe strides in. Monroe, a junior-college player recruited as a linebacker, has been moved up to the defensive line, in part because he struggled with the mental responsibilities at linebacker. "Twenty-two may be as academically challenged a player as there is in America," Thompson says, citing Monroe's uniform number. "You can tell him something ten times and ask him the same question ten minutes later and he'll say, 'Huh?' At Alabama, you ought to be able to find players with athletic talent who are smart."

Still, Thompson likes him. Monroe has never met a haircut too outlandish. Today the sides of Monroe's head are shaved and his hair is high atop his head, like a pillbox hat that Jackie Kennedy rejected. "Your homosexual lover do that for you?" Thompson asks. "I'm going to get mine done like that." To the rest of the team, Thompson says, "He looks like Aunt Bea."

Kenny King, the end who hurt his shoulder for good the previous day, walks into the meeting in street clothes. Thompson tells him, "Go to the doctor in Atlanta and get it taken care of. Life is more important than football."

Thompson locks in on Means, on the end of a row of players sitting along the wall. "Albert Means, Parade All-American," he says. "You know what we call him? 'Moonpie.'" The other linemen smile. "During the Tennessee game, some guy in the front row throws a Moonpie at him. He ate it at halftime. Two years from now, when we go back to Tennessee, I'm going to buy you a whole box of Moonpies."

Means isn't laughing. He's glaring. Thompson turns to the entire group.

"Grasp the situation," he begins. "Tough situation, all right? We got a lot of young guys. This game is the first game of next season. I may be here. I may not be here. We didn't have much good preparation as a group yesterday. We had some individuals who had good preparation." He begins to challenge them, echoing DuBose the previous day, although Thompson cloaks the challenge in a veil of reason. "Who is this game important to?" Thompson asks. "Guys, there is nothing at all wrong if it ain't important to you. You just got to let me know, because I ain't going to play you.

"You've got to play physical. Can you play physical Saturday without playing physical Tuesday, Wednesday, Thursday? Can you?"

Video of the Monday's practice rolls. Thompson turns his laser pointer toward White's body on screen. "Kelvis, I still want your ass up in the air. I want your weight forward."

They watch the scout team offense run its tailback off tackle toward White. "If this is Rudi," Thompson says, "and he's coming from seven yards back, we will not make that tackle. He will break that right over tackle. Kelvis, you got a job. I want you to jack him up." Out of a one-back set, Thompson says, "They went in the B gap thirty-six times. They went in the A gap thirty-three times. They do a good job of balancing the one-back set. Nose guard," and he means White, "that's important. I want you attacking the inside part of that guard. He can never block you. You ought to make tackles four or five yards behind the line."

Thompson turns his attention to Odom, the freshman defensive end. Auburn offensive video appears on the screen. "Antwan Odom," Thompson booms, "this guy"—the laser pointer lands on Auburn right tackle Colin Sears—"is the best blocker they got. The tight end (six-six, 254-pound freshman Robert Johnson) looks like Zeus. He plays like Athena." Funny line. None of the players laugh. They don't know Zeus and Athena from George W. and Laura Bush. After the meeting, Thompson says, "I do it to keep myself entertained."

He continues to give a quick scouting report on the Auburn offensive line. "The center [sophomore Ben Nowland] and the left guard [junior Hart McGarry] are the two weak legs," Thompson says. "Eighty-seven [Robert Johnson, again] is a good-looking guy. He doesn't like to get hit in the mouth. Forty-nine [starting tight end Lorenzo Diamond] is a physical guy. If he gets a chance to rock you, he will."

The video begins to show Leard dropping back. "Guys," Thompson says, "we're going to start pressuring these guys. When you start pressuring, they don't handle it well. They don't handle it." The video zeroes in on Leard being blitzed. "He's got to pay attention to the hot," Thompson says. A "hot" is the receiver a quarterback is trained to look for when he sees a blitz. "They help us because they play a nonathlete at quarterback."

After the meeting, Thompson is talking to running backs Ivy Williams in the hallway when a meeting guest walks by. "See why I get special ed pay?" Thompson says.

Williams looks at the guest with incredulity and bellows, "You were in there? Special ed? I wouldn't last twenty minutes with those guys."

After another practice in bone-chilling weather, DuBose praises the players for concentrating on the task at hand. Thompson hustled off the field and went home to steal a couple of hours with his wife, Stacy, and their three daughters before he returned to his office to call recruits. He ate dinner, read stories to his two oldest girls, and kissed their seven-week-old. Stacy went into labor early on the morning of September 30, which fortunately happened to be the day of Alabama's home opener against South Carolina. Thompson went to the hospital with DuBose's blessing. Shortly before the game, doctors told him the baby wouldn't be born for a while. He decided to go to the stadium. Ronnie Cottrell's wife, Jean, stayed with Stacy.

Early in the third quarter, Jean called the press box. Graduate assistant Mike Bloomgren answered the phone. "It's a girl and everyone's fine," Jean told him. Bloomgren looked over at Thompson and repeated the message.

"He didn't react," Bloomgren says. "He just said, 'Okay,' and went back to what he was doing."

Thompson admits now, he wonders if he should have stayed with Stacy. Coach Bryant used to say, "The price of victory is high—but so are the rewards." That was another generation. Thompson, an honors graduate in mathematics and education at The Citadel, is bothered by the numbers. There are eleven games every season. He and Stacy have only three children and he missed the birth of one of them. The price of victory is high, indeed.

AUBURN

Soon after the three quarterbacks arrive in the offensive meeting room at 6:00 A.M., Ben Leard is already getting razzed by reserve Daniel Cobb. "He was at Chili's last night talking about his wedding plans, not studying," Cobb says about Leard, who recently got engaged. Backup QB Jeff Klein is chatty, even though he spent much of the night studying for a linguistics and a Latin exam. But conversation ends when offensive coordinator Noel Mazzone puts three biscuit and egg sandwiches on the table. Breakfast is spent studying Alabama's game against LSU.

Next up is UCLA, the Tide's first opponent of the season, a time when Alabama's grand hopes for a national championship were still alive.

"This is a different team from the one now," Leard says.

"Right there, they were No. 3 in the country until they screwed up their quarterbacks," Mazzone says. Mazzone then goes over the defenses the Tigers will see to stop Rudi. "They'll put seven in the box," he says, motioning to the big screen with his red laser pointer.

Today the players are given their scouting reports, a fifteen-page primer on Alabama. For the offense, the scouting report lists Alabama's defensive statistics—how many yards they've given up, how many first downs they've given up, how much passing yardage, how many sacks, who's the leading tackler, plus the depth chart, and the base defenses the Tigers will see against their base formations and base blitzes. It highlights Alabama's standout defensive players, defensive end Kenny Smith and linebacker Saleem Rasheed.

After the 6:00 A.M. position meetings, the team gathers later for media day, which is held in a trophy room off the main lobby of the athletic complex. There, ten television stations, from places like Huntsville, Birmingham, Montgomery, and Columbus, have set up ministudios around the room. About twenty print reporters are present as well. Everyone, of course, wants to talk to Rudi, even though he's not likely to deliver a catchy soundbite.

Q: Rudi, since this is your first Alabama game, how is this different from any other week?

A: Just the atmosphere, and all the people, all the hype, and everything.

Q: Did your teammates from the state tell you what to expect?

A: Auburn has many players from Alabama. Seniors and everything like that. I mean even players who are not playing in this game who are like redshirts and stuff like that, they even plan on, like, stepping up in practice.

Even though Rudi may not fill a notebook with witty stories or interesting observations, it doesn't matter to the room of reporters. He is the star. The chant "Rudi, Rudi, Rudi," echoes throughout the stadium during games. Rudi is also popular because he's as humble as a third-stringer.

Typical Rudi: After Auburn beat Northern Illinois in early September, Rudi was approached by a kid wanting a souvenir. Since Rudi had already handed out his wristbands and gloves, he handed the boy the only other memento he had: the game ball.

This afternoon, Rudi makes the rounds going from TV station to TV station. The same questions. The same answers. Five feet away from him, in the center of the room, is Bo Jackson's 1985 Heisman Trophy. Rudi was too young to remember what Bo did at Auburn, but he remembers Bo's NFL career. He even met Bo at Homecoming this year.

"He told me things that'll make me a better football player," Rudi says. "Told me to keep my feet moving. Always fall forward. Enjoy it while you play. Try to keep my nose clean off the field. Be an all-around person."

Rudi is already being mentioned as preseason favorite for the Heisman next season. Sometimes, when he's in this room, he'll take a look at Bo's trophy and dream. "I think about it a lot sometimes," Rudi says. Then he catches himself and reverses field. "I try to maintain my focus on winning the games. Everything else will fall into place."

"I can't imagine a player being more important to their football team than Rudi," Tuberville says, addressing the room full of reporters. "Because we wouldn't be 8–2 if it wasn't for Rudi. We all know that in here. The players know that. He's kept our defense off the field and to me, that's what you look at—you look at a player not how he handles himself or what he does on the football field, but what he does for his entire team. I would have hated to go through this season without Rudi."

In nine of Auburn's ten games this season, Johnson has gained at least 100 yards. He is having the best year by an Auburn running back since Bo in 1985. Last year, the Tigers finished last in the SEC and 112th nationally in rushing. This year, the Tigers are second in the SEC and 35th nationally. All because of Rudi, who was discovered by Auburn's coaches by accident.

Last year, Noel Mazzone was recruiting quarterback Daniel Cobb out of Butler County Community College in Kansas when Cobb suggested that the Tigers take a look at Rudi. "Noel went and watched Daniel play and said, 'You know it doesn't look like Rudi's doing anything and all of a sudden at the end of the night he's got 180 yards,'" running backs coach Eddie Gran says. "So Noel said, 'Eddie, you need to go down and look at this guy.' And after that, I started recruiting Rudi like he was the best running back in the country, because we had to have one. Noel and I flew down to Utah to watch his national championship game last year. And he had 40 carries and 375 yards and 7 touchdowns. It's hard not to want that guy. And thank goodness we have him."

Rudi landed at Butler because of his poor grades in high school in

Ettrick, Virginia. Butler, of course, wasn't what Rudi imagined his college career would be like. "We had dirt for our practice field. By the second or third game, it was already torn up for the rest of the year, so we basically practiced on dirt," Rudi says of the field everyone called AstroDirt. Another practice field sloped downhill. Another had rocks lining the outer edge of the sidelines.

In Rudi's two seasons at Butler, the team won two national championships. After word spread of his seven-touchdown performance in the title game, highly ranked Division I-A schools, such as Oklahoma and Kansas State, came calling. For Johnson, the decision came down to Auburn and Colorado, the two schools that had recruited him the longest. "I visited Auburn during the Alabama game. I went through the Tiger Walk and all that. And that just kind of blew my mind right there. That's all it was. Last year, they didn't have a great year; they were, what, five and six? But it didn't matter after I saw that."

Before interviews, linebacker Alex Lincoln walks over to the stadium so a TV station can shoot a weepy goodbye piece before the senior's final regular season game. "They told me to be upset and real sentimental about the place. So I tried to do the best acting I could. But people were cutting grass and noise was blowing through the stadium. So it wasn't a very emotional scene," Lincoln says with a laugh.

Lincoln came straight to media day from his Medical Technology and Policy class. Today's topic of discussion was football. "Everyone wanted to know about Alabama. Everybody is excited. And our teacher brought a newspaper clipping about me into class," Lincoln says. The story was about Lincoln's friendship with a Pennsylvania boy who wrote him, whose name is also Alex Lincoln. Auburn's Lincoln invited the boy to the Georgia game and the two finally met on Saturday.

"All the other kids in class love me because we talked about football instead of class," Lincoln says.

The press conferences are followed by a special teams meeting, which basically consists of coach Eddie Gran reviewing the Georgia tape and screaming things like, "Catch the bitch right in the head" or "Look there, they got their dumb-ass hats on," or "Hit 'em in the mouth and stand over them and say, 'Game over.' "

Afterward, an academic adviser gives a lecture on academic dishonesty and academic fraud. "Desperate men will do desperate, stupid things," the adviser says. "As of today, some of you are in very, very desperate situations. I'm going to share with you what you can do about your desperate situation. You should run like hell, hard as hell, to your professor to get out of that situation. And if you can't get out of that situation, do not compound it by doing something stupid or very desperate. Take your whooping, take your beat-down like a man. It will cause you embarrassment; it will cause your team embarrassment; it will cause the Athletics Department embarrassment; it will cause the University embarrassment, if you do otherwise. . . . One thing you can remember, we've got fourteen days left of class after today, that's fourteen days. That's not a whole lot. But there's still time to change those F's to D's, still have time to change those B's to A's. I mean, this is it, crunch time. We've got to keep our focus, whether you've got one or two tests left, this is it."

Then wide receivers coach Greg Knox addresses this team. Each week, a different coach speaks.

"All right, this week we've got Alabama and one thing you've got to remember is we're playing for the title. They're not. All right? It doesn't make a difference if we're playing Alabama, if we're playing Ohio State, we're playing UCLA, or we're playing Miami. All right? We're playing for the title. They have nothing to lose, right? They have nothing to lose. They were preseason No. 3 in the country. Preseason, all-world team. Nineteen stars returned on that football team. Kenny King, Kenny Smith, Darius Gilbert, Tony Dixon. Favored for the national champions. Preseason favored for the national championship! But you know what they're lacking? You know what they're missing? They don't have what you got! They didn't go through what you went through. They played their season on a piece of paper. We played ours here, right here, in our heart," Knox says, thumping his chest. "We made our season mark with guts, with attitude, with effort. They don't have it in here, but we got it. Come Saturday, they're going to see it, right? We worked in the preseason. We don't have any preseason All-Americans like they have, or so they say. But we've got it in here [thump, thump]. They got it on a piece of paper. We laid it on the line. When it was hot, when it was 102 degrees on that field, on that dusty field, that dry field, we got up, we got dressed. But you know what they did? They took time off. They read every magazine. They read about how they were preseason national champions and that's why you see them at three and eight. But come Saturday, we win the game right here. Because we've got more heart."

With those inspiring words, the Tigers dress and then walk to the practice field, which is directly behind the athletic complex. On the sideline is the usual cast of characters, among them Tommy Williams, Tiger Walk director, as the embroidered script on his shirt points out. Williams gets goose bumps just talking about the Tiger Walk. He says that in the 'sixties, he and a few loyal fans started meeting by the oak tree near the stadium to greet the team as they walked by. Gradually, the gathering grew into a pep rally featuring the band, the cheerleaders, and thousands of fans. This weekend, Williams expects 18,000 fans will greet the team's buses when they pull into Bryant–Denny Stadium.

Williams holds a detailed map in his hand. It's his game plan, he says. He grabs Tuberville for a moment to go over the details. "On Saturday, I'm going to be on Eighth Street. I'm going to pull right into these apartments right here," he says, not sparing any bit of minutia. Tuberville nods, then moves on.

Of course Norman Barrington, Class of '44, is on the sideline. He's been here every day without fail for the past fifteen years. "The day he doesn't show up is the day I don't want to be here, because that means something bad happened," longtime equipment manager Frank Cox says.

At 150 pounds, Norman played both ways at end for the Tigers' freshman team in 1940. After a career of coaching high school sports and working in the insurance business, Norman, who's eighty, decided to spend his retirement on the fields of Auburn. He still pulls down a paycheck, too—as a bouncer. He works the south end gate of the stadium where the team runs from the tunnel to the field. "I'm the one who keeps the people from coming in that don't belong," says Norman. "This is part of my life and I enjoy it. I guess I still got something to do and this may be it. 'Cause I try to encourage all these kids, even when they are down, try to keep them feeling good about themselves, about this university. Once you have the Auburn spirit, you never lose it."

Since he's at every practice, Norman knows what to expect on Saturdays. "I know what they are gonna do before they do it. I've seen it ten times already in practice. Having coaching for fifteen years, that helps a little bit, too. I know what options they're gonna do," he says. This year's team is one of Norman's favorites. "The seniors on this team are tremendous people. Ben, he's the leader. Two years ago, before Coach Tuberville came in, he wasn't playing any. Because he wasn't so-called good enough. He's so intelligent. A really smart young man. A wise young man because he doesn't really act like he deserves the position and leadership, but he does. He earned every bit of it."

After a spirited practice, Tuberville gathers the team on the 50-yard line. He doesn't have to say much. Playing Alabama should be motivation enough. "If it's not important to you, it's going to be a long life," Tuberville says.

This senior class, which Norman so admires, thinks about its legacy often. At the start of the season, they said they didn't want to be remembered as a losing team, a team that went 3–8 and 5–6 and did little else.

"We want to be able to come back here and hold our heads high," Ben Leard says after practice, as he lounges on a couch in the trophy room surrounded by a few of his closest friends. "And we want people to look at us in a different light."

"That basically was our charge," Cole Cubelic says. "We were charged with the mission to turn this thing back around. We didn't want to leave here saying we didn't get it done. It's a good feeling to start it back in the right direction."

Rob Pate may be the quietest senior on the team, but he is also the most perceptive. When he speaks, everyone usually learns something. "I just think we're going to be remembered as the guys who laid the foundation for a successful program. I think we're going to be remembered as the guys who bridged the gap," Pate says.

"That's what I'm thinking," Leard says. "We realize we're not gonna go to the national championship. We want to give the young guys a foundation to build on. I don't see any problem saying that within three to four years, Auburn will be in a major bowl and in the national championship."

Last season, the football team was slightly appalled when Auburn's highly ranked basketball team stole the spotlight and made the cover of *Sports Illustrated* in the preseason. "Auburn is a football school," Leard says with a smile. "Let it be said: There is no basketball. This school is about football. For one short period of time, they were everything and that was not something we enjoyed."

Adds Alex Lincoln, "And that was another reason why we needed to get this thing back."

"When we first came here we were winning, eight, nine games," Leard says. "People knew who you were. They recognized you, and everything. You played football and they said, 'Come on in.' Then once all this basketball success happened, they shut the door on you. Some of us probably had to pay extra to eat some places. It was just a different thing. Now, fortunately, we've been able to get back to where we were at one point. It can only get better."

The players leave the athletic complex around 7:00 P.M., but for the coaches, who eat just about every meal at the office, the night is just beginning. They arrived in the darkness around 5:30 A.M. and, as usual, they will leave in the darkness, sometime before midnight.

To stay awake, some coaches will stand and watch film so they don't doze off. When Tuberville was the defensive coordinator at Miami, he would be exhausted by 3:30 P.M., before practice even started. To stay alert, he chewed on coffee grinds during practice. "People thought I had chew. I never had chew all my life. I don't drink coffee, either. I just did that to make it through," he says.

"Being a college football assistant is tough because you have two seasons," says Tuberville. "You have the season that starts in August that hopefully ends in January. And then you have the season that starts in January and ends at the end of May, which is recruiting and then spring practice. When you're a coach, you really don't know anything else because you come to work very early and get home late at night. And your family has to be very understanding. A coach is a nomad. I've been very fortunate. I've moved five times in twenty-five years. I've known coaches who've moved twenty times in twenty-five years. And so you really have no life. But being an assistant coach is totally different than a head coach. Now I travel a lot, but they are gone recruiting all of the time. I can selectively do it. But there are so many responsibilities. They say your number one responsibility, of course, is to win games, but to win games you have to recruit. In order to recruit you have to spend hours on the road. And when you are not on the road, you are at home, talking to recruits on the phone for three or four hours."

The long hours become routine. "I just can't believe that the season is over with," defensive tackles coach Don Dunn says. "It almost gets mechanical. I'll bet you five dollars that Monday morning I'll get up at 5:00 A.M. and I'll be bored to death by 10:00 A.M. It's like you're on auto pilot. You do the same thing on Monday, the same thing on Tuesday, Wednesday, Thursday, Friday, Saturday, and Sunday. We do that nine straight weeks before we have an open day."

Tuberville's assistant coaches range from age thirty-two to fifty-two, from different backgrounds. Some came from eclectic backgrounds, such as defensive coordinator John Lovett, from New York, who worked as a truck driver before he went into coaching; and running back coach Eddie Gran, from California, who was in insurance. Others went straight into coaching when their playing days ended. After offensive coordinator Noel Mazzone finished his record-setting career as New Mexico's quarterback in 1980, he became a graduate assistant at the school. After offensive line coach Hugh Nall won the national championship at Georgia in 1980 as the team's center, he became a student assistant at the school.

All but two coaches worked with Tuberville at Ole Miss. There, the staff inherited a losing-program hit by NCAA sanctions and probation. In the staff's first season in 1995, they guided the Rebels to a winning record, despite having just sixty-one players on scholarships. (The NCAA allows eighty-five scholarships.) By their third season, the Rebels were playing in a bowl.

"We had gone through some tough times at Ole Miss. We played in the toughest conference in the country with limited scholarship players. I think these guys kind of grew closer together because of that. And when I put this staff together, I wanted them young because I knew we were going to have some tough times. And older coaches sometimes let those problems go over their heads. Anyway, we survived at Ole Miss.

We were the first coaches at Ole Miss that left in fifty years who have not been retired or fired. What we've gone through, nobody ever wants to go through in coaching. When we walked out on the field the first couple of years at Ole Miss, it wasn't whether we were gonna be beat but by how much. We actually pulled some games off. I was amazed. We just took the mentality that we were not going to accept this. We're gonna do the best we can. We're gonna make it fun for the kids.

"I've been fortunate, lucky, that it's worked out. And I attribute it not to me, but because of the assistant coaches, their demeanor, and how they handled situations. And again, coming here in a tough situation, people said it's going to take us three or four years to get back to a bowl game. And here we are playing for the conference championship in less than two years."

The tough times were made easier because of the friendships that developed. If you spend eighteen hours together each day, it helps if you get along. At least most of the time.

"The only thing that drives me crazy about him is that he snores too damn loud," defensive ends coach Terry Price says of his on-the-road roommate, Don Dunn, the defensive tackles coach. "One night I threw a shoe at him. And I got size 16 shoes."

Price is thirty-two and black and played defensive end at powerhouse Texas A&M. Dunn is forty-seven and white and played center at Lees-McRae Junior College and East Tennessee State. Dunn has a deep, booming voice that can fill an entire field. Price's coaching demeanor is more reserved. Though different, they have become close friends during their six years working together.

At Auburn, even the coaches' wives get along, which is no small miracle. The families spend plenty of time together, and after each home game, a different coach hosts a party. Back at Ole Miss, a few of the coaches formed a barbecue team called the Pigskins. For fun one year, they decided to enter the four-day world championship barbecue contest in Memphis. "We turned our stuff in, then the judges cut it down to three finalists and we didn't think anything about it," Dunn says. "We were having a good time, partying and raising Cain. People were coming by and we're giving our barbecue sauce out, we're eating. All of a sudden, the judge comes by and says, 'We're gonna pick up your sauce now as a finalist.' Well, we didn't have any left. We had to make it all up again. We did then we all stuck our finger in it for good luck before we took it before the judge." When the judge told the Pigskins they won, the group broke up in hysterics.

"We didn't have a clue what we were doing," Dunn says. "We went up there and we won the championship for the best vinegar-based sauce. I mean, the world championship! There's thousands of people at this thing. I've got that big trophy in my house. It's like the Stanley Cup. We pass it around. We haven't lost it yet. We've misplaced it a few times, though."

Such closeness has helped the group get through the worst of times, too. Last season, running backs coach Eddie Gran and his wife, Rosemary, found out that their infant daughter, Sydney, had a rare brain disease, Holoprosencephaly, known as HPE, in which the brain stops developing during early pregnancy. Then in October, one of the twins born prematurely to Terry Price and his wife, Kenya, died. His wife is still in the hospital with his son, Alexander, who is six weeks old and struggling. After every home game, Price drives two hours to Birmingham, spends the night at the hospital, then drives home for Sunday's 9:00 A.M. coaches meeting.

Chette Williams, the team chaplin, says the tragedies have drawn the entire team closer together.

"One day I went over to Terry's house and he told me, 'Chette, the last two days I haven't even changed my clothes.' I mean, he was sleeping in Birmingham at the hospital and driving to practice," says Williams. "And for Eddie, I mean, every day they wake up, they don't know with their daughter, you know. My philosophy is that when tragedies come, they can either draw you closer to the Lord or it can drive you away. In both cases, it's drawn this team closer. One day, Terry said, 'Chette, think of the worst possible scenario in your life, that's where I'm at.' And what can I say? You know, just 'Man, I'm praying for you. I'll be here if you need anything.' That's all the Lord asks from any of us. We can't save anybody. God saves. So I think faith has just been unbelievable on this team. Just what the team's been through, with the coaches and the tragedies—it's built a lot of faith."

"We're all a family," says Tuberville. "I can remember finding out about Eddie's baby. He told me over at his house. We both broke down and cried. It's just when you deal with kids; we deal with older kids and we see their problems—to see this happen to babies. With Terry's situation, Terry for a month wouldn't say a word—even before it happened, because he knew something bad was gonna happen because the doctors told him. His wife's been laying on her back for a month. And then they have to take the babies. One passes away and the other is struggling. . . . Eddie and Terry are kinda like brothers to me. I've seen both of them grow up—a lot. You mature a lot when you go through something like that. Again, we all came together as a bunch of young guys at Ole Miss. Everybody who has had a problem since that time, we've kinda gone through it together. It's good because everyone has someone to kinda lean on, ya know?"

Wednesday

ALABAMA

It is equipment manager Tank Conerly's turn to give the devotional at the morning staff meeting, one in which he quotes from a piece written by a doctor who describes what Christ endured medically during the crucifixion. His point: "There isn't any one of us who is not going through some kind of uncertainty." As he goes through the grahpic description, DuBose, Charlie Harbison, and Dabo Swinney, three of the more religious members of the coaching staff, cup one hand over their eyes.

When Conerly concludes, DuBose goes over the day's schedule, then lists the "travel" squad. SEC regulations maintain that the home team in a conference game may dress out eighty players. DuBose goes over who he has already decided to put on the squad: three quarterbacks, three fullbacks, three tailbacks, two tight ends, twelve wide receivers, ten offensive linemen, five outside linebackers, two inside linebackers, twelve defensive linemen, eleven defensive backs, two punters, three snappers, and three kickers.

"I got nine left," DuBose says, then begins to quiz the assistant coaches about who among the walk-ons and redshirted freshmen should receive this honor. Though no coach would jeopardize a redshirt's eligibility by playing him, coaches like to have young players, such as offensive linemen Wesley Britt and Justin Smiley, experience a game weekend, from start to finish. DuBose includes them with seven walk-ons. The head coach goes over the schedule for Friday and Saturday, asks for changes, then dismisses the coaches.

A few minutes later, the four Alabama defensive coaches are watching the Auburn offensive video again and teasing each other—again.

"If you had just lost Leslie Williams [a backup end] instead of Moorehead, we wouldn't have this problem," Ellis Johnson says to Lance Thompson.

"If you had told me I'd lose those two," Thompson says of Moorehead and Kenny King, "I would have gone to Washington." Last winter, Thompson discussed a job with the Redskins.

He thinks about it for a second and says. "That's not true. I would have lost my friend Rouzie."

While none of the Alabama coaches has a new job, Johnson gets a call today from his alma mater's athletic director, Les Robinson, to gauge his interest in being The Citadel Bulldogs' new head coach. Johnson is interested. In the meantime, he stops for a moment to call media relations secretary Brenda Burnette. The rumor has reached Tuscaloosa that Auburn tight end Robert Johnson has broken his wrist. The Alabama defensive coordinator asks Burnette to find out what's going on.

Leard appears on the screen again. "The only time he is going to go deep is if he is pressed," Rouzie says. "He doesn't have the arm strength."

Secondary coach Charlie Harbison chimes in, "Leard threw nine passes to Z [one of the wide receivers]. Seven were curls."

A couple of minutes pass. The phone rings. Ellis Johnson picks it up. "Hello? Yes, ma'am." It's Burnette.

"I want the inside scoop," Johnson says, a bit exasperated. "Not the media scoop. They tell the media what they want the media to hear."

Johnson hangs up. "I'm trying to find out what happened and she tells me what's in the Birmingham paper. It sounds to me like the kid can't play, but they're trying to act like he will."

The video continues. "If you look at the formations, Eli," Thompson says to Johnson, "Noel is incredibly balanced on where he runs."

"He does a good job," Johnson says admiringly.

"To me," Thompson says, "if he looks at us, he'll run away from Albert."

On the screen, Georgia middle linebacker Adrian Hollingshed runs right past the hole he is supposed to fill. Rudi Johnson goes over his left guard, through the gap Hollingshed leaves for a sizable gain. Thompson clicks his laser pointer and zeroes in on Tigers left guard Hart McGarry, the same player he described as a weak link to his defensive linemen on Tuesday.

"He's gotten a lot better since last year," Thompson says.

"They all have," graduate assistant Kevin Sherrer says.

"Ol' 32 makes them look better," Ellis Johnson says of Rudi.

"LSU ran a stunt and it should have stopped Rudi for a loss of two," Thompson says. "He gets three. One hundred of those and you got 500 yards."

The coaches watch a little more of Rudi, discuss who should start on their defensive line, then start watching the Auburn passing offense again. Coaches must walk a line between assessing an opponent honestly and hopefully. One half of a defensive coach's mind must prepare as if the offense is as good as the St. Louis Rams. The other half, the one that must convince the players on a 3–7 team that they can win, must prepare as if the opposing offense couldn't score against air.

"I don't think they are scared of Leard getting hit," Ellis Johnson says. "I don't think he throws that well."

"He does the right thing with the ball," Thompson says. "He does it in the right place. He doesn't throw the 15-yard wide. He won't stand in there and let the play develop. He throws anything to get it out of there quick." On the screen, Mississippi State crowds the line, then rushes only two men. Too late, Leard thinks more are coming and gets rid of a wobbly, underthrown ball that falls incomplete.

"That's what I'm talking about," Thompson says. "See how that ball dies?"

The hallway on the second floor of the Alabama football building is rectangular with offices all the way around. Another hall bisects the floor. At the far end of the middle hallway is the office belonging to running backs coach Ivy Williams. He is sitting in a chair in front of his desk, his feet propped up, and his head buried in a *USA Today*. More important, his chair is placed so that he can glance down the hallway and take his measure of what's going on. It is remarkably quiet on the floor.

"This week," he says, "we keep all the scouts out. They're looking at film, asking the same questions. It started with Stallings. He said they couldn't come to Auburn week. On other weeks, if they came, they had to leave the field after we started practice. Mike said they can stay the whole practice. They got a job to do, too."

They just can't do it this week.

On Monday night, wide receiver Freddie Milons spoke to the media for the first time in weeks. "It's the best week of practice," says Milons, the preseason Heisman Trophy candidate who has had a lackluster season. "There's no reason to hold anything back. Nothing else matters now. Nothing matters but beating Auburn. My confidence is at a good high. A lot of things in my personal life, struggles—I took some tests and passed them. In the second half of the LSU game, I put everything else aside and just played. I feel I'm healthy enough. I'm focused enough. I'm fortunate enough. I feel great. I have nothing to save it for. I want to put all my effort into this."

The face of disappointment for Alabama fans is a friendly one. It belongs to a junior who, at first appearance, is built no differently than half the students on campus. Milons is listed as five-eleven, 188. To the naked eye, those numbers are generous. On the field, in helmet and shoulder pads, Milons appears even smaller, so small that he gets to one place, then suddenly disappears and shows up somewhere else. Milons can start and stop like a Looney Tunes character. In 1999, tailback Shaun Alexander may have been the offensive bread and butter, but Milons spiced up everything the offense created. He caught 65 passes for 733 yards. He rushed 15 times for 178 yards. That's right: Milons averaged more per rush (11.9) than per reception (11.3). Milons, a quarterback at Starkville High in Mississippi, also completed three of four passes, including a 66-yard touchdown pass against Arkansas. Many of his runs, including a 77-yard touchdown in the 34–7 victory over Florida in the SEC Championship Game, occurred after he lined up at quarterback.

Milons did not draw a lot of national attention as a recruit. Regionally, however, he became the focus of a fierce battle between Ole Miss, Mississippi State, and Alabama. He has the personality that one would ascribe to the fourth of seven children. He gets along with everybody. He loves to care for plants, a green thumb he inherited from his father, Freddie Sr.

Milons began the season as a Heisman Trophy candidate. The first time he touched the ball this season, after the Alabama defense held UCLA to three downs and out on the opening possession of the game, Milons returned a punt 71 yards for touchdown.

No one knew, of course, that the punt return would not only represent the high-water mark for Milons but for the entire Alabama team as well. With four days left in the season, which had started with high hopes and higher expectations, Milons is trying to absorb the troubles he endured as lessons.

"It's been the perfect year for a young man in collegiate sports," Milons says. "It allows you to see life at its greatest. Life is not perfect. It will knock you when you're down and keep hurting you. You have the choice to fix whatever you want to fix. This game is the perfect opportunity. If you want anything, you got to go out and take it."

Milons hasn't always been so mature in his outlook. He spent most of the season in a funk. His receiving numbers for the season are not all that dissimliar from his 1999 numbers. In nine games, he has caught 31 passes for 278 yards. However, he has rushed eleven times for only 44 yards. Since the punt return against UCLA, he has returned only five more punts for 41 yards.

In other words, Milons has been a little better than average. He may not have caught enough passes, but he caught a whole lot of hell. When the Crimson Tide faltered, Milons suffered the wrath of the disappointed faithful. He became the subject of rumors—for instance, upset with his diminished role in the offense, he had refused to get off the team bus before the game at Arkansas and gotten into a shouting match with DuBose; that when he sat out of the Ole Miss game with a partially torn medial cruciate ligament in his right knee, he was, according to whom you believed, either jaking it—pretending to be hurt—or being held out of the game by the university because he had had some dealings with an agent.

"I've had plenty of opportunities to quit, to listen to everything said of me," he says. "I've stayed humble. I've stayed confident. I've stayed with the team concept. I haven't changed my role. Everybody knew that if we had won all our games, there would not be a change. The questions about my personality would not have been asked."

But as he continues to talk, it becomes apparent that Milons hasn't stayed confident. When attacked, Milons reacted the way most sensitive twenty-year-olds would react; he shut down. He quit talking to the media. He quit calling home.

It began, Milons says, when he awoke on September 18, the Monday after the humiliating 21–0 loss to Southern Mississippi. He found that his green 1994 Mazda MX-6 had been vandalized. It was obvious it was not a random act of vandalism. "Someone felt the need to spray paint all around my car," Milons says. "Spray-painted my number on my car . . . a big 15. What kind of good neighbor am I fooling with? I don't trip with someone's emotions like that. Someone was just pissed off. That person is still out there. He could be living in my neighborhood. He could be handing out my equipment at practice. That person is still just walking around."

Two weeks later, Milons injured his knee during practice on Thursday, October 5. Alabama didn't have a game that Saturday, which gave Milons a better chance to be ready for the Ole Miss game on October 14. However, his knee didn't respond and he didn't play. "Then I read in the paper that my knee was just a cover-up because of dealing with an agent," Milons says. "I didn't go home when we had the weekend off. I stayed on campus to get treatment to get ready for Ole Miss. I knew what I had done to get ready. That kind of hurt my feelings right there."

Milons went to the game and saw the offense, without him, give by far its best performance of the season. The Tide steamrolled the Rebels, 45–7. Afterward, as Milons walked home, he heard a fan at a concession stand praise the team for winning without Milons. "Freddie," the fan says, "is an 'I' player." This time, Milons didn't turn the other cheek.

"I walked up to him," Milons says, "and said, 'Excuse me. I am an 'I' player? Thank you for telling me.' " One of Milons's teammates quickly pulled him away. "It really bothered me," Milons says. "With the things

I've sacrificed, that was just like a spit in my face. We had just won. It was a big victory. The last thing on my mind was a negative."

He wouldn't talk to the writers, but he couldn't stop the questions from classmates, from neighbors.

"Freddie, why aren't you getting the ball?"

"Other people are making plays. My job is the play that is called."

"Freddie, why aren't you making plays?"

"I'm not getting the ball."

He sensed that even the coaches doubted him. In the three-receiver formations during the 1999 season, Milons usually lined up as the inside receiver of the twosome, where he could use a teammate to block or pick off his defender. This season, he lined up wide on the opposite side by himself. He wasn't getting open. "I felt like, 'Just prove yourself in practice. If you do it in practice, they'll call your number in a game,'" he says. "I picked up my practice intensity." By the LSU game, when he caught three passes for 38 yards, the last for a touchdown—in a two-minute drill that pulled Alabama within 30–28 in the final seconds—Milons had begun to look like the 1999 Milons.

More indicative of what happened in the 2000 season was the Mississippi State game. Milons's knee injury had kept the coaches from using him at quarterback. Once Milons proved in the LSU game that he had regained his quickness, the Tide coaches tried putting him behind center again. On the first attempt, however, as center Paul Hogan began to send the ball between his legs to Milons, the blunt end of the football got stuck in the ground. The result: a poor exchange. Milons picked up the fumble and was tackled for a loss of two yards. Milons didn't play at quarterback for the rest of the game.

Milons believes he is no longer the player who will be bothered by not playing enough at quarterback. He believes he has matured. It will be a long time before he forgets the reaction he and his teammates received when they lost the Homecoming game to Central Florida.

"Hearing those fans boo was a slap in the face," Milons says. "Like Coach Swinney always says, people have a short memory. Remember how loud it was in Atlanta [after the SEC Championship Game]? Everyone stayed in the stadium to cheer. Those same fans are booing us. That's not right. There's nothing right about that. That's reality. That's life." He shakes his head. "There are so many lessons about this year. We feel as if we're in part responsible. The coaches don't have the opportunity to go out and show what they did. All they can do is trust in us. We are in part responsible. It's just amazing how the chips fall. If we had just won the majority of our games, the subject would have never come up."

Milons leaves to go get dressed for the 2:30 P.M. team meeting. As the coaches and players start to get ready, graduate assistant Mike Bloomgren is sitting at his desk watching a videotape of Auburn playing Florida. However, Bloomgren isn't watching the coaches' video, which shows only the play and the scoreboard; he is watching a videotape of the CBS telecast. Why? Television directors love to use a shot of the coaches on the sideline between plays. "They go to the coach for a reaction," Bloomgren says. "When they do, sometimes you can pick up play signals."

He resumes watching the tape. If only the Pentagon were as thorough in our national defense as coaches are in football defense.

When 2:30 P.M. arrives, the team meeting room is warm. In fact, though the weather outside has been frightful, the building has been overheated all week. The consensus among the staff is that calling maintenance will only make it worse.

All the bodies congregating in the meeting room are making it warmer, too. Wednesday is the day when the assistant coach "in charge" of the game gives his scouting report to the players. For this week, DuBose has assigned his former teammate and longtime friend, Neil Callaway. He played in the rivalry as a Crimson Tide offensive lineman from 1975 to 1977, in the middle of Bryant's nine-year winning streak against Auburn. From 1981 to 1992, Callaway coached the offensive line at Auburn for Pat Dye. In those twelve seasons, the teams each won six times.

"It's a big, big ball game," Callaway says. "I felt strange my first game at Auburn, really the first two years, when Coach Bryant was still here. Mal was on his staff. Dee Powell, who was my position coach, was still here. Most of the other coaches were here when I played. In this business, the loyalty is to the people you work for and work with.

Coach Dye had recruited me. And I still think a lot of him. Sure, you have a tremendous amount of respect for Coach Bryant and a strong feeling of love. But that's part of the game. We still wanted to win the ball game. The first year, we really had a chance to win, and ran out of time [Alabama won, 25–18, giving Bryant the Division I-A record for coaching victories with 315]."

After Dye resigned, Callaway went to Houston for four seasons, then returned to Tuscaloosa with DuBose, who had won two out of three from the Tigers. Of the five coaches who have worked at both schools, Callaway has the most time on both sidelines: twelve years at Auburn as a coach, eight years at Alabama as a player and coach.

"The tailgaters—I got a friend of mine with a budget of eighty thousand dollars," Callaway says. "I'd like to tailgate, but I don't think I'd enjoy watching the game from the stands." Though a lot of veterans of the Iron Bowl wish the game had never been moved from Legion Field, Callaway thinks the move to the two campuses has ratcheted up the intensity. "That scene in Auburn in 1989," he says. "After the game, one of our friends had a party. He owned the bookstore there. He didn't get to his party until midnight. The bookstore was open, and he made five hundred thousand dollars that night." He is asked about the emotions of the week, his final one at Alabama working for a man who has been a close friend for more than half his life. Callaway's eyes widen. He shows a tight smile and gives a look that begs to change the subject. "I'm not going to go there," he says. "That's been a big disappointment. It's a shame. I love Mike to death. But he's the boss and it's his responsibility."

Before Callaway speaks to the team, Moore comes in and speaks briefly to the players. DuBose thanks him and cedes the floor to Callaway. The entire room is focused on him. Clemson coach Tommy Bowden, who has been an assistant coach at both schools, says one trait that both teams display during Iron Bowl week is attentiveness. "You don't have to repeat yourself," Bowden says. "They're early to meetings. Study halls aren't a problem. They aren't going to do anything to jeopardize that game. In a typical meeting, you're right around seventy to eighty percent of attention level. Auburn–Alabama week, it jumps to ninety-eight to ninety-nine percent. You get it all week."

Callaway brings the team's attention to the screen at the front of the room. "I want everybody to look at that right there," Callaway says. "Look at it. Look at it."

AUBURN UNIVERSITY VS. UNIVERSITY OF ALABAMA
NOV. 18, 2000
TUSCALOOSA, AL

"You older guys know that it is always a big game," Callaway says. "This year is going to be the biggest one ever, for several reasons I'm fixing to tell you about. It's not only the biggest ball game ever; it's the biggest one ever in Tuscaloosa, the biggest in the state of Alabama for a long time. Everybody will be here. Everybody in the country will be watching. Not only a big game, a big event. It's the first time ever played in Bryant–Denny. Never been played in your home. Never been played on your field. It was always played in Legion Field or in the last few years in Auburn. For ninety-nine years, it's never been in Tuscaloosa.

"It's the first time ever, and hopefully the last time ever, that the senior class will play their bowl game in Bryant–Denny. Why? It's the first time, and hopefully the last time, a senior class's last ball game will be in Bryant–Denny. You younger guys think about that. Think about what they have to live with for the rest of their lives."

Callaway pauses a moment to let that sink in.

"Let me give you overall a history lesson here. They talk about Oklahoma–Nebraska. Texas–Texas A&M. Nothing compares to this. Our overall record is 37–26–1. When Coach Bryant was here, his record was 19–6. The last seventeen years, it's 9–8. I'll tell you why I'm telling all this. I was at Auburn twelve years. I got a good feeling for what those people think about. To be honest, I enjoyed it. No question, they have an inferiority complex. Every year, the talk is not about winning a national championship, the conference championship. The talk is about beating Alabama. Around here, we talk about national championships. You know what they talk about? 'How many times did you beat Alabama?' They look at Pat Dye's record. How many times did he beat Alabama? They went nine years with Coach Bryant that they never won.

"How many of you were here in 'seventy-two? I wasn't even here then. They still talk about that as if it were yesterday. That's their mentality. That's their problem. We don't have to live with that. It's not a problem here. We take care of business. In 1984, the University of Alabama was 4–6. Auburn went 8–3. Alabama won the game 17–15. Auburn had the best athlete ever to play college football: Bo Jackson. My point is, Alabama got after our ass. In 1989, Alabama was 10–0, ranked No. 2 in the nation. Auburn was 8–2. Auburn won the game 30–20. This is 2000. The University of Alabama is going into the game 3–7. Auburn is going into the game 7–2 [*sic*]. We're going to play at two-thirty Saturday in our house. How are we going to respond?"

Callaway then began to get into the specifics of playing the Tigers.

"First thing you got to remember: You can expect anything anytime from the special teams. Opening kickoff, expect anything, anytime. Coach shouldn't have to remind you, watch the onside kick, watch the popup. Damon Duval, second in the SEC, does a good job kicking off and has a strong leg. He's capable of putting it in the end zone.

"The kickoff return guy is Tim Carter, 24.3 yards. He's very dangerous. The punt returner is Clifton Robinson, 6.8 yards. To be honest with you, he's been catching the ball inside the 10. We ought to have a chance to make something happen.

"The Auburn defense. They have got a defense that is not overly impressive as far as talent. They do a very good job of running to the ball. The best defensive lineman, without a doubt, is DeMarco McNeil, 323 pounds. Their best linebacker, Alex Lincoln, an overachiever, going to be around the football. The secondary, they are very high on their two corners. We'll have to wait and see. Offensively, we ought to be able to control the ball because of their soft coverage.

"Their offense: Veteran offensive line that plays hard, will get after you and play hard. Talented group of receivers that we're going to have to make damn sure we know when they come out and what they are doing. The fullback, a big, physical guy who will beat you when he runs the ball. The quarterback is not having quite the year throwing the ball. They made a commitment to run the ball. His numbers are not the same. The offense relies on the run to win the game. They are capable of throwing and catching the ball."

Callaway isn't telling the players anything they haven't seen on video, or from the scout team. In fact, as far as the Auburn players are concerned, he doesn't tell them anything they can't read in the paper. When he stops talking about personnel and starts in on the personal, his already hoarse voice begins to clog with emotion.

"The game is about our fans and our rivalry," Callaway says. "Your family. Most of all it's about you. You're the guys who have got to deliver. It's our family versus their family. It's the University of Alabama's family versus Auburn University's family. You older guys who have been in the ball game know it. It's a whole helluva lot funner when you win the game. This is very important about how you are going to win the game. I'm going to tell you how we're going to kick their ass. Just like 'eighty-nine, their players and fans were not going to disappoint their family, we're not going to do it here either. Most of all, we're not going to disappoint yourself. This is going to be a very emotional ball game. Whether we're 17 points behind or 17 ahead, it don't matter. We're going to play every play to kick their ass.

"The kicking game, we're going to have perfect execution in every phase of it. We're going to gain field position by it and we're going to score points with it. When was the last time we had a kickoff return for a touchdown? When was the last time we had a punt return?

"Defense, we're going to win it up front. You're not going to stop the running game, you're going to control it. By no means am I saying we want to kick him out of the game. I am saying we want to get after him and kick shit out of him every chance we get.

"Offense, we're going to make big plays in the passing game, taking care of the coverage. Bottom line, whether it's 3–0 or 45–44, you're going to score more points than they score. You're writing your book. This is the final chapter. The book is going to close Saturday night. Are you going to be known as a team that has disappointed or a team that has disappointed that had enough character and chose to win. What are you going to be known as?"

With that challenge hanging in the air, Callaway stops and walks to the side of the room. DuBose stands before his players and issues another challenge.

"What's important now? Do you see yourself doing it for sixty minutes? Give yourself your best opportunity to do it," he says. "Today's practice, you need to be prepared to win the football game."

The players break up and head to their position meetings. They go from those to special teams meetings. Auburn has been effective all season with onside kicks, which take advantage of the return team not paying attention. When the Tigers attempt an onside kick, their formation is different and the kicker is different. Ivy Williams is meeting with the Tide kickoff return team and going over the details on video.

"If the ball's going to be kicked, check the lineup," he says, looking at the alignment of the ten members of the Auburn kicking team with kicker Damon Duval on the screen. "Four, three, and three. Left-footed kicker, see? Anytime that changes, Draper, the ball is coming to you. Don't matter what point of the game it's in."

In practice, the hitting is as brisk as the chill. Steve Webb, a linebacker who played for Bill Curry and Gene Stallings from 1987 to 1991, is one of a few former players at practice. Webb works in the juvenile justice system in Tuscaloosa. He doesn't attend practice every week, but then Alabama isn't playing Auburn every week. Curry went 0–3 against Auburn. Stallings went 5–2, including his first two years, which were Webb's last two in a crimson jersey.

"One of the big things was mental. Curry was a very good coach," Webb says, "but he didn't motivate us in the best way to beat Auburn. It was just different. We felt more confident under Coach Stallings. He knew how to beat Auburn. He let us go. Under Curry, we were held back. No fighting, no taunting. When it came down to Auburn, everything goes. Like wrestling, no disqualification.

"Coach Curry didn't want us to taunt. He didn't want us to late-hit or fight. Stallings understood that you have to win the game. He told us, 'You go on the field and you play and I'll deal with it after. When you're in the game, you shouldn't have to think.' Stallings said, 'Go full speed. Play your best game and I will deal with it later.' Can you get too emotional? We never got out of control. No matter what Auburn did, we still kept our tempo."

Webb is confident that this week, Alabama's 3–7 record is irrelevant. "It doesn't matter who is the better team," he says. "It's much better that way. I know what people in the military feel like when they are defending their country. You're going to war with Auburn. It's the North and the South."

After practice, DuBose sounds cautiously upbeat. The pace of practice picked up. When a coach seals himself off from the media, as DuBose has in recent weeks, the impromptu press conferences are ragged. The media members don't want to waste their only opportunity of the day with the coach, so the questions are a little more direct and a lot more disjointed. Follow-up questions are barely allowed, because another writer wants to take advantage of the short time with DuBose and ask his burning question. The players trudge through the double doors and head down the hallway to the locker room. As with the forty-hour work week, Wednesday is hump day for a football team. The most physical work of the practice week is done.

At the far end of the same hallway is the training room, as far from the practice field as it can be. That's how coaches want it. Quarterback Andrew Zow, freshly showered and dressed, lays cantilevered on a table, his right elbow iced and his right arm connected to a "stim" machine, which provides electronic stimulation to the injured area. "Against LSU, I went down and hit my elbow and it jammed back up," Zow says, gesturing up toward his shoulder. "It originally happened against Virginia Tech [in the 1998 Music City Bowl] and it's been messing with my shoulder ever since."

Daily treatment such as this can be a daily reality in college football. The treatment usually makes the pain dissipate. Getting hit every Saturday, however, keeps Zow's arm from healing completely. "This week it's really starting to bother me," he says. It is one more nagging ache in a season that has been full of them. The only player vilified as much as Milons this season has been Zow, the quarterback who hasn't made the offense go. He has completed 108 of 220 passes, with 13 interceptions and only six touchdowns. His passing efficiency rating, derived from these numbers through a complicated NCAA formula, is 101.6, which is not even mediocre.

Zow has been buffeted this season by harsh winds: the injury, DuBose giving him the starting job and then taking it away, which resulted in a loss of confidence that haunts Zow to this day. Three days before the game that could salvage his season, as well as his team's season, there is a tentative quality about Zow that makes it obvious he has suffered.

"The part that frustrates me the most is that it hasn't been fun," he says. "The high expectations. We put so much into this season. Me personally, it really shocked me. I put so much into it. I believed in the team, that we could win a national championship, be undefeated when we played Auburn. You want to be undefeated so bad. I believe the team had the talent to be undefeated. But no, we lost the chance."

It wasn't so much the loss at UCLA as what the loss meant to the team's hopes that killed the Tide. The team never refocused on lesser, attainable goals. "That's all I wanted: a national championship," Zow says. "It's something you have to put behind you. It's hard. It frustrated us. We have so much talent. It frustrated the coaches. Things went downhill so fast."

After the second game of the season, a 28–10 victory over Vanderbilt, DuBose yanked Zow out of the starting lineup in favor of Watts. In 1999, Zow and Watts answered the experts who maintained that two starting quarterbacks are never as efficient as one. However, they shared the job only because Zow sprained his ankle against Tennessee. He never regained his former mobility and as such, Zow never regained the efficacy he had before the injury. A healthy Watts stepped in and made plays, leading Alabama to victories over Southern Mississippi, LSU, and Auburn.

In 2000, Zow lost the job before he injured his elbow. He kept his opinion to himself. "I'm not the type of guy to run to coach to gripe," Zow says. "I'm going to play and I'm going to get my chances. I don't go to the coach. I go and tell them what I'm thinking. Whatever the coaches say goes. To go and tell them, 'I think I should be playing,' that's not me."

Watts tore the anterior cruciate ligament in his left knee during the 45–7 rout of Ole Miss. The offense belonged to Zow again, without the pressure of a job competition.

He played as if he had been freed of a burden, completing 18 of 22 passes, including 12 consecutive—a school record, for 261 yards. Given how poor his season statistics were, including the Ole Miss game, his performance sets in stark relief what Zow is capable of and how far short he fell of achieving it. Nevertheless, his teammates remain solidly behind him. When center Paul Hogan and left guard Griff Redmill talked of Zow, you could hear the admiration in their voices: "He's held up good," Hogan said.

"I never can undersand why he ends up being the butt of so much criticism," Redmill said. "He's won a lot of big games here. He's a good quarterback."

"That's just the nature of the position," Hogan said. "If one of us has a terrible day, nobody knows. That's the same guy, in the Ole Miss game, who completed 80 percent of his passes. The following week, they're telling him, 'You suck.' "

"When he gets off to a good start," Redmill said, "he plays great. When the crowd was booing him, he actually came back and played good and gave us a chance."

"Yeah," Hogan said, a hint of bitterness creeping into his voice. "They were cheering for him then."

"He never quits," Redmill said. "He never gives up. I respect him more than anybody else on the team for what he does and the way he handles the criticism. Ninety-nine percent of it is bull. You never hear him say a bad word about anybody. He comes every day to learn and to play a ball game on Saturday."

Zow says the booing and the losses embittered his wife, Ambriess. "She holds a grudge against Alabama a little bit," Zow says. What about him? Does Zow hold a grudge? On the one hand, he says, "Things are going to work out for Andrew Zow. Andrew Zow is going to be okay." On the other hand, Zow says he no longer has fun in the football building. "I'm to the point right now, I don't stay here long. I get a tape from coach. I go home and watch my film. I come over here and do what I have to do. I don't come here for joyful things."

These are thoughts that he has kept away from his teammates. He understands his role as the offensive leader. He believes the offense can play as it did against Central Florida and LSU, when Alabama scored a combined 66 points, and not as it did last Saturday at Mississippi State. "I know how people react to negative things," Zow says. "Misery likes company. I'm trying to be positive. We're at a low point right now. I still try to be positive no matter what. I try to let them see me being positive. On TV or in the paper, my religion has shown me to be a positive guy. I want to be that light for them, on and off the field. I'm going to show my light."

That is the public Zow, the Zow that says, "No, we're motivated. We're ready to play 'em. We should be a national championship team but it's a big game and we need to win it. It would help the team. It wouldn't fix anything in the past."

The private Zow, the one that goes home to his infant son A.J., allows as how he does daydream about what might have been. In this case, however, he's not thinking about the national championship at Alabama. "I could have made a simple decision to go to Central Florida," he says. "Two hours from home, be in a program that would have been less competitive. Play. I could have gone to a D-III school and went out there and played. I sit back and think, 'What if I did this?' What if I hadn't gotten my knee hurt in high school? I would have been somewhere else. I've enjoyed my time here. I'm not second-guessing anything. It's just, 'What if?' "

AUBURN

At 6:00 A.M. the running backs meeting is about to begin, but Rudi is not in the room.

"I knocked on Rudi's door," backup Michael Owens says. "I knocked and I knocked and there was no answer. I was getting cold so I stopped knocking."

"I tried his phone," fullback Heath Evans says. "It's been off the hook for four days. It's been busy for four days. It must be broken."

Rudi walks in the room at 6:05.

"Hey, Rudi, we appreciate you showing up," Coach Gran says. "There's a sandwich there for you. You're late."

Rudi looks at Gran but says nothing.

"Had your extra minutes of sleep? Well, we'll get Coach Yox to handle it."

When players are late, the next morning they run sprints, stadium steps, or endure other torture from strength coach Kevin Yoxall.

"It's six," Rudi says.

"You're late," Gran says, his voice growing louder.

The five running backs in the room are reviewing yesterday's practice tape. After twenty minutes, Gran notices that Rudi is fading.

"Sit up, Rudi, get off your arm," Gran says. "Sit up, Rudi. Put your arm down. I'm tired. Everybody's tired. My wife's tired. My children are tired. My feet are tired. We're playing Alabama, Rudi. So you can't be tired, Rudi."

Back to the tape. "What's that they're running?" Gran asks.

"Four–three," a few players say. The quiz continues, as Gran tests the players on formations they will likely see.

"Keep your eyes open," Gran says. "They might do something that says, 'Screw you, coaches, you're leaving.' So you don't know what's going to happen. They might punch you in the mouth, Rudi. Okay? You know what they'll try to get you to do—they're going to try to get you thrown out of the game. We've seen all that crap this year, right? Get up. Hand the ref the ball. Let them get thrown out. Class. Class. We've done it all year. We've done it with class. Just keep it that way.

"But there is one thing I don't ever want to have happen again. Okay, Rudi? Losing. You were at the Alabama game last year as a recruit. You've experienced the ambience, the electricity here. The one thing that you have not experienced, Rudi, is the hate that we have for Alabama. I was sick and I've been sick for three hundred and sixty days. I don't want that feeling ever again. I can't stand them. We recruit against them. It's all about this state, the pride, the people of Auburn, this university, your families. So you just better get your ass strapped and ready to go. And it don't have to happen today. I understand all that. It starts building up. Like a damn pot of coffee. Boiling water. It just gets hotter and hotter. I would save that energy. Be mentally sharp in practice today. Because that's what got us there last week. Right or wrong? The preparation we had last week? Good preparation. You guys did a hell of a job. It was sharp, you were mentally focused. Then you all let that emotion out. And you get ready to play football again. That's what we're going to need. Man, it's going to be a battle. That first half is gonna be a battle. We've won four games this year in the fourth quarter, right? Four games. That's nothing to us. Don't worry about the crowd. You have to throw them on their ass to take that crowd out. Take that crowd out, you will have the best fourth quarter you'll ever have. Make them quit. Come ready to go."

At the start of the 9:00 A.M. coaches' meeting, the team chaplain, Chette Williams, delivers a devotional entitled, "Finishing Strong."

Williams, the team's full-time minister, attends all the practices, travels with the team, and holds weekly devotions and services. Williams is also a former player at Auburn who played for Pat Dye from 1982 to 1984, but was kicked off the team for drinking and doing drugs. Williams turned his life around after he discovered Jesus, graduated from Auburn, and became an ordained minister.

"On one day, Jesus told his disciples, 'Let's go over to the other side of the lake,' " Williams says. "So they got into the boat and went to the other side. As they were sailing, He fell asleep. There was a squall, a strong wind that came down from the lake. So the boat was being swamped and they were in great danger. The disciples went and woke him saying, 'Master. Master, we are going to drown.' Jesus got up and rebuked the wind and the raging water. The storm subsided. And all was calm. Here's what Jesus said when He got out. 'Where was your faith?' he asked. His disciples in tears and amazement asked, 'Who is this? He commands even the winds and the waters and they obey him.'

"When storms arise in our lives, when difficult times arise in our lives—and they will, guys, they will arise, it's no doubt. If you profess to talk the talk and walk the walk, you're gonna have storms coming in your life. What does Jesus teach His disciples in this storm? Don't worry. Don't worry. God has everything under control."

The devotional lasts longer than any other part of the meeting, including the injury update and academic report. Afterward, the academic adviser lists the players who have papers and tests this week. Rudi is doing a paper on affirmative action and must show the adviser his progress on a daily basis.

Before the meeting wraps up, Tuberville says, "We've got an NCAA drug test tomorrow. Testing for steroids. Shouldn't be a problem. . . . But if they checked our strength coach, that would be a different story."

Everyone laughs, even Coach Yox, who looks like he just stepped out of Gold's Gym, with his bald head and dark goatee.

After the meeting, the coaches return to their meeting rooms and Tuberville goes to his office. Tuberville's door is always open. At 10:25 A.M., defensive coordinator John Lovett peeks inside and says, "We need you."

"It's nice to be needed," Tuberville says, walking down the hallway.

"Now I can stand on the sideline on Saturday, thinking I had something to do with it."

A football game takes roughly three hours. Not counting the players, approximately seventy-five people are involved with Auburn's preparation. That includes coaches, graduate assistants, student managers, student trainers, video handlers, team doctors and trainers, secretaries, business managers, the weight-room staff, recruiting coordinators, and the media relations staff. Consider that the average graduate assistant works seventeen hours a day, which means a GA works about 102 hours a week before game day.

The ten coaches and four GA's work about twelve hundred hours a week combined. Figure that the rest of the staff puts in forty-hour weeks. That's a total of thirty-eight hundred hours of man power. All for a three-hour game.

The GA certainly has the most varied job description. He's coach, gopher, den mother, attendance taker, and whatever else needs to be done at the moment. A rite of passage, it's how every coach usually begins his college career.

When Don Dunn arrived for his GA job interview with Johnny Majors at Tennessee in 1983, the Volunteers coach was in the shower.

"Send him in here," Majors said.

So with his new suit and shiny shoes, Dunn walked into the bathroom.

"I'm standing at the edge of the shower, the place is filled with steam, and I'm already a nervous wreck. And he's soaping himself and I am talking to him and all he said was, 'Are you ready to be a Volunteer?' And I said 'Yes, sir.' And he said 'Go up and see so and so.' And that was my interview.

"So I leave and my wife picks me up on the corner. So she said, 'Did you get the job?'

"And I said, 'I'm a volunteer!'

"And she goes, 'Oh, honey, that's great. I've always loved the Tennessee Volunteers.'

"And I said, 'No, you don't understand, I'm a *volunteer*.' So I went to work at my first big job for no money."

• • •

Levorn "Porkchop" Harbin's primary responsibility is to make sure players go to class. In the mornings, he is a human wake-up call in charge of about thirty of the players housed in Sewell Hall, which is across the street from the athletic complex. The younger players and those who have academic problems aren't allowed to live off-campus. At 7:00 a.m., Porkchop (who is called Porkchop just because Tuberville thought he needed a nickname) wakes the players. They have until 7:30 a.m. to be in the cafeteria downstairs. Otherwise, they face Coach Yox.

Porkchop, who played for Division II national champion North Alabama in 1995, has heard every excuse there is. "Sometimes kids like to tell their coaches that they didn't hear me knock," he says. "But I kick that door real rude. And if that don't get them up, I got a key to get in their room. I just kind of go in and turn the lights on and start yelling and all. Shaking them up. Actually, I have a bullhorn. With the real heavy sleepers, I open the door and I just blow the horn in the room."

During the day, Porkchop shows up at various classes to check on the twelve players he is responsible for. "Sometimes I get lucky and I get maybe two or three kids in one class. If not, I have to be all over campus. I got a little golf cart to do that.

"I'm not their favorite person. But the thing about it, when I first came in, they didn't like me. But it's different now, since they know that I'm doing it because I care, and I'm fair about it regardless of who you are. I turn you in regardless—if you're Rudi Johnson or a redshirt freshman, it don't make a difference."

Of course, if they don't show up at class, Porkchop offers them up to Coach Yox. "My first victim when I first got here was [wide receiver] Ronney Daniels," says Porkchop, "and you know, Ronney Daniels last year was having a great year. And the week of the Florida game, we ran him in the stadium and he couldn't walk for three days. So that was pretty funny. And Coach Tub, I mean, it don't matter who it is or what time of the season, he'll punish you regardless."

Tony Levine is not your average GA. Not just because old-time coaches say to him, "In all my years, I ain't never coached with a Jew before."

But also because he's from Big Ten country and played wide receiver at Minnesota in the mid-nineties. Truth is, Minnesota and Alabama are about the same as lox and grits.

On staff since March, this is Levine's first Iron Bowl. "This whole year has been unlike anything I've ever seen," Levine says. "Football in Minnesota isn't anything like football in Alabama. That might be for a couple reasons. People say that in Minnesota you have the Vikings, the Timberwolves. Here you just have Auburn and Alabama. I thought this past week in playing Georgia was the most unbelievable thing I had ever seen. People stopped me in the hall this weekend and said, 'You think that was big, wait till Saturday.' In Minnesota, we thought Minnesota–Wisconsin was a big deal. It doesn't compare to this. I was talking to some people in town last night. They were saying, 'Yeah, we're going to Tuscaloosa and I'm picking up my friends and their friends and we're taking three cars with us.' I said, 'Where are your seats?' She says, 'Well we don't have tickets, we're just going.' Well, no one would just go to Madison, Wisconsin just to go and not have Minnesota–Wisconsin tickets. Those Auburn fans are just gonna go and tailgate all day. Go to the bar and watch the game, be there and just support the team. In that respect, it is just so different.

"My parents and my brother, they came down a few weeks ago for Homecoming. I was telling them, 'Now be prepared. You can't see grass on our campus for a home game. 'Cause there are so many cars parked.' And they couldn't picture it. I told my dad that there have been campers here since Tuesday. They can't imagine it. I was telling my mom, 'When we win, people go out of their house and throw toilet paper over a tree. And they have to close the streets off.' They really couldn't picture that. I don't want to make Minnesota sound like a bad deal—but at Minnesota you get to the game when the game starts and you leave when the game is over. Here, you get here two hours ahead of time, and then you got to hurry up and get into the stadium so you can get in to see the eagle fly."

Levine had to further explain to the folks back home both the toilet paper and the reason why the Tigers have an eagle for a mascot. After wins, fans head to Toomer's Corner, where College Street intersects Magnolia Avenue in the center of town, to roll the trees with toilet paper. After such a celebration, Toomer's Drug Store, which has been serving its famous lemonade ever since John Heisman coached at Auburn in 1896, looks like it's been hit by a blizzard. It's safe to say that no other town in America has a line in their budget for toilet-paper cleanup, as Auburn does. The next morning, workers painstakingly hose the trees and sweep up the soggy wads.

As for the eagle, legend has it that the nickname came from an Auburn student who was fighting in the Battle of the Wilderness in Virginia in 1864. The Confederate soldier was wounded in battle and when he regained consciousness the only living thing around him was a baby eagle. The soldier brought the eagle back to Auburn and named him War Eagle. The soldier later became a member of the faculty. In 1892, the eagle came to Auburn's game against Georgia. When Auburn scored the first touchdown, the old bird broke free and began to soar above the field. Fans looked toward the sky, saw the familiar figure, and shouted, "War-r-r-r Eagle." At the end of Auburn's 10–0 win, the eagle collapsed and died and the battle cry, "War-r-r-r Eagle" was born, as the story goes.

At practice, the linebackers can easily tell this isn't any ol' week by looking at their coach's eyes. Last week before the Georgia game, coach Joe Whitt was so emotional, he couldn't even talk. After the win, he embraced several of his players and cried. This week means even more. Whitt tells his players that he doesn't think winning a national championship would be better than beating Alabama. And he means it. "He does have a hatred burning in his heart," linebacker Alex Lincoln says.

"He's big on being tough," Lincoln says. "He feels he's a tough man and we ought to be tough, too. He tells a story about if we ever see him in the woods and he's fighting a bear, that we'd better help the bear out. A lot of times before practice, before a big game—and he knows it's going to be a physical game—he'll come out and sing, 'There'll be blood on the saddle . . . ' And he always uses his hunting dogs as a reference to linebackers. 'You don't have to make a hunting dog go hunt,' he'll say. 'A linebacker should want to hit just like a hunting dog wants to hunt.' "

Linebacker Rob Pate had a good day at practice as the weather was cool. The group went over how to cover Alabama's stack-I formation with three wide receivers. Other than that, Pate says, "It was a regular old practice. Same old stuff." It's mostly about mental preparation now. "About now, I start getting a little bit of butterflies, not thinking about class so much. I like to come over here and watch a bit more film. Just so I recognize everything, because when we get out there in a game, it's just so much more faster than what we see in practice. You just have to react. You can't second-guess yourself. You just have to go out there and make the play."

After practice, all the players are given their allotment of four tickets to the game. Pate's family is lucky because brother Philip, a redshirt freshman linebacker, is also on the team, which means his family gets eight tickets. Since the Pates are from Birmingham, which is about forty-five minutes from Tuscaloosa, they could certainly use more.

For Pate, it will be strange not to play at Birmingham's Legion Field. "It would have been neat to have played my last game in my hometown against the team I grew up watching and loving," he says.

At the venerable Legion Field, there will be another Saturday game going on, a youth football game called the Shug Bear Bowl. Instead of the estimated crowd of 100,000 that usually rolls in for the Iron Bowl, there will be around 1,500 parents and kids in the stands. There will be no vendors lining the streets or kids hustling cars for five dollars, parking them in the empty spaces of neighbor's yards. Even the Tide and Tiger bar, which is jammed on Iron Bowl Saturday, will be closed.

"You know, this last one's the one that I've thought about all my life," Pate says. "But to be able to play in Tuscaloosa, I think that's gonna make it, you know, all the more sweeter if we can go in there and get a victory. They beat us here for the first time ever last season, and if we could just go back, and do the same thing then that would mean everything."

Thursday

ALABAMA

If the bulk of the physical work is done on Tuesday and Wednesday, the mental work begins on Thursday. As the players and coaches bring their focus further to bear on Saturday, they need the comforts of food. No one eats like a college kid, except maybe a college coach. DuBose's secretary, Dee Gibson (ironic, yes, but no relation to the secretary with whom DuBose had the affair), keeps dishes full of hard candy and small candy bars on the front of her desk. On Thursdays, secondary coach Charlie Harbison's wife, Gloria, bakes cookies and breads for the afternoon meeting her husband conducts.

The coaching staff has breakfast together every Thursday morning in the players' lounge across the hall from the locker room. Along one cinder-block wall is a table with steam trays of cheese grits, ham, and biscuits, as well as a bowl of sliced fruit and coffee and juice.

In one corner of the room, *SportsCenter* is on a television set up above eye level. Ivy Williams asks if anyone knows whether Arizona State fired Bruce Snyder on Wednesday. "I got two calls from the West Coast last night," he says. "Coaches send up smoke signals." Williams eats and leaves before *SportsCenter* confirms the rumor. At another table, coaches Dabo Swinney and Charlie Harbison and video coordinator Don Rawson challenge graduate assistants Kevin Sherrer and Will Friend to find a teammate for a three-on-three game next week. Instantly, both sides dub the matchup "old guys versus young guys."

Swinney gets up from the table to refill his plate. High on the wall behind the food table are cardboard pennants with the insignias of the other SEC teams. Directly above one steam tray is the insignia from Auburn. One side loses its contact with the wall and sways precariously. Then the whole insignia falls to the floor. "It's an omen!" Swinney proclaims. "They're going down!"

The staff finishes up and assembles upstairs for its last meeting. Williams looks up at the wall he has looked at every morning since he arrived to work for Stallings nearly seven years ago.

"There's a picture missing—Dwayne Rudd," he says, referring to the All-American linebacker at Alabama who played from 1994 to 1996. "They got legs."

Friend chimes in, points at a blank spot on the wall. "A picture of Bryant–Denny was right there."

"I ain't touching nothing," Ellis Johnson says, "until I got somewhere to hang it."

Rawson, who's been fretting about giving the devotional at this meeting for days, comes in, sits down, and nervously clears his throat.

DuBose comes in and sits down. "There's a Unity Rally tonight at Calvary Baptist," DuBose tells the staff. The religious event is meant to bring the university community together with the student and faculty of Stillman College, a predominantly black institution near campus. "Jeremiah Castille [another former Alabama All-American] will be the speaker. You will be blessed by being there. We're trying to develop oneness, bring people together."

DuBose nods at Rawson, who begins to speak, reading quietly from a three-paragraph passage entitled "Today."

"Those servants who refuse to get bogged down in and anchored to the past are those who pursue the objectives of the future. People who do this are seldom petty. They are too involved in getting a job done to be occupied with yesterday's hurts and concerns. Very near the end of his full and productive life, Paul wrote: 'I have fought the good fight. I have finished the course. I have kept the faith.' What a grand epitaph! He seized every day by the throat. He relentlessly pursued life.

"I know human nature well enough to realize that some people excuse their bitterness over past hurts by thinking: 'It's too late to change. I've been injured and the wrong done against me is too great for me ever to forget it. Maybe Paul could press on, not me.' A person with this mind-set is convinced that he or she is the exception to the command to forgive, and he is determined not to change.

"But when God holds out hope, when God makes promises, there are no exceptions. With each new dawn there is delivered to your door a fresh, new package called 'today.' God has designed each of us in such a way that we can handle only one package at a time . . . and all the grace we need will be supplied by Him as we live out that day."

Rawson needn't have worried. The reading is entirely appropriate.

DuBose goes over the practice schedule for today and informs the staff that he has scheduled a light workout on the practice field for Friday afternoon. He adjourns the meeting without mentioning that they will not meet in this room again.

A few minutes later, the defensive staff meeting begins, although linebackers coach Jeff Rouzie is not in the room. Johnson is sitting close to the screen, slowly drawing out the game plan for Saturday. The work he is doing could be done more quickly and efficiently on a computer by most coaches. Johnson, however, is computer-illiterate.

"Look," secondary coach Charlie Harbison says, "I wanted to say something."

"Don't say anything you'll regret after the game Saturday," Johnson teases.

"I've enjoyed being on the staff," Harbison says. "I'm a better coach when I leave than I was when I got here."

Being men, and football coaches at that, they treat Harbison's show of emotion as if it were a soiled diaper. There are mumbled responses and the meeting continues. Thompson, sitting at the other end of a long table from the screen, announces tendencies as they appear on screen.

"Second and nine, ten or eleven and they just threw an incomplete pass," he says. "They run the ball on the next play a high percentage of the time.

"Third and 5-to-9, they run streak route."

"We'll just sit on them with man [coverage]," Johnson replies.

Harbison begins to sing a gospel song in a nice tenor.

"Cheese, go get with Jeff and get him up," Thompson says. "His spriits are a little down."

"His singing ain't going to help," Johnson teases. After a moment, he returns to his task. "Auburn has done a helluva job," he says. "It's an average football team. They've learned how not to lose before they learned how to win."

From behind the closed door of DuBose's office comes the sound of masking tape being ripped off its roll. Administrative assistant Cedric Burns emerges from the office, goes into a supply closet, and grabs a couple of plastic garbage bags.

"What are you doing?," Burns is asked.

"Packing," he says.

Back in the defensive meeting, the more video Thompson watches, the more he is convinced that his defensive line can take advantage of Auburn left guard Hart McGarry. Thompson, watching Auburn's offense on third down and four-to-seven yards to go, points his laser at McGarry's image on screen. "This kid here ain't very good and ain't very strong. There's no way he can block Aries."

Johnson asks Thompson if he can shift the alignment so that McGarry must block Monroe, one-one-one. "If we're smart, we could do so much with him." On screen, Leard, the Auburn quarterback, chooses the wrong receiver. Thompson yells at the screen. "That's third and nine and he throws a two-yard route. A two-yard route!"

Johnson looks up from his work scripting defenses. "He never throws anything of length," Johnson says. "They do such a great job of protecting Leard. Not pass protection. I mean, keeping him from having to do things. I think the quarterback has gone backward. Maybe it's because of the run." A couple of more pass plays appear on screen. "If we keep 32 [Rudi Johnson] around sixty yards," Johnson says, "and they get two hundred fifty yards passing, we got a chance to win."

The room goes quiet for a moment before Johnson says, "Tommy, with all that, comes out smelling like a rose." He is referring to the preseason problems Tuberville had. "A kid with a gun charge [Deandre Green], he comes out smelling like a rose.

"That Deandre Green, we had him in camp at Georgia Tech,"

Thompson says. "He's not a bad kid. It's the environment he grew up in. You get in his face and challenge him, he'll respond."

Harbison is gone, perhaps to cheer up Rouzie. Thompson, just before he leaves Johnson in the room by himself, teases him about The Citadel job. "I'm going to be Eli's director of football operations "

" No, I'm going to tell Les [Robinson, The Citadel athletic director] to hire you as coach. I'll go down there and be your consultant and draw my one twenty-five [$125,000 salary Johnson will be getting through June 2002] from here."

Thompson thinks for a moment and says, "Maybe we should just drive there and open a bar."

As the defensive coaches split up, Ronnie Cottrell's Deputy Dawg countenance is drooping a little more than usual. All the recruiting groundwork he began laying last spring went for naught on November 1, when DuBose and his staff were fired. Cottrell, like Johnson and Charlie Stubbs, is under contract through June 2002. However, none of them has any guarantee that a new coach will retain them.

Back in his office, Cottrell asks, "Have you thought about the running of this deal? On one hand, you're fired. And on the other hand, you're asked to recruit guys when you don't know if you're going to be here. The guy who fired you is asking you to help him." He catches himself. He understands what is expected of him. "Professionally," he says, "it's the right thing to do." That doesn't make it easy. "Ever since we been fired," Cottrell adds. "I can't answer the [recruits'] questions.

" 'Are you going to be there?' I don't know.

" 'Can I play defensive line?' I don't know. You need to ask the new coach.

"Of all my twenty years of coaching, I don't know if there's a more helpless feeling."

Actually, Cottrell knows a more helpless feeling. On Friday night, November 3, six days after the loss to Central Florida and three days after he was fired, he and Harbison walked into a high school game in Troy, Alabama. Cottrell's cell phone rang. He and his wife, Jean, who have two children, had been preparing to adopt. "It was our attorney in California," Cottrell says. "The birth mother decided she wanted to keep the baby."

Cottrell stops himself from talking about his problems. "There are guys around here who, without question, won't be here," he says, referring to other assistants. "The Cottrells are going to rebound. We'll know where we're going to be and what we're doing. We're going to bounce back."

Cottrell's phone rings. It is Mac Tyler calling from Milford, Connecticut. Tyler, who graduated from Jess Lanier High in Bessemer, just outside of Birmingham, is another heralded defensive lineman in Cottrell's class of 2000. Tyler didn't qualify academically to play this year, so he enrolled at Milford Academy, in Connecticut, an infamous prep school known for being a good place to park nonqualifiers or partial qualifiers.

"Mac, you still committed to here?" Cottrell asks. "We need you to come here. Are you going to hang in there?"

Cottrell puts his hand over the mouthpiece of his office phone. "He just told me he's going to stay committed."

He speaks to Tyler for a little while, then transfers him to someone else in the athletic department. "It's just hard to express the frustration in trying to do a good job in recruiting when you're somewhat powerless. You're trying to do a good job when your family is worried about where you're going to be."

Shortly before noon, Johnson, Thompson, and Rouzie go eat lunch. Every Thursday, they drive over to the Hooters Restaurant in Tuscaloosa. It's a chance to blow off steam more than anything else. They swap recruiting tales, coaching gossip, and just relax. As they await the check, Thompson suddenly looks at Rouzie and says, "Don't forget to get your teeth checked." Rouzie says he's going Tuesday. Thompson's concern for Rouzie's dental health is touching. However, it has more to do with financial health. "The truth is," Thompson says, "the team dentist cleans our teeth for half price and we're not going to be here too much longer." He shrugs and smiles embarrassedly.

Walk-on kickers are the witness protection program for college football. You can't be any more anonymous and still be wearing a uniform. Freshman Gabe Giardina is five feet six inches tall, skinny, and wears glasses. In a locker room filled with guys who could use him for dental floss, Giardina looks like he should be pushing a laundry cart. That's not the only way in which Giardina is out of place. He grew up at Penn State. His father Frank is the director of radio and television for the Nittany Lions. One of Gabe's best friends growing up was Jonathan Ganter, the son of Penn State offensive coordinator Fran Ganter.

Frank Giardina is active in the Fellowship of Christian Athletes in the Happy Valley. His son is a quiet, deeply religious young man. Gabe can't really say why he decided to visit Alabama. He had been set to walk-on at Marshall. Coach Bob Pruett had been encouraging about the possibility of getting Gabe a full scholarship after his first season. He had also looked at Virginia Tech and North Carolina State. However, the first time he drove on the Tuscaloosa campus last April, Gabe says, demonstrating with a sigh, "It was just a little bit easier to breathe."

He met with a few walk-ons who were still on a high from the A-Day Game a few days earlier. They told him about the reaction of the fans. "Out of the tunnel, forty thousand people were there and they were cheering for us and we were nobodies," Gabe remembered them saying. He smiles. "The fans see that crimson jersey and it ignites a fire. It doesn't matter who it is."

While on campus, Giardina met with three coaches: Ronnie Cottrell, Charlie Harbison, and Ellis Johnson. Their interest in him struck a chord. "When I was being recruited at Marshall, I met Coach Bobby Pruett, a good guy. Later, I said hello to him and he just didn't remember who I was. I came down here and I wanted to hate it. I wanted to do the easy thing and go to Marshall. I thought, 'I don't know what's going on, God, but You're really opening a feeling in my heart.'"

Most of all, Gabe says, he was attracted by DuBose. Frank says his son took an interest in the Crimson Tide because of DuBose's very public marital problems and his spiritual rebirth. "I knew he was hurting," Gabe says. "It was a very hard thing to go through. I had seen how he had come through that. I had read a lot of things and talked to certain players. I thought, 'Man, I want to be a part of what's going on down there,' because of Coach's new attitude, the way he had been changed. He is a much more genuine, humble guy, how God had broken him. That's a man of God. That's who I want to play for. I want to play for a Christian coach."

On the first day of classes, the first day that walk-ons may practice, Cottrell called Giardina and told him he would be on the 105-man roster. "If my five-six frame could dunk a basketball," Giardina says, "I could have done it then. I was just flipping out. And I walk into the locker room and see my nameplate and see my helmet. The helmet, I think of the Derrick Thomases and the Shaun Alexanders and the Ryan Pflugners who have come before, and I thank God for the opportunity."

The decision to include Giardina was made by DuBose, who took a shine to the earnest young kicker. In September, DuBose spoke to a Fellowship of Christian Athletes meeting. That afternoon, Giardina told his head coach he was looking forward to hearing him speak. The last thing Giardina—a self-described "sixth-string walk-on nothing" who had been on campus less than a month—thought he would hear was a personal response.

"I was expecting, 'Thanks,'" Giardina says. "Coach said, 'Well, Gabe, that means a lot that you say that. I hope you'll be praying for me.'"

On the Thursday night before the Tennessee game, DuBose opened his home to his team to hear a woman "give her testimony," that is, to speak of her Christianity. Giardina says twenty players showed up, "a pretty good mix of walk-ons and scholarships."

"They fed us pizza and sodas," Giardina says. "We went out and sat on his deck and he came out and sat and talked to me like he was my uncle. Not about football. He was talking in front of his fireplace about life." After the woman spoke, each player in the room took turns praying. Just remembering what happened chilled Giardina. "She saw into my heart a little bit," he says. "She said, 'Mike, pray for him,' and I turned around . . ." Giardina paused to try and dislodge the emotional frog from his throat. "Coach hugged me for three or four minutes. Guys put their arms around me. He just prayed for me for three minutes. I'm sitting here embracing him and praying for him as another guy, not a head coach but for my Christian brother."

Giardina took DuBose's firing hard. "It was a hard thing to accept at first because I love him so much and everything he's done for me," Giardina says. "This is God's plan. God doesn't make mistakes. I know where I'm supposed to be. He's shown me so much going through this 3–7 season."

Giardina arrived at the interview with a camera in his hand. He had gone into DuBose's office to see him, say goodbye, and get a picture of the two of them together. "He knows this is what's supposed to happen," Giardina says. "That comforts him. He knows God is in control. This is His plan. Something good is going to come of it."

The chilly, gloomy conditions that have predominated in Tuscaloosa all week have only gotten worse. A steady rain forces DuBose to move the last full practice of the year into the indoor facility. The noise reverberates off the walls. The spectators, including a smattering of former players, trustees, and CBS-TV analyst Todd Blackledge, line the near sideline, keeping one eye on the footballs that fly back and forth between the bored walk-ons who are also on the sideline.

Watching football practice is never easy for anyone who isn't intimately associated with the depth chart. On this day, it's impossible. Many of the players, as part of a celebration of the final practice, are wearing someone else's jersey: receivers Jeremy Drummond and Sam Collins have swapped jerseys, as have tight end Shawn Draper and right guard Will Cuthbert. Antonio Carter is wearing Freddie Milons's No. 15, while Arvin Richard is wearing Carter's No. 2. Though it's cold and wet outside, the air in the facility is light. Enthusiasm is high. DuBose, at the close of practice, confirms that, as every Crimson Tide fan hoped, Auburn week has been the curative tonic for a broken team spirit.

"We have been more focused this week than any week all year," he says. Seconds before, DuBose gathered his team together for his final postpractice talk. As he finishes, the players break the huddle with a whoop. The underclassmen grab the seniors and hoist them up for a ride to the locker room. The larger seniors are shared loads, with underclassmen clinging to each leg as if they were trying to toss a caber. As the players leave the field, they are met by members of the student government association, including president Emily McMurphy, who are handing out goody bags filled with snacks. "We want them to know the students are behind them, win or lose," she says. That bright sentiment isn't exactly shared by her 19,000 constituents, but it's the thought that counts.

DuBose meets a handful of waiting beat writers who ask him one more time if he has decided what he will say to his team before his final Iron Bowl. "I've thought about it," he says. "I've thought about how I'm going to say it. I'm not sure I can say it. But they know it."

An hour or so after practice concludes, Paul Hogan limps out of the training room after taking treatment on his bad ankle. He will share in the responsibility of trying to hold off Auburn's massive freshman tackle, DeMarco McNeil. He has been studying the Auburn defensive line all week. Tonight, however, he isn't going to look at a single videotape. Instead, he says as he walks to his truck, he will "chill out; play Nintendo. You think about the game tomorrow. We'll have a meeting tomorrow night. I mean, you got to have some time off. You can't constantly think about it. Everything is in. You know exactly what they're going to do. I watched a little bit of everybody. McNeil's a good player. I'm going to be there, ready to hit him."

For months, the city of Tuscaloosa has been planning a parade for tonight to kick off the celebration of Auburn's return to Alabama. They planned for the parade to travel down University Boulevard from campus to downtown. They planned for floats to be constructed by the students. They arranged for fireworks to be set off over the Black Warrior River.

They didn't plan for nearly an inch of cold rain and a fandom depressed by a 3–7 record. The crowd for the parade could be measured in the hundreds. On the Strip, the portion of University Boulevard near campus where the students converge on most Thursday nights, the parade patrons stand in the bars to stay dry and go out when they see the floats approach. The bands still play. Fire trucks cruise by, dragging toy Tigers in their wake. The fireworks, diffused by clouds and smoke, seem representative of the night and the entire season. They are a mess.

On Thursday nights during the season, the football team reserves the recreation room at the Highland Apartments, where many of the players live on the northeast corner of campus. Graduate assistant Mike Bloomgren brings several game videos over from the football office and lures the players to come watch them with hot hors d'oeuvres,

cake, and a cooler full of soft drinks. Though it's raining, and the parade might have lured the players away, Bloomgren is beaming.
"Thirty kids came to eat and watch football," he says. "It's amazing,
knowing that they went to the parade." It's the most players that have
shown up in weeks—another sign that the players are focused and
preparing mentally to play. There haven't been a whole lot of those
signs in recent weeks.

Bloomgren brought five tapes of Auburn playing LSU, Mississippi
State, Florida, and Georgia, as well as a copy of the Tide's victory over
the Tigers a year ago. "I was watching the defensive ends and the linebackers," tight end Shawn Draper says. "When the linebackers walk up
[toward the line] the defensive ends always come wide."

As Auburn sophomore wide receiver Tim Carter scores on a 37-yard
pass against Arkansas, Bloomgren says, "He looks like Freddie [Milons]
used to."

Draper defends his teammate. "Freddie is back," he says. "He looks
good."

"Yeah," defensive end Kelvis White says, "he didn't trust that knee
for a while. He couldn't cut."

A buzz remains in the room. The players know that it's their last
chance to redeem themselves.

"May as well hang it all out," White says. "Go out. Have fun."

"Ain't got to watch film Monday," chimes in Draper.

"No one to critique you," White says.

As they talk, Bloomgren nods in agreement, but he's also a little
miffed. "I think we're going to play. I think that every week," he says.
He points at them, "If you motherfuckers cared as much as Coach
did . . ." Bloomgren leaves the sentence unfinished.

The coach starts to clean up. The players help, in their own way.
There are still soft drinks in the cooler. The players carry as many as
they can hold away to their rooms. Within a matter of minutes, the
cooler is empty.

Not far away, DuBose spoke at the Unity Rally over at Stillman College. Rawson, the videographer, set up and locked in his camera on the
podium, then went home to eat dinner with his family. He returned at

the end of the evening, long after DuBose had concluded. The coach didn't speak long. In fact, he admitted that he almost decided not to speak at all "with what was going on." But he came in sports coat and sports shirt, Bible in hand.

"I am proof," DuBose said, "that God hates sin but loves sinners. He has forgiven me.

"I want to ask you a question," he said to the largely young crowd. "Who is your God? Or what is your God? I've read and heard this week where the game coming up this coming Saturday is the biggest event that has ever happened in the city of Tuscaloosa. That is a sad statement. That is a sad, sad statement for this city to make. The most important event this week is this rally right now. If there's one life changed, this event is greater than any Alabama–Auburn game ever will be."

It's not surprising to hear that statement from a man of God. It's not a statement you would ever expect to hear from the head football coach of the University of Alabama, even a lame-duck coach fewer than forty-eight hours away from his final game. DuBose is so new to his faith that he has yet to figure out how to keep one foot in the religious world and the other in the football world. He is convinced that he is a better man and a better coach now that he has found God. When athletic director Mal Moore is asked if DuBose's religious fervor interfered with his ability to win football games, Moore almost blanched. It may be merely a coincidence that as DuBose reached deeper into his religious well, the team fell deeper into its own hole. In truth, the losses could have just as easily pushed DuBose to lean more heavily on his faith. It's a line that Florida State coach Bobby Bowden, who often gives his testimony on pulpits across the southeast, straddles with the grace of the late Gene Kelly. DuBose has yet to hear that same music.

"We pull up to the stadium and I see literally thousands and thousands of people cheering with such passion for the team and passion for the game," DuBose continues. "I get a pain in my heart. They don't have the same passion the next day in church. They don't have the same passion for Jesus. They don't have the same passion for serving God, and they have made football their God. I can relate to it. For a long, long time, football was my God. I put it before my family. I put it before everything. Because of the grace of God, it is not my God anymore. God is my God. My family is second. My job is third."

DuBose then used football as a metaphor to reach his audience. "There is Satan's team and there is God's team, and you're on one of the two. You can pull for Auburn. You can pull for Alabama. You can pull for somebody else. I'm telling you, as you are sitting there right now, you are serving Satan or you are serving God. This book," he said, waving his well-worn black Bible in his left hand, "does not lie. The last chapter tells you: God's team wins. If I could recruit a young man and I could guarantee him without a shadow of a doubt . . . that if he came to our team, he would win the national championship every year, what would he do? He'd come, wouldn't he? You would, too. That's what He's telling us. My prayer when you leave here together is that you'll be on God's team." With that, DuBose exited the stage to his right.

AUBURN

It is 5:30 A.M. and Alex Lincoln is trying to pee. He is standing in the locker room, facing the man administering the NCAA drug test.

"Can I turn around?" Lincoln asks.

"No. I need to make sure it's your sample."

A few minutes pass.

"So you like Mobile?" the man asks.

"Buddy, if you want anything to happen, you better shut up," Lincoln says. Then Lincoln closed his eyes and thought of waterfalls.

Afterward, Lincoln goes to the training room for treatment, as he does twice a day, in the morning and before practice, for about an hour each time. Throughout the day, players file in and out of the trainer's room, an endless stream of deep thigh bruises, concussions, and ankle sprains.

Therapy for both of Lincoln's injured shoulders consists of ice, electric stimulation, time in the whirlpool, range of motion exercises, and limited weightlifting. And then more ice. "I'm not used to being on so much ice," Lincoln says. "I feel like a dead fish."

Because of the concussion he suffered on Saturday, the team doctor checks his balance and asks about any headaches. After Lincoln was knocked out in the game's final minutes, the trainers learned that his concussion wasn't very severe. To test his awareness, they asked Lincoln to name the U.S. president. "We don't know yet," Lincoln told them. "They're still counting the votes in Florida."

Lincoln is fortunate that his concussion wasn't as serious as the one suffered by wide receiver Tim Carter in the second quarter of the Georgia game. Carter caught a pass and was struck on the top of the helmet by a tackler. Medical personnel ran to him, an ambulance drove on the field, and the game was stopped for fifteen minutes. Auburn's players gathered and knelt in prayer. Georgia's players did the same thing. Then both teams came together in one huddle and prayed. When Carter returned to the sideline later in the game, everyone exhaled. However, he won't play on Saturday.

"Just seeing that replay of that hit on Tim, man, it just scares you," Lincoln says. "You know, it's such a violent game. You never know when something like that is going to happen to you. My heart goes out to him because I know how he must feel. And I'm happy my concussion was not so severe and that I am going to be able to play, because this is going to be my last chance at this. And that's why we've worked so hard with treatment this week to get it one hundred percent. I feel like my team needs me out there, plus I want to be out there for them. I would like to say that I'm three times as good as I was after the Georgia game. I expect to get even better. I expect to play with a little soreness. That's just going to be part of it. I have my range of motion back. I can get my hands over my head and I don't have any problems. It doesn't hitch when I'm moving my arms, as opposed to Sunday when I could barely move around. I was just a big stiff board. You can't play linebacker like that. You can play with a little pain, but you want to have that movement."

At the 9:00 A.M. coaches' meeting, the staff goes over the usual topics, including the status of Rudi's paper (he's progressing) and the status of Rudi's ankle injury (it's improving). As usual, the coaches don't talk much about X's and O's in the morning meeting. They discuss what warm-ups to wear. Tuberville reminds everyone that practice tapes must be collected and erased. The weather report is given. It's expected to be cold and rainy.

"Do we receive or kick?" Tuberville asks.

"Kick," Gran says. "The wind's not supposed to go hard."

"I guess we'll see how the temperature is," says Tuberville.

Equipment manager Frank Cox is playing close attention to the forecast because he's responsible for bringing the rain gear and heaters. One thing he hasn't worried about lately is the team's Popsicle supply. "I get an ass-chewin' if we don't have Popsicles in the freezer," Cox says.

The first time Cox handed in his expense report after Tuberville was hired, the business office took notice.

"Um, Mr. Cox, is this a mistake: twelve hundred dollars for Popsicles?"

"No ma'am," Cox said. "We have a head coach who likes Popsicles."

This afternoon, practice is moved to the indoor facility because of a steady rain. Though center Cole Cubelic practices with the first team most of the time, he still doesn't know if he's going to get the start.

"When it's a situation like this, they usually tell you real late, like the day of the game," Cubelic says. "Which makes the situation worse, because you think about it a lot. I try not to worry too much."

Everything now is in place. "I want Thursday to be my best day of practice because it's the last time you're gonna do something until it's time for the game," quarterback Ben Leard says. "If I mess it up on Thursday, I'm afraid I'm gonna mess it up in the game. Sometimes, if you don't do well on Thursdays, it's in the back of your head. It sets my mood for the rest of the week."

Norman is at practice, of course. He watches Leard and the rest of the group as they leave the field. "I have a good feeling," Norman says. "I've seen a lot of practices and they're ready. I can tell from the intensity and the emotion."

On Thursdays after wins, the players eat dinner at their coaches' houses. Tuberville started doing this so the players would get to see a different side of their coaches. "Players need to see you as a parent, not just as a guy who just screams or hollers at them all the time," Tuberville says.

At the defensive line dinner at coach Don Dunn's house, the players go through six bags of potato chips, four pans of macaroni and cheese, ten ribs each, four pieces of chicken each, plus baked beans, bread, and dessert. There are never any leftovers, either.

"They bring their Tupperware along," Dunn says.

At the linebackers' dinner at Joe Whitt's house, Joe Jr. entertains everyone with stories about his father. Joe Jr. speaks in a whisper so his father, who is in an adjacent room, can't hear. Some Mr. Tough Guy, Joe Jr. says, as he tells the story about the time he pinned his dad against the refrigerator and his dad pleaded for mercy.

Suddenly, a voice from the other room is heard. "That did not happen," says Coach Whitt. "He's lying."

Everyone laughs.

All the while they devoured ribs, chicken, Brunswick stew, sausage, baked quail, potato salad and then ice cream and cake. Since Whitt is a hunter, every week he tries to serve some game animal. "Basically, quail tastes like chicken, but it's neat to watch guys who are from Miami, like James Callier, who never been exposed to any of that kind of food," Lincoln says. "They look at a little piece of meat and pick around it."

Every Thursday night, Tuberville does "Tiger Talk," a radio show broadcast live from the Auburn University Club. Though it's a call-in show, mostly it's a comment show. Fans suggest plays and Tuberville listens.

When fans arrive at their reserved tables, they are greeted with this memo: "The live show will be broadcast over the speakers in the dining room. You will hear the phone calls as they come in. We encourage you to react to any comments you hear with Auburn enthusiasm. Your applause will be heard on the air. Be sure to return every War Eagle from callers, guests, etc.! YELLING WAR EAGLE IS APPROPRIATE AND ENCOURAGED! IT WILL BE HEARD ON THE AIR!"

Coach Terry Price remembers the first time a fan greeted him with a handshake and a hearty, "War Eagle." At the time, Price didn't know Auburn etiquette. He didn't know "War Eagle" was a salutation that was expected to be returned.

"War Eagle!" the fan said.

"Hi, how'ya doin'?" Price said.

Silence.

More silence.

"Um, War Eagle?" Price said and the fan finally left contented.

"Tiger Talk" begins with the host asking Tuberville about the cold and rainy forecast.

Tuberville: "We don't worry about it. The coaches and players can't control it. What we do is prepare for it. We prepare for cold, rain, and hot. We have warm heaters for the sidelines. We have big-fan air-conditioners. You just don't worry about it. You just talk to your quarterbacks mainly. The quarterback and your center are the two guys you are concerned about.

"As for practice, it's gone well. We've just come off of a win against Georgia. We had to break the guys down a little bit on Tuesday. We're not just going through the motions. We've had contact today. We had to go indoors today. Defensively, we look like we've got our legs back right where we need. We just had several guys go out with injuries. We've had a few concussions and some guys with some shoulder problems, but it looks like we are ready to go. We're one hundred percent and everybody is looking forward to it."

HOST: "Let's go to the phones. We have John in Mobile. Go ahead John."

JOHN: "We've got to stop Alabama's offense. We've got to stop their quarterback."

TUBERVILLE: "John, don't give our game plan away. [Laughter.] Alabama has a good football team. They're 3–7 but they recruited well. Everybody knows about the great recruits they have had for the last three, four years. The thing, of course, that we're going to have to do is to give the ball to Rudi. There's no secret to that. We're gonna run Rudi and we're going to see if they can stop him. If they can, then we'll throw. I think that our players will be up for the challenge."

HOST: "James from Birmingham, you're on *Tiger Talk*, go ahead."

JAMES: "The talent we have in receivers, we should be able to throw the ball deep against Alabama's secondary. Are we going to?"

TUBERVILLE: "We're going to throw the ball deep. Of course last week we threw the ball deep seven times in the first half only. And that's a lot of times to get the ball down the field. That's always in our game plan. It just depends what people try to do to us. We ran several reverses this season. We always try to fit it in, in an opportune time when people don't expect it."

MARY FROM FLORIDA: "War Eagle!"

CROWD: "War Eagle!"

MARY: "We drove all the way up here in the rain today, just to be here. We're going to a basketball game tomorrow night and then we're going to Tuscaloosa to Tiger Walk. We don't have any tickets to the game, but if anyone knows where any are. Last week we thought at the Georgia game whomever put the "Eye of the Tiger" music on, it was great and we thought it brought a lot of enthusiasm. So, everybody, enjoy the Tiger Walk. I'd like to say War Eagle to all my friends in northwest Florida and south Alabama. War Eagle!"

CROWD: "War Eagle!"

HOST: "We've got a question from the audience."

A girl, about eight years old, goes to the podium and asks what turns out to be the best question of the day.

KELSEY: "Do you think our defensive line will get to their quarterback?"

TUBERVILLE: "Our defensive line will try very hard to get up to their quarterback. Every play. That's a good question. We've probably have improved in that area as much as any area all year long. Our coaches have done a super job of teaching these guys, especially the younger players. Some of these younger guys, I can see it in their face all week long that they are kinda in a little bit of a daze getting ready to play this game, because they grew up in this state and they've seen this rivalry."

NEXT CALLER . . . RICHARD: "Just want to give you guys a big War Eagle and let you know you're doing a great job. You seem to have a real affection for the players. It's amazing with all the team's success this year, it seems to be a team effort. You don't see a lot of individual stars, even as good as Rudi is. And I think that's probably what makes this team so special. I have a couple of questions since a lot of the others didn't have any questions. One is in reference to Rudi. You do a great job of finding talent. I'd like to know what areas are you emphasizing next year. The other question I have is on offense. Why do we do the lateral pass so much? It seems to me that the risk outweighs its benefits. We don't really seem to get all that much on it, but it comes up to be intercepted. Another caller earlier also wanted more downfield passing. On defense, I thought that the pressure was really good Saturday night. The defense played real good. They played real tight. It's good to see them placed closer to the line of scrimmage. They seem to do worse when they are playing so far back. Overall, I think the game plan that we used against Georgia will work against Alabama. I'll be there Saturday. I'll be there yelling and screaming. I would like to say that we need a loud stadium on Saturday. If they want to sit and watch the Jumbotron, they can do a better job staying at home."

TUBERVILLE: "You about got it all down, I guess. From Rudi all the way to watching the Jumbotron. The lateral pass is the pass that we have several options on. We throw the ball down the field. We'll throw out to the wide receiver. And that's basically up to Ben Leard, so I'll let you take that up with him. On recruiting: We are recruiting in all areas this year, but mainly on the offensive and defensive line. We've got to get some more to go along with what we have. I think that recruiting's going along great."

DAN FROM MOBILE: "I'd like to tell everybody War Eagle! I have a question about a player on the team, one of the more exciting players, Tim Carter. . . . I know that he got hurt at the game. I heard he's all right. I just wanted to see how he's doing in practice this week and what's his status."

TUBERVILLE: "Tim's been doing fine. He didn't do a lot this week. What they do when you have a concussion is evaluate you as the week goes on. He's a very lucky guy. Getting hit on the side of the head. Watching it on TV, it's not a pretty sight. But fortunately, he's fine. Our doctors do a great job in those situations. He's an inspiration to the other guys. He's going through a lot. He was injured the last two years."

BRYON FROM GEORGIA: "War Eagle, Coach."

CROWD: "War Eagle!"

BYRON: "My question has already been answered but I have a new one. What chance does Rudi have to come back his senior year, and what kind of record can he break for next year?"

TUBERVILLE: "Well I hope Rudi comes back. But he'll have to make that decision after the season to see if he wants to come back and get his degree. He's much improved from what he began. He's had a great year. His offensive line is doing better. Most of them will be around next year. Just being around Rudi, he's not a selfish person. He always gives everybody praise. He is pleasant to be around. He's got a lot of improving to do. But thank goodness for Rudi this year. He is a potential leading candidate for the Heisman Trophy next year."

CASEY: "War Eagle, Coach."

CROWD: "War Eagle!"

KEVIN FROM MOBILE: "Coach, I just want you to know I'm an Alabama fan all the way. I can see the twinkle in your eye from that loud crowd you got there. Basically, Alabama recruited a lot of egos, instead of talent. But you could be outcoached this weekend." Click. New caller.

CROWD: "War Eagle!"

KEN: "War Eagle! I was at the game at Birmingham ten years ago. I walked into the game about two and a half hours before kickoff. That's what I'd like to do this year. Get there two and a half hours ahead of time and get a pep rally going. Take that Alabama crowd out of it. So that we can get a good start."

TUBERVILLE: "That sounds good, Ken. We will arrive there at twelve. Tiger Walk is at Gate 19. We'll start our pep rally. We'll just carry it inside of the stadium at two-thirty."

GARY IN COLUMBUS: "War Eagle, Coach."

CROWD: "War Eagle!"

GARY: "I'll be there Saturday. Auburn used to be a tough, physical football team. They whooped everybody at the line of scrimmage. And I saw that with Georgia last week. And that's why I'm not afraid one bit to go to Alabama this week. People talk about them getting up for this ball game. But I don't have any doubt that we're gonna knock them right back down like we should and like we used to do. It's just great going to ball games now. This is your era. With Coach Dye, I was never afraid to lose a ball game. It's great for you to get those physical athletes in there. We manhandled Georgia, the way I saw it. I just wanted to ask you one thing. There were a couple games this year, road games, I thought if we could have used the two-minute offense. Do we have that in our offense, or is that something you think about or you ever use when your team has a sort of rhythm and you can stick to them in that two-minute offense?"

TUBERVILLE: "We used to run our two-minute offense quite often. We run it everyday in practice. You just have to run it at the right time. The problem when you are on the road, to run the two-minute offense, you have to be real good with your signals because of the crowd noise. You usually run it more at home. We do have that in. It just depends on how the ball game goes, whether we'll run it or not. As you said, as you get the momentum, sometimes you want to get into a no-huddle offense and just see if they can keep up with you. That's a good question. Hopefully, we'll get to run it this weekend."

HOST: "Coach, we wish you the best of luck this week. We'll be at Tiger Walk at twelve."

TUBERVILLE: "We're looking forward to the challenge."

While "Who Let the Dogs Out" plays in the background, Tuberville steps down from the platform to greet his wife, Suzanne, who is sitting at the front table. After a few minutes, he leaves to return to the athletic complex for the team's 8:30 P.M. meeting.

The players are already in place in the green squeaky chairs and roll has been checked. Tuberville begins: "We leave at three, so make sure that you are ready to go. We got to get on the road. We don't want to get caught in traffic in Birmingham. About the game. One: It's the first time over at Tuscaloosa in one hundred years. There'll be a lot of people there causing a commotion. We are there to play a football game.

We're not there to get caught up in all the hype and all that stuff that is going to happen before the game, before kickoff. I'm talking composure. Like we've played all year. I want you to go in there with a level head, know what you are getting into. Think about the things we did during the week. Don't get caught up in all that hype over there, anything but playing the football game.

"When the game starts, we don't want anything to cause us to lose this football game because of fifteen-yard penalties, or anybody getting kicked out of the game. Normally, in a traditional game like this, you don't have any problems. But they've had problems all year long. They've had a lot of frustration, a lot of frustration. They don't have a coaching staff that has a whole lot of control over there with their players. So, we don't need any fifteen-yard penalties. Especially you guys on the kicking team. You guys don't get out there very often. There's going to be a lot of pushing and shoving. Don't get caught up in a lot of that stuff.

"Weather: It's going to be cool. I want you to have everything that you are going to need to wear. Everybody is going to look alike. Everybody's going to have to wear the same thing. We're going to wear the blue tights or the white tights, I don't care what. We're going to wear white uniforms so that everybody looks the same. We don't want to look like a bunch of little children going over there and dressing with a bunch of different colors. We're going to be cold, that's fine. We'll have hand warmers on the sidelines. We'll have heaters on the sidelines. Main thing is that you stay ready to play, stay stretched out.

"The game: This is an important game. Number one, because it's Alabama. Number two, because we have a chance to play in the conference championship game. We can't control anything that they do. We're gonna control what we do. We're going to play our game. Everybody's going to be fired up, jumping up and down, and that don't mean a hill of beans. You win the ball game when you play sixty minutes, not the first fifteen, not the first thirty, not the first forty-five. You've got to play sixty. Ask Georgia. They played a good thirty minutes last week. That didn't mean anything. You got to play sixty minutes. And this week we're going to have to play all the way down to the end. It doesn't make any difference what happens. We jump ahead

14-nothing, they jump ahead 14-nothing. The ball game will be won in the last fifteen, ten, five minutes. It's just how these games work out. We can jump ahead 21-nothing, but you better be playing the same the last quarter as you did the first quarter. I promise you that this thing is going to come down to the end. We got a chance to jump off and make something big out of this game. That doesn't make any difference to them. They are going to fight. They won't quit, I promise you that. They do not want to be embarrassed. National TV, first game in Tuscaloosa, they're 3–7. This will be the worst season that they will have in fifty, sixty years. And they're gonna lose it. They are going to lose it because we are going to go over there and play our game. The best team normally wins this game, and we are the best team. We're going to take care of business, be the most physical football team. Whatever it takes, we'll win the game. We're going to play better than them the whole game. We're 8–3, we're going to a bowl game. And you deserve it. Let's go take it. It's been a great privilege for me to be a part of this team this year. We got it done this year."

Tuberville then asks the two seniors, offensive tackle Colin Sears and linebacker Alex Lincoln to address the players. The coaches leave the room.

Sears walks to the front, next to a long table. "Go out and play our game and get it done," Sears says succinctly.

Lincoln then takes over. "I'm not the type to throw a stool," he says, referring to Cole Cubelic's antics earlier in the week. Then he pauses for dramatic effect. "I'm going to throw the whole table." And in exaggerated WWF fashion, Lincoln heaves the table a few feet.

The room breaks up in laughter. The meeting is over.

Friday

ALABAMA

Thirty-three secretaries and other staff members in the Alabama football office are all wearing a special crimson sweatshirt, a tradition for the day before the Auburn game. "It started out five or six years ago with five or six secretaries," equipment manager Tank Conerly says, dryly. A list for free clothes never gets shorter.

There are other, more public, unmistakable signs that Game Day is nigh. The *Tuscaloosa News* prints a map showing where University Boulevard will close for tonight's pep rally. The *News* also has a front-page story showing the deflation in Iron Bowl ticket prices. Tickets that went as high as $300 only a week earlier are now available for half that. Student tickets that sold for $125 are going for $55. The weather is bad. The morale of the Tide fans is worse.

The contested vote count in Florida for the presidency has remained a steady hum of background noise during the week. Literally background noise—Don Rawson has kept a television in the video room tuned to Fox News Channel all week. No one has watched it for any length of time, but members of the football staff have stuck their heads in the doorway to catch a headline. As the various state and federal judges have considered the recounts, it has become evident that the courtrooms will be open on Saturday and that the national news networks will be there, too. Hence, the problem—if the judges make news on Saturday, then CBS could very well interrupt its telecast of the

Iron Bowl. There isn't a telephone switching system built that could take the pounding that would ensue from irate fans in the state of Alabama. CBS News president Andrew Heyward, after frantic calls from the state, gave the network's permission for the state's affiliates to utilize a split screen. The headline in the morning's *Birmingham News* says: WIAT WON'T INTERRUPT IRON BOWL FOR ELECTION.

The republic may not have a president, but the state of Alabama has been saved.

Outside Coleman Coliseum, the parking lot is startlingly empty, looking as if it were adjacent to a mall at 4:00 A.M., not in the middle of a campus about to hold one of the biggest games in its history. The lot is awaiting the motor homes that will have been stashed elsewhere in the city or on the outskirts of campus all week. At 9:00 A.M., the motor homes may enter the lot. By 10:00 A.M., the lot will be full. An instant village will appear, with crimson flags waving and folding chairs and tables set up under the canopies.

Mike DuBose arrives at his office a few minutes after 8:30 A.M., later than usual. He finds two gifts waiting for him—one is a Beanie Baby, with a beatific smile, closed eyes, and hands clasped in prayer. It is named Hope. A woman in the athletic department has left him a leatherbound copy of the former inspirational bestseller, *Tough Times Don't Last, Tough People Do* by Dr. Robert Schiller. DuBose puts the book on his desk and takes an admiring glance at it. The office no longer looks like his. The brick wall behind him, which had been adorned by large framed photographs of his family, is bare.

Friday mornings are a time of reflection for a football staff. The game plan is in. The players have been coached on the field. For DuBose, it's not just any Friday morning; it's his last day in his office. Perhaps that's the reason, when he asked about the rivalry, that he feels unbound to say what he believes. Or it might be his newfound passion for his religion. Whatever the reason, he sits behind his desk and says what few officials connected to the game will say publicly.

"It's the kind of game I didn't enjoy playing in," DuBose says. "The game is never over. You kept repeating it and repeating it and repeating it. You couldn't help but be around the fans. It's never over until you play it again the next year. It's a great game. But it's a game. For too many people, it's been their life, their goal. I don't want to diminish the significance of the game. It should be big. But it's still a game. There are families that can split over it. There are people that die over it. If we had that kind of passion for serving God and for taking care of our families, this would be a much better place. There are things that are bigger and more complicated. We need to understand that."

DuBose's lack of enjoyment stems from his sophomore season at Alabama. In 1972, he played on the team that lost to Auburn, 17–16, in the "Punt Bama Punt" game. He played defense when the Tigers' drove for their only offensive points, the field goal that pulled Auburn within 16–3.

"It was very difficult to go home," DuBose says. "Opp [his hometown in southeast Alabama] is probably a little more for Auburn. There's so much agriculture. That may have something to do with the way I feel about it. That [1972] game, today, is still being played. I didn't play a lot. I had gotten hurt two weeks before. I didn't practice at all. I didn't start in 'seventy-two. But I played. I was in the drive that Auburn kicked a field goal. I didn't play well in that drive. I don't know if it was because I was not getting as much work. When it comes down to five, six, seven plays that decide a game, especially in that game, [if] I did something in that game, maybe Auburn wouldn't have that opportunity. That's the one they remember. The play you didn't make. Defensively, we only gave up three points. Still, three points is the difference between winning and losing. The objective is to win. If they score 17, you got to find a way to score 18. If we score three, we got to find a way to let them score 2."

Down the hallway, graduate assistant Mike Bloomgren is assembling the bound game plan that will be handed out to each of the defensive players. On Thursday morning, he had recalled reading an essay written by an Alabama fan that describes why Crimson Tide football stirs the passion that it does throughout the state. "We need to play with that passion," Bloomgren said. "We need a fan to come in here and kick our guys' asses."

Eventually, Bloomgren digs it up and makes it the first page of the bound scouting report. The essay is entitled, "This is Alabama Football." The piece begins, "It is Wallace Wade. It is Paul "Bear" Bryant. It is not Bill Curry. It is the Rose Bowl. It is hearing Keith Jackson call an

Alabama game. . . . " Among the lines especially relevant to the Auburn game, it reads, "It is hearing the first notes of 'Sweet Home Alabama.' Sorry, UAB and Auburn, but that isn't your song. It is the desire to beat Auburn at any competitive event that exists. . . . It is watching the Bear get No. 315 against Auburn [how appropriate]. . . . It is almost coming to tears whenever Alabama loses to Auburn or Tennessee. . . . . It is pulling for any team that's playing Auburn. It is pulling for any team that's playing Tennessee. It is hoping that the stadium blows up when Auburn plays Tennessee. . . . "

The defensive scouting report, fifty-eight pages of computer print-outs, statistics, hand-drawn plays, charts, and inspirational writings, is all but a waste of paper. Alabama knows what Auburn is going to do. Quarterback Ben Leard is going to turn around and hand the ball to tailback Rudi Johnson. The defensive game plan has nothing to do with the defense. Alabama's plan to stop Auburn has more to do with the Crimson Tide offense. If Alabama keeps the ball, Johnson will never get it. The plan is to control the ball. Move the chains. More important, move the clock.

"We have to use Dustin, especially in short-yardage situations," DuBose says, referring to bull-necked fullback Dustin McClintock. "We had four opportunities against Mississippi State to make a first down [in short yardage] and didn't make them. That's an opportunity for at least twelve more plays. We got a 250-pound guy. If you get Dustin to the line, he's going to get a yard. It's important to utilize him on early downs to [prevent] the linebacker from running outside at the [tailback]. One of the big factors is how many first downs we can make. We're not big enough, not physical enough in the defensive line. We would like to play thirty, thirty-five guys on defense. With the injuries and the people who didn't qualify [academically], we get to play twenty-five."

A year ago, with Chris Samuels at left tackle, making room for tailback Shaun Alexander, Alabama ran wherever and whenever it liked. "Dustin's going to get it quite a lot," running backs coach Ivy Williams confirms. "We'll go to him early in short-yardage situations. Our plan is to keep ridin' him. We were able to do it with Shaun. Just grind 'em up. Last year, we were really left-handed with Chris. Now we're oriented to the wide side of the field. Try to stay away from the boundary, to give a guy some options."

The plan is a gamble, not because of McClintock, a fifth-year senior who may be the toughest guy on the team. But the Crimson Tide has not been able to sustain such a running game against the tough teams all season. Alabama rushed for 44 yards against Tennessee. Last week, at Mississippi State, Alabama rushed for 31 yards. As the season wore on, the Alabama offense held the ball for fewer minutes. The Crimson Tide hasn't held the ball as much as thirty minutes in any of its last four games, averaging only 26:35. Still, it is equally clear, as DuBose points out, that the defense is young, undersized, and understaffed. Alabama will have to depend on the wave of emotion that will accompany the Auburn game and DuBose's farewell to boost the performance of a team that has withered with every passing week.

DuBose says he does not know what the future holds for him. He has some speaking engagements in the next couple of weeks that he will honor. He says he has offers to go into business. He has heard from NFL teams and other colleges. He may travel to spread the word of God. He doesn't know. "Before we feel the need to do something and make the wrong decision," he says, "I'm praying and trusting the good Lord. His time is not our time. He doesn't feel the urgency that we feel, the need to find something. You try to get Him to hurry up and He doesn't feel the need to hurry."

The rivalry always looks different from inside the football building. It goes without saying that the coaches want to win as badly as any alumnus. But the coaches see the human side of the rivalry, too. They understand that jobs and mortgages hang in the balance. Linebackers coach Jeff Rouzie's closest friend during his playing days at Alabama was fellow linebacker Wayne Hall. After making All-SEC as a junior in 1971, Rouzie and Hall were in a car that was broadsided by a utility truck. Rouzie never played again. Rouzie became a coach at Alabama. Hall became Dye's defensive coordinator at Auburn.

"You don't even want to get too close to the enemy, as far as having feelings," Rouzie says. "This game is an emotional one. That's the way I feel about it. It's a war. That's what I do. It's a war. You are going out there to compete for the same players. You are going out there to sell your program. You're lining up against them every day and competing. You're just not on the football field. That's the way I look at it. Those guys are very competitive. Just because we're not lined up on the field, it doesn't make any difference."

After practice one evening this week, DuBose said he didn't believe the outcome of the game had much effect on recruiting. "I don't know that it's ever had the impact that people think it would have," DuBose says. "Auburn and Alabama go head to head on very few guys. The game doesn't play a significance from that standpoint. The young men are making decisions based on opportunity to play, academic evaluation."

When the premise is presented to Rouzie, he gives a succinct assessment. "That's bullshit," he says. "If there's a top-ranked player, we're both looking. You got to win the majority of those instate battles. That's your ball team. It's critical. For somebody to say that, it's not. Certain kids grow up Alabama fans and certain kids are Auburn fans. But you're going to recruit the heck out of them. In a state our size, when it comes down to ten or twelve kids [who can play Division I-A football], you better get your share. Coach Bryant said, 'I can get all the coaches I want that can do X's and O's. Ninety-eight percent of the game is recruiting, and don't forget it.' "

Rouzie recruits the southern part of the state and says he counts longtime Auburn assistant coach Joe Whitt, who recruits the same area, as a friend. "You sit together in the stands [at a high school game], eat popcorn, drink Coke," Rouzie says. But he is careful about spending free time with Whitt. It wasn't until Dye retired that Rouzie went to visit him. "I went down to Coach Dye's place with Neil [Callaway, the Alabama assistant who coached for Dye for twelve seasons]. We went hog hunting and quail hunting. Ol' Joe Whitt, we've talked about him coming up and fishing with us. We haven't done it. He and I talked about it. People would say, 'Say, we saw Joe Whitt hanging around down there with Neil and Jeff.' I worry about that, what rumors you can get yourself mentioned in a New York second."

To an outsider, that might seem ridiculous. Rouzie acknowledges as much. It doesn't change how he feels.

"The game affects business. It affects attitudes. I know that sounds silly," he says. "The importance of it can't be overstated. The players handle it better than anybody. When the game is over with, there's a lot of camaraderie. That's one of the good things. You never see the players with anything but respect. I wish I could say that for some fans."

Friday practices are usually a monument to killing time. Special teams run through what they need to do. Otherwise, it's a way to help players let off some steam before the game. However, DuBose has called for a short practice at this hour in order to go over some things one more time. Before the work commences, DuBose uses the rally at which he spoke on Thursday night in order to give his players an example of what they can achieve. "The singers sang individually," the coach says, "then all of a sudden, they came together. Collectively, as one, they were unbelievable. Absolutely unbelievable. That's what is awaiting us. Coming together as one. That's what we've talked about all year. We've got an opportunity to seize the moment. It's going to be a lot of fun. If you come together as one, we'll win!"

The players work crisply. If one is interested in omens—and anyone rooting for a 3–7 team will take any help available—the sun emerges from behind the clouds for the first time since Monday. Within twenty minutes, the practice is over. The players dress and disappear for a couple of hours before they are to report back for dinner and the team movie.

It's a testament to the staying power of friendship—or perhaps the bonds of matrimony—that a smattering of Auburn hats and parkas can be seen at the Alabama pep rally. The police closed off traffic on University Boulevard at 5:30 P.M. A large stage has been erected in a parking lot adjacent to the Sigma Nu house on University Boulevard. A couple of morning "radio personalities" introduce the emcee of the rally, Ken Stabler, the former Alabama quarterback who is now the analyst on the radio broadcast of the games.

"The season starts tomorrow," Stabler declares. He implores the crowd to greet Auburn fans with courtesy and kindness. His civility is impressive, until he finishes the thought. Alabama fans should greet Auburn with courtesy and kindness, Stabler says, because "we gon' beat their ass on the field tomorrow."

Stabler rouses the base emotions of the Tide fans, then introduces Dr. Andrew Sorensen, the university president. He is, by all accounts, as intelligent a man as you would expect. He is also so socially stiff that he can stop a conversation at twenty paces. Sorensen leads the crowd in a "Roll, Tide, Roll" cheer. Sorensen is the first of several dignitaries to be introduced, all of whom remain aboveboard in the nature of their cheering, until Keith Page takes the stage. He is the president of the University of Alabama alumni chapter in Lee County, home of Auburn University.

"It's so good not be in Auburn," Page begins. He continues that this weekend is a "Get Out of Auburn Free" card for the Alabama alumni who must leave there. The Tiger fans in the crowd can be heard muttering "Traitor" and "Classless," although they take care not to say it too loudly. Page's enthusiasm signals an increase in spirit, which Stabler maintains by introducing Shaun Alexander to the crowd. The fans roar, and Alexander keeps them roaring when he informs them that the NCAA has informed him he has one game of eligibility left.

"Auburn made the biggest mistake of their lives [by coming to Tuscaloosa]," Alexander says. "They're gonna want to tear up the contract. I know they can't read down there but they'll want to tear it up, anyway, because now they're in Tuscaloosa." Alexander tells the crowd that they are important players in the game Saturday. They have to be as loud as humanly possible for all four quarters, so Ben Leard can't call a single play. "If you do that, " he says, "I guarantee you that my little brothers"—his former teammates—"will whip Auburn up and down that field."

It says volumes about the Tide's 2000 season that Alexander received the biggest cheer of anybody.

The first competition of the weekend does not bode well for Alabama. Across the street from the Sheraton Four Points Inn in Tuscaloosa, the Crimson Tide's headquarters for home games, the Auburn men's and women's swimming teams swept their rivals by lopsided scores. Of course, the Tiger men, winners 184.5–109.5, are ranked second in the nation and the women, with a comparable margin of 186–112, are sixth.

In the lobby outside the Sheraton's meeting rooms, the Alabama coaches are milling about, waiting for the team to return from the movie *Men of Honor*, the story of the sailor who overcame the odds to become the first African-American Navy SEAL. Defensive line coach Lance Thompson says, "I think we're going to play well. Just from the answers I've been getting, they're paying attention at practice."

A few minutes later, the players rumble in. Fans young and old in the main lobby stop them for autographs. The chairs in the meeting room, which combines the Arthur Bagby and Benjamin Fitzpatrick ballrooms, are lined up and waiting. So, too, is a portable screen. Rawson, the video coordinator, has put together a tape to get the team in the proper frame of mind. He has blended scenes of the 1999 victory at Auburn together with scenes from *Braveheart*, in which the underdog band of militants led by William Wallace, as portrayed by Mel Gibson, defeats the better-equipped warriors of King Edward I. He shows Wallace riding his horse back and forth before his motley band of soldiers, imploring them not to run but to stay and fight for the freedom they profess is important. Rawson inserted his own narrative into the film. "WILL YOU FIGHT?" appears on a blank screen, followed by scenes from Braveheart.

"SOME SAY NO."

More movie.

"ONLY YOU KNOW."

More movie.

"THE WAR IS HERE."

Then the video cuts from the movie to footage of Auburn coach Tommy Tuberville shaking hands on their pregame Tiger Walk, to the movie, to the mascot eagle, and as Gibson yells "Now!" and unleashes his troops, the video begins to show Alabama dominating the game at Jordan–Hare Stadium. After a few scenes of Wallace's men, and the Alabama men winning their respective battles, Rawson lets the soundtrack swell to a crescendo then inserts the slogan "RUN OR FIGHT?" onto the screen.

As the tape ends, DuBose stands in front of the team. All week, he has been asked what he will say to the team. He begins to deliver his message.

"Come together and fight," DuBose reiterates. "So many people are trying to steal your dream. In the movie tonight [*Men of Honor*], a lot of people tried to steal his dream. He refused. He absolutely refused. He could have let them. He refused. There are people willing to steal your dream. The question is, will you let them? They're trying to steal mine. They can't steal it. It's not about winning a game. It's not about winning a championship. It's about oneness, together. Regardless of race, religion, color. I really believe when this team becomes one, this team has a chance to reach its premium potential. Think of your mom, your dad, your girlfriend. Don't let people steal it, guys. I love you."

The defense stays on one side of the room. The players pull the dividers down the middle of the meeting room and the offense gathers on the opposite side. Offensive coaches Neil Callaway, Ivy Williams, Dabo Swinney, and Ronnie Cottrell stand in front of them as the video of the Auburn defense plays. Callaway and Williams speak, one after another, without interruption but without pause, bombarding the position players they coach with messages.

"One thing to say," Callaway says. "Does anybody have any doubt about what this is about?"

"Until this game," Williams says, "we haven't made a big deal about time of possession. We need to hold on to the football. Brandon [Miree], Dustin [McClintock], you're going to get the ball. Move the chains."

"They're not a big 'dog' team," Callaway says, using the slang for blitz. "They're going to bluff you at times."

"They're going to be in white jerseys," Williams says. "Knock the shit out of someone in a white jersey."

"No excuses for having pressure, men," Callaway says to his linemen. "They are not talented pass rushers. Make 'em run down the middle of you. Give the quarterback all the time he needs. Also, tackles on the left side." Callaway directs his comment to Dante Ellington, the replacement for All-American Chris Samuels, as the offense watches on video Samuels open holes against Auburn a year ago. "See how they are all on their ass on the ground? I guarantee that's sticking in their craw. Everybody all year has been talking about it. Go ahead and stick it up their ass again. Griff [Redmill, the left guard], make 'em run down the middle of you. Keep shuffling your feet."

Quarterbacks coach Charlie Stubbs chimes in from the back of the room as they watch Georgia quarterback Cory Phillips complete a pass against the Auburn defense the week before. "Quarterbacks, give your receivers a chance to make the play. This kid does," Stubbs says.

"They're not a big-pressure team," Callaway repeats, watching a rare Auburn blitz, "but when they do, they're going in."

"You can tell they're coming by where the safety is," Stubbs reminds his quarterbacks. Williams is more emphatic. "Get your hat on these pencilnecks and knock the piss out of them. Don't cut [block] them."

"They were [in a] 3–3 [formation] against Arkansas and Florida," Callaway says of the Auburn line and linebackers. "They'll be a 4–2 team eighty to ninety percent of the time [on Saturday]. Always look for the changes."

The video ends. "Get after this ass, men," Callaway says. "Offensive line, I'll see you tomorrow morning."

The lights go on. The players get up and walk into the meeting room at the end of their hall on the right, where they have a late-night snack of pizza, hamburgers, and ice cream. In the defensive meeting room, as their teammates chow down, veteran strong safety Marcus Spencer and freshman linebacker Donnie Lowe sit with coach Jeff Rouzie and go over pass coverages one more time.

AUBURN

Tommy Tuberville is relaxed, as usual, as he sits in his office answering some e-mails. His new contract rests on his desk, unsigned. "I'll sign it before the game in case we lose," he jokes.

A few of the coaches, carrying garment bags, shut their office doors and walk across the street where the buses are idling in front of Sewell Hall, the dorm which houses most of the younger players. Don Dunn lags behind. He pauses in the lobby of the athletic complex and makes a detour into the Lovelace Athletic Museum to pay his respects to ghosts of the past. When asked if he does this every week before a game, he says, "No, because this isn't any other week."

Inside the museum, Pat Sullivan's 1971 Heisman Trophy is immediately on the left. A video of Auburn athletic highlights, nearly all of them football, runs continuously on a large screen in the center of the room. A clip from a 1960 Rat Pack movie, *Ocean's 11*, is included. "I've got great news for you," a woman gushes in the clip. "Auburn beat Alabama by twelve points."

There are pictures of Fob James, an All-American halfback for Auburn in 1955, who was elected to his first term as governor in 1978. There is a Camel cigarette case which was given to students trying out for the football team in 1947. There is a box full of tickets from the 1905 season. There is a 1937 football playbook. There is a recreation of Toomer's Corner, complete with a rolled tree. There is toilet paper salvaged from a tree after the first Auburn–Alabama game at Jordan–Hare in 1989. There is a toilet paper roll from Toomer's which graced a family's Christmas tree for years before being donated to the museum.

There are life-sized dioramas of Pat Sullivan talking with Coach Shug Jordan, both looking eerily like the real thing. There are also life-sized mannequins of Pat Dye, Bo Jackson, Charles Barkley, and Frank Thomas.

In one display case, there is a handwritten letter dated March 14, 1961, from Athletic Director David Housel, who was fourteen at the time, to Auburn All-American Ed Dyas, who played fullback, linebacker, and kicker.

> *Dear Ed,*
>
> *I hope you're the right Ed Dyas, the one that played for Auburn, but if you're not please disregard this letter and return it to me, so I may mark off your name in the telephone directory in my search for Ed Dyas, Auburn's fullback. A friend of mine who was in Mobile recently got a telephone directory and copied the Dyas column out of it, that's how I got your address. Ed, would you please autograph a piece of paper for me? I would appreciate also if you would give me a few field goal kicking tips.*
>
> > *Thanks and War Eagle.*
> > *Yours truly,*
> > *David E. Housel*
> > *Box 22*
> > *Gordo, Alabama*

Next to the letter is one from Ed Dyas, dated November 4, 1994.

> *Dear David,*
>
> *I am sorry I have been so long in getting back to you. Almost 34 years have slipped by since you wrote to me this letter in which I am returning to you. I found it 3 years ago in a box of old Auburn things. You must have been a high school freshman when you wrote it and I had just graduated from Auburn in March 1961.*

You have had a remarkable career at Auburn. I have become
an orthopedic surgeon and have had a long career in Mobile.
Auburn and life in general has been very good to both of us. We
have always been and will always be strong Auburn men.
    I look forward to seeing you at the upcoming Georgia game.
              War Eagle,
              Ed Dyas

"That letter shows how dreams can come true far, far beyond whatever you realized. I wrote Ed Dyas wanting to learn how to be a kicker.
I remember writing it in study hall in the eighth grade. I don't know
that he had ever dreamed his life would turn out as good as it has, but
I could never dream that my life has turned out as good as it has.
Auburn has been a far greater part of it than I could have ever
dreamed. And I had big dreams about Auburn. My only goal in life at
that time was to come to Auburn. I hate to think of what my life would
be without Auburn. Auburn born, Auburn bred. When I die, I'll be
Auburn dead," Housel says with a laugh.

The first Auburn–Alabama game Housel saw was in 1956, a 34–7
Auburn victory. After the game, Housel, then ten, wrote to both school's
publicity directors to request media guides. Auburn's Bill Beckwith sent
Housel a media guide with a nice note. Alabama sent him a media guide
with a bill enclosed. The gesture made an impression.

The next year, Housel watched Auburn thump Alabama, 40–0, and
capture the school's first and only national championship in 1957.
"The dye was cast after that," Housel says. Housel majored in journalism at Auburn, then worked in the ticket office, taught journalism, and
then served as the sports information director.

Sports information director was the only job Housel ever dreamed
of having. But in 1994, university president William Muse turned to
Housel to be the school's athletic director in the wake of NCAA probation. (The NCAA found that an Auburn assistant coach and recruiting
coordinator under Pat Dye made cash payments to former player Eric
Ramsey. A booster also gave Ramsey cash and merchandise.) "I didn't
seek this job, it sought me," Housel said at the time.

In Housel's pocket is a key to Jordan–Hare Stadium. Sometimes late at night, when there isn't a soul around, Housel drives across the street to the stadium, sits in the hallowed place, and remembers. "You just think about all the people who have played there, all the wonderful things you have seen there, the various stages of your life you have experienced, to some degree, there," he says.

When Housel watches a game, he becomes a kid again. "If we are doing something good and I happen to be like this," he says, folding his hands, "and we make a first down, I would stay that way." Against Alabama last year he determined that if he took the lineup card, folded it, and held it a certain way, it helped the Tigers. "I am not superstitious but I don't want to take any chances," he says.

When he was married in 1985, his wife, Susan, gave him a gold wedding band inscribed with these words: DAVID, I LOVE YOU. 6/15/85. BB.

"You know what 'BB' stands for?" Housel asks. 'Beat Bama.'

"When we got married, I'm not sure whether she thought I would rather marry her or beat Alabama," he says, letting loose a belly laugh.

Normally, Housel rides in the third or fourth bus, but today, for Auburn's first trip to Bryant–Denny Stadium, Housel is in the first patrol car. After the Tigers' final trip to Birmingham last year, he thought about this day, about being in the first car.

"I was born an Auburn man. I grew up an Auburn man. And when Auburn marches into Tuscaloosa—not when we're dragged in there, but when we march in there—I want my foot to be one of the first Auburn feet to touch that campus," Housel says. "And to me, in my heart of hearts, it's going to be symbolic. For all of those Auburn men and women who went before to make this moment possible. Coach Shug Jordan, Coach Beard, Marvin Price. All the Auburn people, I mean, I'm a product of them and I just want to go as somebody who went to school here, who grew up here, I want to go and represent them. When my foot touches that soil, it will be them touching that soil. And I'm going to feel that way in my heart of hearts. This is a heart thing for me. It's not an ego thing. It is a heart thing. I came from the Auburn people to this job. But I'm going to represent those Auburn people who are not here to represent themselves. We're going to march in there with our flags flying and our band playing and our colors held high, and we're going to represent Auburn. And then, we're going to get after their butt."

Housel, fifty-five, lists birds, books, and Broadway as his hobbies. However, Auburn is his passion. His office is decorated with both Auburn and Broadway memorabilia. In fact, in 1992, Housel made his Broadway debut in a production of *Five Guys Named Moe* at the Eugene O'Neill Theater in Manhattan. To Housel, Auburn is the Everyman. He wants his foot to be first for all the other dreamers who came before him.

Dreamers such as Shug Jordan. "In the 1970s, Coach Jordan said that he didn't like artificial grass, and he was talking about bringing the Alabama game to Auburn's campus," Housel says. "All the Alabama people made fun of him and ridiculed him for being too old and out of touch. When he said college football was meant to be played on the college campus, on grass, on a Saturday afternoon, they made fun of him. Well, November the eighteenth, the year 2000, proves Coach Jordan right."

Dreamers such as Jeff Beard, Auburn's former athletic director. Beard fought to have a stadium big enough and a program good enough to invite every SEC teams to campus. His wish finally came true on December 2, 1989, when Alabama became the last SEC team to come to Auburn for a football game. "It was meant to be," Beard said that day.

Dreamers such as Marvin Price, who was a pharmacist in Housel's hometown of Gordo in western Alabama, which is about twenty miles from Tuscaloosa and 180 miles from Auburn. To get to Auburn from Gordo, you have to drive through Tuscaloosa. In the drugstore on Saturdays, Price was tormented by boastful Alabama fans if the Tigers were trailing.

When Price died in 1985, Housel, the school's poet laureate of sorts, wrote these words about his old friend: "Coming out from the flowers on his casket, was an orange-and-blue ribbon. On that ribbon was the word 'Auburn.' Underneath, there was a football. . . . Marvin Price never played football here. He never attended Auburn. . . . M. R. Price's name will never be recorded in the annals of Auburn history. He never gave a scholarship, he never built a building, he never did any of the things that cause people to be remembered. All he did was give Auburn his love and loyalty for more than seventy years. It is entirely appropriate that his casket bore Auburn colors. For he was a great Auburn man."

When Housel speaks about his alma mater, it's as if he's composing a love sonnet. "There are things that remind me of what a special place Auburn is every day. It can be an orange and blue sunset. It can be a something somebody says, something somebody does. A word of care: I think the Auburn people, the whole Georgia game, the way the eagle flew. The Auburn people around that game. Everybody has their own special feeling and their own picture and image of Auburn. And you can't snapshot that. I mean, you can't snapshot one's heart. And you can't snapshot one's life. But you can look at a series of snapshots and be reminded of the totality of it all. I bet if you can look behind me right now, you'll see a beautiful blue sky and some gold trees. And, you know, I think about Auburn when I think about those things. Another day in paradise."

"It's showtime," Alabama state trooper Randy Byrd says, as he puts his car in drive. At 3:15 P.M., a motorcade of state trooper cars and motorcycles leads the team buses out of east central Alabama for the 116-mile trip northwest to Birmingham. Throughout the drive, the troopers entertain themselves with Alabama jokes over their radios.

"What's the difference between a maggot and Alabama?" Byrd asks.

"They've both been living off the Bear for twenty years."

The troopers keep the trip interesting by bullying cars out of the caravan. When an unsuspecting motorist switches lanes into the motorcade, the troopers respond as if it's an enemy invasion. Motorcycle cops blast their sirens, surround the intruder, and force him to switch lanes.

"Get your ass outta here," Byrd yells. "Some drivers are just crazier than a runover dog."

The motorcycle troopers speed ahead of the motorcade to block off incoming traffic. Throughout the journey, they radio each other traffic, play-by-play. When Bus No. 2 is too far behind Bus No. 1, they radio bus driver No. 2 and ask him to speed it up. And so the drive goes, north on 65, past a billboard which reads: IF YOU DON'T GO TO CHURCH, THE DEVIL WILL GET YOU. A devil with a pitchfork looks down menacingly from the sign.

When the team buses arrive at the Sheraton Perimeter Park South in Birmingham, the Tigers are greeted by the lights of TV cameras and the photo flash from fans. The music of Jock Jam's "Let's get ready to rumble," blasts from the speakers as the Tigers walk through the lobby. For Alex Lincoln, the scene is nothing like Division III Mississippi College, where he spent his first two seasons.

"When I was growing up that's how I pictured college football," says Lincoln, who turned twenty-three today. "A lot of movies glamorize it, about staying in all these real expensive hotels, and sometimes you know, maybe it's different in Alabama, but we don't always have a good hotel. When we're playing in Starkville, Mississippi, they don't have any of those five-star hotels around there. Coming in here and being in a nice place, people playing music and reporters everywhere, that's how I see college football. Man, I just got so excited. I just can't imagine how it can get any better, and I know it is going to be ten times that tomorrow. I had a ball. I didn't want to go to my room. I wanted to stay in the lobby. I was like a big kid there. That's how I was, growing up. When I would look at a football player, I would stand in the corner looking starstruck."

Rob Pate smiles as he remembers the first time Lincoln went to an away-game with the team. "I just remember how excited he was just to get on the plane for his first road trip," Pate says. "It was a big deal for him. Better than the game. We're sitting on the sidelines and he was saying, 'I get to go on the plane again.' It was a lot of fun for him. I think a lot of times you take things for granted and then a guy like Alex comes along and you know how special it is."

As Cole Cubelic got off the bus, a fan yelled, "Roll Tide." Cubelic is still fuming about the comment. "It's stuff like that that really makes you want to go there and win badly. Obnoxious people like that don't have any business even being at this hotel, much less saying that in front of eighty SEC football players for the other team," he says. Good thing Cubelic didn't look in the men's bathroom just inside the lobby. Scribbled on one stall was this prediction: "Alabama 28, Auburn 27."

Earlier in the week, Cubelic tried to get in contact with Alabama offensive guard Griff Redmill, whom he's met a few times, and back-up quarterback Tyler Watts. Cubelic doesn't know if either got his message, because neither returned his phone call. "I was just gonna tell them, 'I know exactly what you are going through and if you want to talk about it,'" Cubelic says. In 1998, Auburn faced similar turmoil, when the Tigers lost their coach, Terry Bowden, and far too many games, finishing 3–8.

"It's amazing how similar it is. I think that they had a lot of guys that they depended on last year. And maybe they knew how good they were and how important they were and they thought that they were easily replaceable," Cubelic says. "And we had some guys like that in 1997 in Victor Riley, Takeo Spikes, and Dameyune Craig. You know they are good players, but when they are gone, it's when you really realize how important to the team they were. Alabama lost guys like Chris Samuels and Shaun Alexander. And I think they had some younger guys who, due to the fact that those guys were playing so well, it was a little easier on them last year. Alabama was probably expected to do too much this year.

"Obviously when things don't go your way, you're gonna make changes. Then you start to lose games and then everybody wants to fire your coach. When everybody is talking about your coach getting fired all the time, you don't think about playing football.

"I can remember some team meetings we had and some guys pointing fingers and that type of things. I'm sure that they are seeing some of the same stuff. I've heard rumors, but I don't know for sure—probably won't ever know. But I know we had a lot of 'You need to do this' and 'That's your fault' and stuff like that. That never helps, especially when you are not winning games that you should be winning."

Before dinner, the Reverend Chette Williams talks to the team about finishing strong and reminisces about the Iron Bowl of his senior year, in 1984. "We were 8–3. Alabama was 4–6. We had the best running back in the nation, Bo Jackson. The defense was awesome. We had a quarterback who was experienced, who the players believed in and trusted in. We came in with a lot of confidence. At the start, we drove it right down the field and scored a touchdown. But then they scored, and after that you could just kind of see the emotion start to change. You could see their senior leadership and their players pushing them, you could start seeing them build confidence, and you could see us relaxing, because we were expected to win. The bottom line is, we lost that game. We lost that game not because we weren't physically able to win that game. We lost that game [17–15] because of mental mistakes. Bo went the wrong way on a play, but the game wasn't lost by Bo Jackson. The game was lost because our team, we didn't finish strong. If I had to have a theme for this evening, it's finish strong."

After the prayer, the Tigers help themselves to the buffet. Ben Leard fills his plate with three pieces of fried chicken, a slab of steak, macaroni and cheese, and potatoes. "I have to keep up my masculine figure," he says. Seconds and thirds are followed by bowls of ice cream.

After dinner, the offense and defense meet in adjacent conference rooms. Both units watch highlights from the Georgia game. At the end, "2000 SEC Champs" flashes across the screen. As they study some final film on Alabama, Leard sits directly in front of offensive coordinator Noel Mazzone and nods knowingly throughout.

"I just want to win bad. This makes our season. It's a huge game for us, a huge game for me," Leard says. After four years of listening to the critics, this is his last, greatest chance to prove them wrong. Yesterday, Leard received some hate mail from a Georgia fan, which isn't unusual. "It's pretty rude. It was pretty bad, probably the worst I have ever gotten. It pissed me off pretty bad," he says, without further elaboration. "It's just one of those things. People have too much time on their hands."

As for the game plan, if the weather is lousy, as expected, the ball will be in Rudi's hands, even more than usual. It won't matter that the Tigers don't have receiver Tim Carter, because the field will be too slick for the receivers to cut. Since Rudi isn't a scatback, since he runs up the middle and runs over people, he can barrel straight ahead without losing his footing. The plan is to run Rudi inside the tackles.

On defense, John Lovett talks about the zone coverage the Tigers plan to use. They hope that their four defensive linemen will provide enough pressure on the quarterback so they won't have to blitz much. The weather might make it too risky to blitz, since a defensive back in man coverage could slip and get burned.

The Tigers are mostly concerned with receivers Freddie Milons and Antonio Carter getting the ball. If they don't blitz, they can take away the screen passes Alabama usually throws to both.

Since the Tide has struggled on offense, Lovett is confident that the

Tigers can hold them to 10 or 14 points, especially because the Tide's running game has faltered the last four games. In the rain, their running game won't be able to bail Alabama out.

Special teams go over punt block protection, as they have all week, thinking that Alabama will surely try to block one. Georgia blocked a punt against Auburn last Saturday, which led to an eventual score. After a poor game last year against Alabama, Tuberville announced that he was going to sign a new kicker to replace Damon Duval, who handled both placekicking and punting duties. But Duval persevered this season. His confidence is high entering the game, following last week's three field goals, including a career-long 49-yarder.

After the meetings end, the players stop at a buffet table full of chicken fingers and load up one last time, though the night's not over yet.

As usual, there's the Friday-night prayer meeting, which is organized by fullback Heath Evans. The players, nearly the entire team, and several coaches, sit along the four walls of the conference room, facing each other.

The prayer meeting has drawn the team together, because it's when the players talk about everything but football. They talk about their families and their concerns. Earlier this season, one married player shared his financial problems. At the end of the meeting a collection was made of the ten dollars everyone receives as meal money. The money was given to their teammate who broke down in tears.

Tonight, coach Terry Price talks about his baby son, who is doing better in the hospital. "That's a testament to the power of prayer," Price says.

Lincoln reminds everyone to appreciate the moment. "On November 18, 1996, I had thirty-two people attend my game at Mississippi College," he says. "It was so quiet, my dad could hear the checks at the line. So this, what we have here, is what it's all about."

Lincoln goes on to tell a story about defensive tackle Roderick Chambers. When Lincoln arrived at Auburn in 1998, Chambers gave him a hard time. "Where are you from? From what college? What are *you* doing here?" Chambers would say.

Gradually, Lincoln, who is white, and Chambers, who is black, became close friends, and last summer Lincoln was a groomsman in

Chambers's wedding. "Back where I'm from, if people saw us walk down the street together, people would wonder what we were doing together," Lincoln says.

Several of the seniors talk about their last Iron Bowl game. "It's kinda like, we don't really want to play this game," senior cornerback Rodney Crayton says. "Can we put it off? We're one day closer to the last time we play Alabama as a senior class. It's the hardest thing."

Adds Lincoln, "When I got here two years ago, if you would have asked me if I ever cried, I'd say, 'I don't cry, I'm a mike linebacker.' The last few weeks, I've cried so much I feel like my mother at a movie."

The evening closes with a gospel song called "I'll Follow You," performed by senior cornerback Domincke Haston.

After Cole Cubelic says goodnight to ten relatives who came by the hotel, he goes to his room. His roommate is Ben Nowland, who beat out Cubelic for the starting job this season. The game is almost fourteen hours away, but neither player knows who's starting.

"It will be a game-time decision," Cubelic says. "Coach Nall is back and forth. Nothing against him. He just don't make up his mind too fast."

It's nearly midnight and the day is finally over. All that's left to do is to BB, as Housel's wedding ring says. Beat Bama.

Saturday

The Game

4:00 A.M.: Neil Callaway can't sleep. Actually, it may be more accurate to say that the Alabama offensive coordinator doesn't sleep. Seven hours ago, standing outside the meeting rooms at the Sheraton, Callaway nursed a cup of coffee and said, "I've been known to go into the office at two or three in the morning. I would want to watch film." Those kind of hours, he said, explain why he is holding a cup of coffee. Drinking caffeine so late? "I'll sleep tonight," Callaway said, with a sly smile, "until three."

He didn't get up and out of his house until an hour after that. In Callaway's guest room, Bill Ham Jr., heard the truck drive off, and got out of bed. He phoned Callaway on his cell phone and asked if he wanted company. Callaway circled back and picked him up. Of all the strained marriages and mixed friendships that this rivalry produces, the bond between Callaway and Ham is at the top. Callaway is an Alabama assistant coach. Ham is the mayor of Auburn. They became close in the mid-1980s, when Callaway, then an assistant coach on Pat Dye's staff, lived next door to Ham. Given the tumult that Callaway has been through this season, Ham called him before the game and said, "Look, you got more on your plate then you need to deal with. You're looking for a job. Maybe we shouldn't come."

"No," Callaway said. "I need y'all here more than ever."

So that's how, at 4:00 A.M. on a frosty night, the mayor of Auburn found himself riding around Tuscaloosa with the Alabama offensive coordinator. Their friendship, Ham says, came about because "he and I didn't have to talk about sports. We could talk about life, kids, friends." That said, for the hour or so that they rode around, Ham says, they talked about the game that day. "I figured," Ham says, "he needed to talk to somebody. We talked about how anything can happen in this game. I said, 'You know how I feel and you know I want to beat those guys. If you win, I'll be happy for you.' "

Ham can hardly believe what came out of his own mouth. "There are not many people," Ham says, "that I could say that to."

9:30 A.M.: The Alabama team reassembles and the special teams coaches go over the keys for their respective teams: kickoff return and coverage, punt return and coverage and the field-goal kicking and defending teams. After they finish, DuBose stands before his team again. All season, he has been pleading for this team to come together. The Tide's 3–7 record shows his lack of success. That doesn't mean the team doesn't need to hear it again.

"You know what the key is?" he asks his team. "It's love. If you don't have love, there's no oneness. If you don't have love, there's no team. Guys, it's unconditional love. Why should it start with somebody else? It should start with you. It should start with me. Jeremiah Castille [a former Alabama All-American who spoke with DuBose at the rally on Thursday night] had a brother stabbed to death. His brother wasn't a victim. The person who stabbed him was a victim. Jeremiah went to the prison and ministered to him. It's hard to do, isn't it? That's what changes the world."

As he speaks, he paces a couple of steps in one direction, then the other.

"It's unconditional love," DuBose says. "I'll give anything and do anything as long as it's right for my brother and sister. Let's cherish the moment. It's special. Know that I love you. I want the best for you."

The team breaks up into position meetings. The quarterbacks, led by starter Andrew Zow, congregate in chairs in the back left corner of the room.

"It's going to be a little wet," quarterback coach Charlie Stubbs says.

He turns to backup Jonathan Richey. "Make sure you throw a little bit," he says. And then, to reassure the group, Stubbs says, "It's not going to be that bad." Stubbs then begins to rattle off everything he can think of.

"Remember ball security. Make sure you secure the ball to the back before you carry out the fake. In the red zone, all we're expecting is a little more press. Everything will be tougher. [Number] 10 [cornerback Rodney Crayton] is more aggressive than 24 [Larry Casher]. Always key to the safeties. They really tip it. If the linebackers get close, key to the safeties. If they stay back, the linebackers will pull out of the blitz. Key to the 25-second clock, always. We haven't had a problem. Let's keep going. Look to Jonathan [Richey on the sidelines] quick for signals. I want to keep a tempo. . . . No turnovers. Stay with your reads. Don't assume nothing is there. Don't predetermine. . . . Andrew, you play best when you're a little loose. Let the game come to you. Enjoy the experience. You got a great opportunity. We've got to throw the ball down the field to make sure they don't squat on the run. Let's have some fun."

When the players walk out, they find a massive buffet awaiting them: sweet rolls, scrambled eggs, bacon, grits, french toast and warm syrup, toast, fruit, and cereal.

Outside, the rain has begun to come down. The weather reports have been saying that the precipitation won't settle in for good until after the game. Right now, however, the rain is exacerbating the cold rawness of the day.

9:30 A.M.: At the Sheraton in Birmingham, Auburn breaks up for position meetings. There's only a few meeting rooms, so the defensive linemen move into the hallway, across from a phone bank and the rest rooms. Five chairs are lined up in front of them, impersonating Alabama's offensive line.

Minutes before the defense meets as a whole, coaches Terry Price, Greg Knox, and Porkchop are sitting at a table with a stack of newspapers. Someone has already gone through the pile, picking it clean of the sports section. Price looks at the lifestyle section. "Mister Rogers is retiring? You gotta be kidding me," he says. "I loved that show, that and *The Electric Company.*"

The coaches are loose. The preparation is done. All that's left is last-minute motivation. "Start strong and finish strong," John Lovett says. "Go for sixty minutes. Seniors, this is your last shot."

There is no talk of what may lie beyond this game. If the Tigers win and Mississippi State loses to Arkansas today, Auburn will capture the SEC West championship and play Florida in the SEC title game.

11:15 A.M.: The Tigers grab their bags and load the bus for the forty-five-minute ride to Tuscaloosa. Athletic Director David Housel sits in the front seat of the first patrol car. Just after noon, the Tigers arrive at Bryant–Denny Stadium. Housel steps out of the car, smiles, as he stares at his shoes.

At Gate 19, Auburn fans are lined up for Tiger Walk. Tommy Williams, the Tiger Walk director as the script on his shirt says, is in front. Tuberville raises his arms and shakes his fists. The crowd cheers as the team snakes through the thousands of fans. War Eagles and hi-fives are exchanged. Coach Hugh Nall spots his eight-year-old daughter, Mary Ashton, and grasps her hand, as she falls into line in front of him for the rest of the Tiger Walk.

12:08 P.M.: The Alabama players take the quarter-mile bus ride from the Sheraton down Paul W. Bryant Drive to Bryant–Denny Stadium. The fans line up several deep along the sidewalk to cheer them as they walk through the wrought-iron gate at the south end of the stadium. The players stride into the locker room and ninety seconds later, emerge from the south tunnel to walk the field, a tradition that began under Bryant many years ago. Senior cornerback Milo Lewis walks onto the grass, a video camera to his eye, and narrates as he heads downfield: "This is what I do when I come out here...."

Near the south end zone, graduate assistant Kevin Sherrer allows an edge of excitement to creep into the calm he usually displays. "It's not been like this all year," he says. "I haven't seen that focus, that look. We may not win. I think we're going to win. I think it will be a good game."

The team takes a lap around the field and comes back to the locker room, a low-ceilinged, cinder-block fortress at the opposite end of the south tunnel from the field. Eight training tables are lined up immediately to the left as you enter the door. The room opens to the right and goes well under the end zone stands. The shower room is at the opposite end. Wooden benches, bolted to the floor, stand before the lockers that adorn the wall all the way around the room.

DuBose reminds the seniors that all of them will be honorary captains. He turns to center Paul Hogan, defensive lineman Kenny Smith, and deep snapper Bradley Ledbetter, the team captains, and goes over what he wants on the coin toss. After they break up, the players return to their lockers. Five defensive backs—Lewis, Kecalf Bailey, Tony Dixon, Marcus Spencer, and Reggie Myles—gather before their lockers and get a manager to take their picture. This is their last game together.

12:15 P.M.: Auburn center Cole Cubelic still doesn't know if he's going to start. Though it is 39 degrees out, he walks on the field in his T-shirt and shorts wearing a pair of headphones. Heath Evans and Alex Lincoln kneel at midfield and pray.

Housel is on the sideline wearing a trench coat and a porkpie hat. "Do I look like the Bear?" he asks with a smile.

In the locker room, the Tigers change, get taped, and stretch. The lockers are gray, the chairs are crimson.

"Seniors, it's on you," Coach Yox reminds them.

There is no noise. The players tuck their jerseys in their pants. Cubelic and Leard apply each other's eye black. Alex Lincoln struggles to get his jersey over his shoulder pads, so a trainer lends a hand.

"This shit ain't just going to happen," Coach Yox says. "They're not just going to say, 'Oh shit, they're 8–2' and lay down and die. They have to be convinced to lay down and die."

"Nobody works as hard as we do. Nobody," Don Dunn says, as he paces a path on the carpet.

Lincoln works the room, pointing at teammates, slapping others on their shoulder pads.

Cublelic is at the training table, getting taped. When Lincoln asks him if he's starting, Cubelic shrugs. "Hey, don't worry about it," Lincoln says.

As if on cue, Coach Nall approaches to deliver the news.

"You're going to start it out," he says.

Cubelic nods.

1:15 P.M.: Alabama quarterback Tyler Watts, recuperating from the knee ligament he tore against Mississippi five weeks ago, is standing in the end zone with only a letterman's jacket to guard against the chilly drizzle. "I'll be right over there on that sideline," he says, looking to his right. "I'll be all right if it doesn't sleet. I won't sit in the stands. People run their mouths. I'd get mad."

The drizzle is no longer intermittent. The forecast that the bad weather wouldn't arrive until after the game has been as accurate as the prediction that Alabama would repeat as SEC champion. Doug Layton, who has broadcast Alabama games for most of the last three decades, peers up at the leaden sky from the south tunnel and says, "It just goes to show you. God doesn't want this game here."

2:20 P.M.: The Tigers gather in the center of the locker room around the Reverend Williams. "Lord, please clear my head of all the distractions. So that I may perform my very best. Lord, please lift me up so through your eyes I may see and have a clear understanding as the game unfolds. With courage, I will meet this challenge. Keep me humble and remind me my strength comes from knowing you. Amen."

Tuberville picks Cubelic to speak to the team. Though Cubelic didn't prepare for this moment, the words flow easily.

"I just want everyone to think about one thing. They think they're better than you. Think about how many people in this locker room got offered scholarships to go to Alabama. I know I didn't. Guys like Pate and Linc and Leard. They they think they're better than you because y'all weren't blue-chip enough for them. This is the Super Bowl, this is the World Series, this is everything. Right now, do me a favor. Go to war with my ass. Let's beat these motherfuckers."

Tuberville takes over. "We gotta go out there and play four quarters. And we gotta make sure that we take care of business the first half. And as time goes on, we're going to get stronger and stronger. Everybody's going to feed off each other in here. We've got about fifteen thousand folks out there and the crowd can be noisy. It's going to be a little wet. It's going to be a little slippery. All you got to do is concentrate. Concentrate on what you're doing. Believe in each other as you have all year long and we'll be fine. We've come a long way. A long way. Concentrate. Remember last year. Let's go."

The Tigers charge out the door and then gingerly jog down the slick incline of the tunnel that leads to the field.

2:20 P.M.: For the last hour, the Alabama players have tinged their comments with braggadocio. "This is my last one, folks," tight end Shawn Draper says. "I'm fixin' to party." Across the locker room, a voice rings out, "Y'all get that in your head right now. We gon' win this game." Painted on the wall just inside the door, in large block letters, is the word "WIN." As the players left the locker room for their pregame drills, each one touches the word for luck. Some swat it with a fist. Some obsessively touch each letter. Some place their palm on it and stop for a moment. Everyone touches it.

Now the bragging has been set aside for a moment. Nearly all eighty players are crowded in the showers at the back of the locker room. A voice from the middle of the tightly packed players competes with the clattering of cleats on tiles and the shuffling of some very large bodies. "This will be the last time some of us strap on pads," the voice says. "The last time we will be together. Think about all the stuff we've been through. We pray that we have the strength to climb up the mountain. When the game is over, we'll look down from the mountain and see what we've been through."

Tony Dixon, the senior safety, took over. "Think about the help you had along the way. Think of all those people. Think of what they mean to you. Think about how much they have done for you."

The players say "Amen" and file back into their locker room. After a few moments, DuBose calls them to the center of the room. "There'a a time for all things," he begins. "There's a time to talk. There's a time to do. A time to do. Sixty minutes. I wish you the best of luck. Never forget this. You go out and make your own luck. Things don't happen. You go out and make your own luck."

The players crowd out the door, again touching the "WIN" sign. Zow headbutts it. The team congregates at the mouth of the tunnel, and as the Alabama Million Dollar Band strikes up "Yea! Alabama!" the Crimson Tide runs to its home on the east sideline.

Shaun Alexander, in a crimson stocking cap, waves the game ball overhead as he walks it out to the officials at midfield. For an SEC official, the Iron Bowl assignment means you've arrived. "It might be the easiest ball game to work," says veteran linesman Ray Moon, who, since he briefly attended Auburn, has never been allowed to work it. "That's the game everybody wants to get. Those kids just get after each other. So many of them played high school ball with each other. You see the friendship they maintain. There's teasing [on the field] but the fans take it a lot harder than the kids themselves."

No player worth his pads starts the game without fist-sized butterflies. When it's your last college game against your biggest rival, it's all you can do to keep your food down. "It's pretty uptight," center Paul Hogan says. "The first quarter, anyway. That's going to be the biggest thing. Not getting uptight: all the hype, wanting to win so bad."

"The hardest thing to do," agrees guard Griff Redmill, "is to settle down and rely on what you've been taught. Before the game, I'll replay every scenario in my mind and how I'm supposed to react."

Auburn won the toss and chose to defer until the second half.

In the stands, Carol Ham sat with Karen Callaway and the other wives of the Alabama coaches. Bill Ham Jr., sits in the stands with his son Forrest, an Auburn freshman.

2:30 P.M.: Virtually the moment Auburn kicker Damon Duval sends the ball in the air, the steady raindrops turn into sleet.

First quarter: On Alabama's first series, Zow moves the ball to Auburn's 28-yard line. On second down, the Tide lines up in I formation. Zow play-fakes and throws to receiver Antonio Carter, who is being covered by Rob Pate and Stanford Simmons. Pate intercepts the pass and returns it 10 yards to Auburn's 11-yard line. Clearly, this cold, miserable weather is perfect for Pate.

On a double tight-end set, Lorenzo Diamond goes uncovered downfield and makes a 20-yard reception to convert a big third down.

With 3:25 remaining in the first quarter, the game is still scoreless.

That's about to change because of an Auburn run. However, Rudi isn't the man with the ball. Fullback Heath Evans, with clearing blocks by left tackle Kendall Simmons and right guard Mike Pucillo, breaks downfield for 34 yards to the Alabama nine-yard line. Two more rushes get the Tigers to the two, but Rudi is stuffed by Todd Whitmore and Kelvis White and pushed back three yards. Kicker Damon Duval comes on to attempt a field goal. His breath hangs like a cumulus cloud in the heavy cold air. The 22-yard kick is good. Auburn leads 3–0.

Second quarter: Clumps of dirt, kicked up by cleats, cover the length of the field. Water drips from the tips of face masks. A steady stream of rain runs off the bill of Tuberville's baseball cap. On the sideline, Auburn players huddle around the heaters. They dangle their feet and hands in front of the heat, as if toasting marshmallows. Most watch the game on the Jumbotron, since it's easier to follow that way.

On Rudi's first carry of the quarter, lineman David Daniel and linebacker Saleem Rasheed knock him back for a two-yard loss. On the Alabama sideline, former All-American defensive lineman Bob Baumhower calls out, "Marty!" His former Tide teammate, Marty Lyons, looks over at Baumhower and nods in appreciation. Nearby, the Alabama offensive linemen, who wouldn't deign to put on windbreakers when they came to the sideline in the first quarter, are wearing them now.

One tackle doesn't stop Rudi. He runs up the middle, time after time. The defensive line, the unit that was much maligned at the season's start, is playing extremely well. The Tide doesn't advance beyond Auburn's 46 the entire quarter. Auburn begins its final possession of the half at its 41, its best field position of the quarter, because Tide punter Lane Bearden is having a poor game. Leard quickly hits Deandre Green on 17-yard crossing pass into Bama territory. Still, there's little excitement in the stands or on the field. Baumhower turns to a friend on the sideline and says, "Does it seem flat out here to you?"

Dull, perhaps, but Rudi does the rest of the dirty work to bring the Tigers to Alabama's 25. Duval finishes the drive off with a 42-yard field-goal attempt. Auburn leads, 6–0. The Tide's Jason McAddley returns the kickoff 24 yards to the Tide 41. Alabama has 47 seconds, plenty of time to get into scoring position, with a two-minute offense. On first down, Zow throws into the left flat to Carter. He's wide open, yet Zow's throw is so off-target that Carter must make a diving catch. The clock continues to run and Alabama must use a timeout. The drive, as has the offense for the entire half, fizzles.

Halftime: As expected, both quarterbacks have mediocre statistics given the weather. But the story of the first half is evident in this statistic: Auburn has 78 yards rushing, Alabama has 12.

Alabama trots into south tunnel. The coaches peel off into a small room on the left. The players keep going and return to the locker room at the far end on the right. Halftime is a study in frenzy, as everyone seems to talk simultaneously.

The offensive coaches go over a couple of blocking wrinkles. After a couple of minutes, they hustle into the locker room. At the grease board in the back of the room, Callaway holds court with his beleaguered offensive linemen. Halftime stats prove how tough they have had it. The theory that McClintock could tough out the hard yards to sustain Alabama's offensive possessions hasn't tested out. For one thing, the feeble efforts on first and second down have left only one third down of fewer than four yards. For another, even McClintock, with a neck as thick and round as a telephone pole, can only do so much by himself. The holes simply aren't there.

"We got to sustain our blocks," Callaway tells his linemen. "We're slipping and sliding. We've got to stay after their ass. We got to knock them off the ball." He switches from scolding to pleading. "All we got to do is do it." Callaway repeats the line. "All we got to do is do it. C'mon, guys! Get mean when you get out there and let's get after their ass!"

At the grease board in the front of the room, the linebackers are seated on the left side and the defensive linemen are seated on the right. Defensive line coach Lance Thompson is charged up and demanding that his players meet the challenge before them. "We have got to get field position," he tells them. "Turnovers or score. Who is going to decide the game? You have to want it. Every snap is going to [hurt us] if you don't hit those motherfuckers on every play. Three and out right here. Tackling is the most important fundamental. This half, gang-tackle his ass."

Linebackers coach Jeff Rouzie, a cooler, grayer head than Thompson, is speaking evenly to his players. "It's there, guys. It's there."

Freddie Milons wanders by, walking off nerves. "Get right, D. Get right. Yeah, that's what I'm talking about."

A digital clock on the wall, in sync with the game clock, ticks off the waning seconds of intermission. DuBose calls the team to the center of the locker room.

"You're going back out there, defense," he says. "Take away the big run [by Evans] and the big throw [to Diamond]. The defense gave up six points because of two plays. We had three opportunities to take the ball away [and didn't do it]."

DuBose turned his attention to the other side of the ball. His tone is even. His words aren't. "Offense, we got five first downs," he says. "We keep talking. Somebody has got to line up and whip somebody, one on one. I wish with all my heart that we could outscheme them. We can't. We can't.

"You got thirty minutes left. Thirty minutes. Last year, we were in the same situation. Chris Samuels and Shaun Alexander took it over. Cornelius Griffin, Reggie Grimes took it on themselves. Somebody has got to say, 'If it is to be, it's up to me. Somebody has got to be willing to do that.'

"Let's go out there for thirty minutes and win the football game. Is that guy across the line better than you? I know you'll give everything you got to this team. We been saying it all year. The offense has got to go up and down the field. Let's go."

DuBose's talk confirms what coaches have said all along. Knute Rockne–like speeches don't exist outside of Hollywood. With thirty minutes left in his coaching career, he is reminding them of lessons they should have learned long ago.

In the center of the Auburn locker room, the team gathers around Tuberville. "Remember last year. We whipped their butt all over the field in the first half. And then they came out, they made their mind up that they were going to win a conference championship. They had the opportunity to win one. So do you this year. They don't. All that running in off-season. All that weight lifting. All that extra stuff, they didn't do that. It's been showing all year long. They've been getting their butt kicked in the third and fourth quarter.

"Now, defense, they're going to try to get an easy on you. Concentrate. The ball game is going to be won here with our defensive line, hitting Zow, legally. He does not throw well if you put pressure on him, as we've just seen. You gotta keep turning it up. Offensively, just keep on keepin' on. We're going to make plays. Kicking game, just keep on doing it. Good field position. This can be your ball game, easy or tough. It's going to be up to you. We get the ball opening up. No stupid penalties on the kickoff. Watch for an onside kick, they're liable to do anything. They're desperate. Hold on to the football. Let's bring this thing back and let's jam it down their throat and get it over with. Let's go."

"Thirty more minutes, and they'll give up," Diamond shouts.

Third quarter: No one seems to notice the rain anymore. As the temperature drops, steam rises from calves and shaven heads. On Auburn's first drive, Rudi, Green, and Diamond carry the Tigers to Alabama's five-yard line. But on second and goal, Leard underthrows a tightly covered Ronney Daniels and the ball is intercepted by Milo Lewis. Tuberville screams into his headset, "What are you doing?" as he questions Mazzone's playcalling. Three Rudi runs might have led to a score, or at least the Tigers could have settled for a field goal.

The Alabama offense, charged with the momentum of a score-killing interception, comes onto the field and can't get off a play before Zow must call a timeout. Exit momentum. On third-and-two at the Tide 28, Milons lines up at quarterback. He starts around left end and sees a wall of Auburn white. He reverses field and loses five yards.

On the first play of Auburn's next possession, Leard is picked off again—this time at the Auburn 39. As he walks over to the sideline, he pats his chest. "My fault," he says. Alabama is handed another opportunity to get back into the game. On second down, DeMarco McNeil and Javor Mills sack Zow for a loss of nine yards. Zow doesn't flinch on third-and-19. He finds a wide-open Triandos Luke in the middle of the field. The freshman bobbles the ball, then drops it. Bearden must punt the ball away. The quarter ends without either team scoring.

Fourth quarter: The stands are still full. It would take more than three hours of freezing rain to send an Iron Bowl crowd of 85,986 home.

Tuberville is pacing along the sideline during Auburn's first possession. Leard completes a 26-yard pass to Diamond. A 31-yard reception by Green puts the Tigers on Alabama's 36. Then, on a play action, the ball slips out of Leard's hands, but he recovers his own fumble. On Bama's 10, Duval comes on again for a 27-yard field-goal attempt. As usual, Leard says to Duval, "Nice and easy." As the ball goes through the uprights, Tuberville throws up his hands in celebration. Auburn 9, Alabama 0.

"Ten more minutes, ten more minutes!" Coach John Lovett yells to his defense. "Just knock their ass off for just another ten minutes."

Arkansas beats Mississippi State in overtime, 17–10, and the news is quickly passed along the sideline. Within a minute, the entire team knows. If Auburn holds on, the Tigers are headed to the SEC championship game.

With 7:53 remaining, Rudi rumbles 16 yards for a first down, using a strategic stiff-arm to stop a bigger defensive lineman, Whitmore, and breaks into the defensive backfield. However, Rudi twists his sore ankle. He leaves the game and then collapses on the sideline, grimacing in pain. Two plays later, he's back on the field. However, the series ends when Tony Dixon's helmet pushes the ball out of Rudi's grip. Kenny Smith recovers.

"Five more minutes, five more minutes," Lovett screams.

With 2:52 remaining, the Tide takes over on their own 24-yard line. Tuberville paces. Zow leads his team all the way to Auburn's 31 on a 13-yard run, but after three incomplete passes, Alabama is forced to try for a 48-yard field goal. As soon as the ball is snapped, several players on Auburn's sideline yell, "High snap! High snap!"

Neal Thomas's kick falls short, bouncing on the B of the painted ALABAMA in the end zone. Auburn's sideline erupts. Thomas trots back over his bench. Charlie Harbison, who coaches the field-goal unit, walks over to give him a hug. Shaun Alexander and backup snapper Tripp Powell pat Thomas on the butt. No other teammate comes near him.

Noel Mazzone reminds the offensive line: "One more series and the SEC championship can be yours."

With 1:48 remaining, Auburn can take a knee twice to close it out. "I'm getting the ball," Cubelic tells Leard. "No, I'm getting it," Leard says. On the Alabama sideline, Redmill is red-eyed, crying in frustration.

As time runs down, the Tigers sprint on the field. "We did it!" Cubelic says to Leard as they embrace. Cubelic, who just played the best game of his career, as his coaches say later, has the game ball in his hands. He cradles it and doesn't let go.

Mayhem breaks loose. Defensive tackle Roderick Chambers, who is 300 pounds, does a chicken dance. Wide receiver Clifton Robinson runs along the end zone carrying a soaked orange flag. CBS interviews Tuberville and Rudi. Rudi is shaking from exhaustion, from carrying the ball 37 times for 130 yards.

Colin Sears finds Ben Leard. "This was worth staying for," Sears says to him.

As Coach Hugh Nall jogs off the field, a few Alabama fans shout, "Go to hell." Nall looks up in the stands and screams back, "I'm already in hell. I'm headed for paradise now."

On the tunnel back to the locker room, Coach Whitt and his son, Joe Jr., hug each other and cry. They walk together, arms around each other, to the locker room.

"We actually did it," Sears says to no one in particular.

Just about everyone is crying. Alex Lincoln and Coach Whitt embrace. "To be able to give that win to him and to see him break down in tears, I'll never forget that," Lincoln says.

Equipment manager Frank Cox knows he should be checking that the $40,000 phone system and all the headphones have been collected, but he can't stop the tears.

Tuberville gathers the team in the center of the locker room. "Take a knee and grab somebody's hand," he says. The Reverend Williams says a prayer. At "Amen," the team breaks out in a cheer.

"Listen up, guys," Tuberville says. "You came to play and you came to play for four quarters. That's the reason we won that football game. There's one guy here we need to take our hat off to. I'll tell you what, the last two weeks he's been the major difference in us being here. Damon Duval."

The team cheers as Leard hands Duval a game ball.

"Congratulations to all the seniors. [Clapping.] Defense, that was about as good as you'll ever see. Give yourself a hand! [Clapping.] Offensively, we got the job done. You know, you can tell that everybody keeps coming together the whole game. Never any doubt. Everybody just kept coming together. [Cheering and clapping.] I'm proud of you. All the coaches are proud of you. And there's twenty thousand people out there proud of you. You guys have come a long way. Unfortunately, you've got yourselves another week of work." (Cheers.)

Someone yells out, "How 'bout them Hogs!" (Cheers.) "Soo-ey!"

"How 'bout them rings we gonna get?" Tuberville says. (Cheers.)

"We're going to take a few days off. We're going to come back to work. We'll get the itinerary to you. And one thing we are going to do for a few days is we are going to live on this victory, because I'm going to tell you something; it's been a hundred years. In the beginning of the year, not one person—not one person outside of this room—gave you a dog's chance to be where you're at. I'm talking about not anybody. You've accomplished something that nobody maybe in history has ever done. You've come from so far down to come so far up. And it's because you're a team. We're not overly talented in a lot of areas, but we've got more heart than probably most of the teams put together. I want to thank you from the bottom of my heart. I love every one of you. You know what I always say—be careful going home! Live on this one. This game we won tonight goes to Auburn University." (Cheers.)

Leard stands up holding another game ball. "This one goes to the SEC West championship head coach," he says. (Cheers.)

In unison, they sing the school fight song.

> War Eagle, fly down the field. Ever to conquer, never to
> yield.

War Eagle fearless and true. Fight on, you orange and blue.
Go! Go! Go!
On to vic'try, strike up the band,
Give 'em hell, give 'em hell.
Stand up and yell, Hey! War Eagle, win for Auburn,
Power of Dixie Land!

Most of the players run back on the field to greet their family members and the Auburn fans still in the stadium. Leard finds his fiancée and gives her a kiss.

Cubelic, with eye-black streaking down his face, walks to midfield. He bends down on one knee and says a prayer. Then he bends down on the other knee, outstretches his arms, and raises his eyes to the black sky . Though he wearing only a T-shirt, freezing rain never felt so good. Auburn has just beaten Alabama, 9–0.

Inside the Alabama locker room, the team gathers in the middle of the room. The players and coaches drop to one knee and recite the Twenty-third Psalm. They finish and remain in that position as they look at their coach.

"It's never quite as bad as it seems. It's never quite as good as it seems," DuBose tells them. "There's truth to that. I'll pray for all of you, especially the seniors. All of this will make you better men, better husbands, better members of the community. All of you deserve better than you're getting. For that, I'm sorry.

"Show your class. Do what we talk about. I want you to keep your head up. Show unconditional love. Dare to change the world. I love you. I love you."

DuBose's voice softened and nearly gave way as he finished. A voice from the group responds, "We love you, too, Coach."

"I appreciate everybody," DuBose says. "I love you all."

Safety Tony Dixon, who made 11 tackles, hugs DuBose. Dixon's teammates line up behind him to hug their coach. Others drift back to their lockers. Defensive coordinator Ellis Johnson spies Kenny King, the injured defensive end, and says, "Be well, buddy. I'll holler at you."

Zow walks over and hugs Smith, the defensive captain who proved with his play what a leader he can be.

DuBose eventually walks over to a folding chair near the grease board at the front of the room and collapses into it. He keeps his head down, trying to have his cry as privately as possible. Sports information director Larry White, who will lead interference for DuBuse into the interview room next door, kneels next to DuBose and puts his right arm around DuBose's shoulders. Athletic director Mal Moore comes in and pats DuBose's left arm. The coach reaches up with his right arm and grasps Moore.

A few minutes later, with White as his lead blocker, DuBose walks down the tunnel and into the interview room. The media is respectfully quiet, yet the adrenalin is surging. This is DuBose's good-bye.

"I'll try hard to get through this," he says. He begins by congratulating Auburn. "They've done an outstanding job. I wish them nothing but the best. They played hard. Very physical, very clean. I wish the outcome had been different."

He loses his composure for only a brief moment, when he is asked about this being the end. "I'm going to miss it. I'm going to miss the university," DuBose says. He stopped, and waved forward the next question. He is asked about the Alabama offense, which finished with 135 total yards and no points.

"When you talk about our offense, you got to talk about the Auburn defense," DuBose says. "They lined up and whipped us at the point of attack. They didn't do anything different. If you had told me our defense would hold them to nine points, I would have told you that we would have won the game. . . . If we didn't make first downs and stay on the field, Auburn would, and Auburn would dominate the fourth quarter. That's what happened." In the second half, Auburn held the ball for 21:43 of the thirty minutes. In the fourth quarter, Auburn had possession for 12:10. The final tally: Auburn 37:45, Alabama 22:15.

Redmill, the senior guard, is not so sanguine. He prefaces what he says with genuine respect for DuBose and the coaches. Redmill sounds more mystified than miffed. "It was the same thing we've been doing all year," he says. "We said all along, on third and short, we would give it to Dustin. We ran the veer [sweep] maybe twice. We didn't run the belly [up the middle]. We didn't run any of the stuff we had for Dustin. It was frustrating. We're working on all the plays in practice and we don't see them in the game. I have all the confidence in the world in the coaches. I just wonder why we don't [use] some of the stuff we work on, that we're comfortable with."

Zow, one of the last players to enter the interview room, says that he didn't have a good grip on the first-quarter interception he threw in the Auburn end zone. He admits that the early mistake may have stayed in his mind. "I may have let it affect me, instead of dropping back and throwing the ball," Zow says. "We lost to Auburn, especially on our turf. It's just horrible. We just didn't execute our offense. It's something we keep repeating, but we just didn't get the job done."

In the middle of the room, senior defensive tackle Kelvis White speaks with composure, a calm he didn't have at the end of the game. "I got pretty emotional," he says. "It might be the last time I put the pads on. I've been playing football all my life. I've been around football all my life." (His father is a football coach.) "I'm from Courtland. Colin Sears [the Auburn senior offensive tackle] is from Russellville. I see him in the summertime. We went to Notre Dame together on official visits. We played in the [high school] all-star game together. He looked straight across the line of scrimmage and told me to keep my head up. He wasn't bragging. When [Leard] downed the ball, Colin said he didn't want to see me crying."

"Yeah, I was crying," White says. "That's what that's all about. After the game, soon everybody was hugging and praying together. That's what it's all about."

David Housel is standing on the side of the room during Auburn's press conference. He has a cigar in his mouth. It's a tribute to Marvin Price, the pharmacist who lived across the street in Gordo. "He, like a lot of us, took a lot of stuff from Alabama people," Housel says. "He was a cigar smoker. He had to smoke a lot of cigars in a lot of pain. This one's for Mr. Marvin."

Tuberville is surrounded by microphones. A white towel is draped around his neck. "This is a game for all of Auburn University. When you play Alabama, you're playing for the rights to brag. To beat them on the road, I mean, it took them ten years to beat Auburn in Auburn. It took us one year. And, you know, it just makes it so much sweeter. But again, I thought we had the best team going in and we got the job done.

"I thought the weather was really conducive to what we do, but we needed to throw the ball a little bit more. They were putting seven, eight, and nine guys out there to stop Rudi, and luckily, Rudi wasn't going to have none of that. You know, Rudi just kept running. And Rudi was Rudi tonight, and again, he got 130 yards and he earned every one of them. I mean, there wasn't any of those—we didn't have a lot of 15- to 20-yard runs. They were all 5-, 6-, or 7-yard runs and again, he's made a big difference in this football game. And I think if you pick two guys that made the major difference, it'd have been him and Damon Duval.

"I thought Ben did a good job. Again, it's very tough in that type of weather, throwing the football. Other than those two interceptions, I thought he played a good game. We just got a lot of confidence as the game went on, and again, Ben, he's not playing perfect. No quarterback plays perfect, but I'll take his efforts every day."

"Coach, as I recall," a reporter says, "that this time last year you said that you were going to find yourself a new kicker. Where did you find this Duval kid?"

Laughter fills the room. "I tell you, he's grown up more than anybody. He's been great to be around. And I told people at the beginning of the year that he worked as hard as anybody—the kickers, I mean, the running backs, the linemen—and all of them are getting better. And I think that mentally he has gotten so much better. He hasn't missed a field goal in at least two weeks."

Clyde Bolton, the *Birmingam News* columnist, asks Tuberville if this is his greatest day as a head coach.

"Yes, sir, Mr. Clyde, this is it."

When Tuberville leaves the podium, Bolton rises from his seat to see what is behind a curtain where the coach was standing. To his surprise, it is a larger-than-life statue of Bear Bryant. As Bolton reported, "He was not smiling."

•   •   •

After the game, the Hams returned to the Callaways, where, Bill Jr., says, "I had bought a lot of steaks. We came back and cooked out." When Ham arrived, Callaway's sons, Clay and Russ, shook hands with their dad's good friend and congratulated the Auburn mayor on his team's victory. Then, to Ham's utter shock, they handed him a game ball. The Callaway boys work the sideline at Bryant–Denny Stadium as ballboys. Bill's son Forrest, a freshman at Auburn, arranged for Clay and Russ to spirit a ball away for his dad. Once the sodden leather dried, Ham sent the ball to Tuberville to have him autograph it.

Coach Terry Price drives to the hospital in Birmingham to visit his wife and son on the fourth floor of the neonatal unit. "Alex is 1 and 0 right now," Price says. His wife watched the game from the hospital, where all the nurses wore Alabama T-shirts. Six babies had had little Alabama caps on. Alex wore an Auburn cap, of course.

"They do take sides on everything, don't they?" he's asked.

"Everything."

At noon on Sunday, Price leaves Birmingham to be back to campus for the coaches meeting. At 3:30 P.M., Tuberville sits in sports information director Meredith Jenkins's office holding his usual press conference.

"Well, what a night," Tuberville begins. "One of those that I'll always remember. It was bad weather. Great crowd. A defensive game on both sides. I thought we played great defense, but after looking at the film, I thought Alabama played great on defense. Couldn't stop Rudi in a couple of situations and Ben made a lot of key passes. Offensively, our offensive line blocked as well as they had blocked all year. I thought Cole had a heck of a game. We were gonna run the football no matter what they did on defense. They played to stop the run. They put seven or eight guys up there to stop the run. Rudi was still gaining yards. If it had been a nice night where we could have thrown the football a little more, I think we could have moved a little bit better through the air. We'll take what we got. It was a good effort, overall, on offense. Receivers caught the ball well. We blocked well down the field.

Ben did make a couple of mistakes, but other than that, he really played well.

"Defensively, Javor Mills and DeMarco McNeil played outstanding. The whole defense played outstanding. Those two guys played as well as any two defensive linemen that I've been around in a while in one game. Our secondary: they challenged their receivers a lot more. I don't know if the difference was that they had a lot more confidence last night. They did a good job. Our linebackers were playing good zone coverage. We didn't blitz one time. If you'd a told me that we could have held them to 135 yards without blitzing, I would have never believed it. It was a superb game. Our kicking game was great. I can't say enough about Damon. He averaged 44 yards a punt in that rain. Kicking three field goals. Now we've got to get ready for another game."

Afterward, in their meeting, the coaches talk about the team's schedule this week, about recruiting, about hunting, about Thanksgiving. All the while, Tuberville's son, Tucker, is sitting on his lap playing with a stick of Big Red gum. As Tuberville talks, Tucker throws the wrapper at his dad. Tuberville picks it up and stuffs it down his son's shirt. Toward the end of the meeting, Tucker is lying across the table, leaning on his elbows. As the coaches talk, Tuberville pokes Tucker in the butt with a pencil eraser. And so it goes. Noel Mazzone is chewing tobacco, Eddie Gran and Terry Price are chewing on coffee stirrers, as usual.

In the bowels of the athletic complex, equipment manager Frank Cox is sitting at his desk. The place smells like an ashtray and is about as neat as one, too. "I come in here this morning and I've got about five voice mails. People just crying, loud. Friends of mine," he says. "Just to see their emotions, it's just so neat. I say it's neat; it's also kinda scary. And I just wonder, why? That's the way it is in this state. That's what you probably got a better understanding of now. It's something that you just can't tell somebody. If you had come down here just today and you listen to me say all of this stuff, you'd walk out and say 'That guy ain't got a lick of sense.' But you experienced enough of it now to know.

"Most of those guys, despite enjoying the heck out of it, don't really know what they did. They'll be a lot older and at a lot more football games and have a lot more life experiences when they do realize it. But those guys that played in that game yesterday are basically going to be immortalized in football lore. I don't think that it is possible for them to understand that right now. I looked around that locker room yesterday, and I was thinking that, golly, there's some guys in here that people are going to be talking about forever."

Epilogue

On December 1, Alabama athletic director Mal Moore introduced his choice to replace Mike DuBose as head coach of the Crimson Tide. Actually, Moore introduced his third choice—Dennis Franchione, fresh off a 10–1 season at TCU. Franchione, who also had built winners at Pittsburg State (in Kansas), Southwest Texas State, and New Mexico, had been set to accept an offer from Arizona State. Moore swooped in and signed Franchione after being jilted by Butch Davis of Miami and ignored by Frank Beamer of Virginia Tech. Davis negotiated with Moore before getting cold feet. Beamer shied away because it became clear after the 2000 season that Alabama would have a difficult time returning to the Top Ten. The problems would not stem solely from the 3–8 disaster just concluded, but from a looming NCAA investigation of Alabama recruiting.

Rumors had been circulating among college football coaches for months that Alabama had crossed the line and begun spending money on players. In January, the Memphis Commercial Appeal quoted a local high school assistant coach named Milton Kirk as saying that his head coach, Lynn Lang, had received $200,000 from Alabama boosters to steer high school All-American Albert Means to Alabama—the same Means that had been a flabby flop as a freshman for the Tide. Lang denied it. The booster most linked to the payment, Logan Young, denied it. Means left Alabama and transferred to Memphis. The NCAA ramped up its investigation. The specter of NCAA probation and scholarship reductions will scare away plenty of coaches. Franchione dismissed it, noting that Miami had rebounded from probation and the loss of scholarships to become a national championship contender.

The lure of tradition helped Franchione overcome such fears. He came to Tuscaloosa to stand on the sideline where Bryant once stood. He displays the intelligence of a man who is aware of a world outside of football, yet he expressed delight at coming to a state consumed by the sport. After a couple of months in Alabama, even Franchione seemed taken aback at the fervor of his school's fans. "They really do eat their young in this state, don't they?" he asked one day.

The whispers of NCAA problems compounded the problems of the former Crimson Tide assistants in getting jobs. Coordinators Neil Callaway and Ellis Johnson, both veterans with established reputations, found new employment relatively quickly. Johnson turned down an offer to coordinate the Maryland defense in order to become head coach at his alma mater, The Citadel. Callaway is coaching the offensive line at Georgia for new head coach Mark Richt. Secondary coach Charlie Harbison hooked on at LSU, while defensive line coach Lance Thompson returned to Georgia Tech, where he was taken as tight ends coach and recruiting coordinator.

Receivers coach Dabo Swinney turned down feelers about the head coaching job at I-AA West Alabama and eventually went into private business. Running backs coach Ivy Williams, was set to take the head coaching job at I-AA Miles College in Birmingham when the Memphis story broke. Williams, who recruited Memphis, denied any involvement but the NCAA wanted to talk to him. That ended any interest at Miles College.

Quarterbacks coach Charlie Stubbs and recruiting coordinator Ronnie Cottrell, both of whom had two-year contracts, remained out of coaching in spring 2001. Linebacker coach Jeff Rouzie appeared likely to remain at the university as a fund-raiser.

Two weeks after the Iron Bowl, Auburn met Florida for the SEC Championship in Atlanta. In the first half, Florida scored touchdowns off of three Auburn turnovers and went on to win easily, 28–6.

In their first bowl since 1997, the Tigers were invited to play Michigan on New Year's Day in the Citrus Bowl. The day before the game, the team elected its permanent captains of the 2000 season: quarterback Ben Leard, center Cole Cubelic, and corner Rodney Crayton. Though Leard set school records, throwing for 394 yards with three touchdowns, the Wolverines edged out the Tigers, 31–28. The Tigers finished the season at 9–4 with more victories than the previous two seasons combined.

In December, the school announced that the senior class of 2000 will be permanently honored in a Tiger Walk area under construction at Jordan–Hare Stadium. "It will be something for what they've gone through, what they've done to get this football program back," coach Tommy Tuberville said. "They've earned the recognition."

In January, junior running back Rudi Johnson, the SEC player of the year, junior fullback Heath Evans, and sophomore wide receiver Ronney Daniels announced that they would enter the NFL draft. Combined with the loss of Leard, Cubelic, Crayton, Rob Pate, Alex Lincoln, Colin Sears, and the rest of the seniors, the Tigers will have a challenging rebuilding job in 2001.

In February, Auburn signed a strong recruiting class ranked in the Top 20 by most analysts. Included among the group was Alabama's Mr. Football, Carnell "Cadillac" Williams, a running back surely needed with Rudi gone.

On February 21, at halftime of Auburn's 72–69 home-court victory over Alabama, a young woman walked onto the basketball court, took a microphone, and began singing the "War Eagle!" fight song. That woman, Emily McMurphy, was the president of the Student Government Association at the University of Alabama. Thus was the annual bet between the two student bodies paid in full.

In March, the Tigers returned to the field for spring practice. Though quarterback Daniel Cobb began the month as the No. 3 quarterback, before the spring game, he was No. 1. Like Rudi, Cobb was signed out of Butler County College. When offensive coordinator Noel Mazzone was recruiting Cobb in 1999, the quarterback mentioned that he had a pretty good running back on his team that Auburn might want to take a look at.

Meanwhile, in Tuscaloosa, Franchione began spring ball by turning the depth chart upside down and shaking. After the first scrimmage, in which quarterbacks Andrew Zow and Tyler Watts combined to throw four interceptions, Franchione promoted Jonathan Richey to the first team. Richey, who says he was ninth-string when he arrived on campus in the fall of 1997, turned down a basketball scholarship to Berea College (in Kentucky) in order to walk on for his beloved Crimson Tide. A week later, Zow had won his old job back. Message received, Coach.

On April 14, both Auburn and Alabama played their spring games, called A-Day. Though it was the day before Easter, sixty thousand fans combined were in the stands to see the Tide in Tuscaloosa and the Tigers in Auburn. Sixty thousand people to hope, to dream, and to count down the days until they meet again.

Appendix
ALABAMA—AUBURN SERIES RESULTS

Alabama leads 37–27–1

1893	Auburn, 32–22;	1954	Auburn, 28–0
	Auburn, 40–16	1955	Auburn, 26–0
1894	Alabama, 18–0	1956	Auburn, 34–7
1895	Auburn, 48–0	1957	Auburn, 40–0
1900	Auburn, 53–5	1958	Auburn, 14–8
1901	Auburn, 17–0	1959	Alabama, 10–0
1902	Auburn, 23–0	1960	Alabama, 3–0
1903	Alabama, 18–6	1961	Alabama, 34–0
1904	Auburn, 29–5	1962	Alabama, 38–0
1905	Alabama, 30–0	1963	Auburn, 10–8
1906	Alabama, 10–0	1964	Alabama, 21–14
1907	Tie, 6–6	1965	Alabama, 30–3
		1966	Alabama, 31–0
1948	Alabama, 55–0	1967	Alabama, 7–3
1949	Auburn, 14–13	1968	Alabama, 24–16
1950	Alabama, 34–0	1969	Auburn, 49–26
1951	Alabama, 25–7	1970	Auburn, 33–28
1952	Alabama, 21–0	1971	Alabama, 31–7
1953	Alabama, 10–7	1972	Auburn, 17–16

1973	Alabama, 35–0	1987	Auburn, 10–0
1974	Alabama, 17–13	1988	Auburn, 15–10
1975	Alabama, 28–0	1989	Auburn, 30–20
1976	Alabama, 38–7	1990	Alabama, 16–7
1977	Alabama, 48–21	1991	Alabama, 13–6
1978	Alabama, 34–16	1992	Alabama, 17–0
1979	Alabama, 25–18	1993	Auburn, 22–14
1980	Alabama, 34–18	1994	Alabama, 21–14
1981	Alabama, 28–17	1995	Auburn, 31–27
1982	Auburn, 23–22	1996	Alabama, 24–23
1983	Auburn, 23–20	1997	Auburn, 18–17
1984	Alabama, 17–15	1998	Alabama, 31–17
1985	Alabama, 25–23	1999	Alabama, 28–17
1986	Auburn, 21–17	2000	Auburn, 9–0

At Auburn: Auburn leads 4–1
At Tuscaloosa: Auburn leads 3–0
At neutral sites: Alabama leads 31–19–1 (5–1)*
    At Birmingham: Alabama leads, 30–17 (6–1)*
    At Montgomery: Tied, 2–2

*Birmingham games counted as neutral site until 1988, when ticket allocation changed.

COACHING RECORDS

Alabama coaches versus Auburn

E. B. Beaumont (1892)	0–1
Eli Abbott (1893–95, 1902)	1–3
M. Griffin (1900)	0–1
M. H. Harvey (1901)	0–1
W. B. Blount (1903–1904)	1–1
Jack Leavenworth (1905)	1–0
J. W. H. Pollard (1906–1907)	1–0–1
Harold "Red" Drew (1948–54)	5–2
J. B. "Ears" Whitworth (1955–57)	0–3
Paul "Bear" Bryant (1958–82)	19–6
Ray Perkins (1983–86)	2–2
Bill Curry (1987–89)	0–3
Gene Stallings (1990–96)	5–2
Mike DuBose (1997–2000)	2–2

Auburn coaches versus Alabama

D. M. Balliet (1892/winter)   1–0
G. H. Harvey (1892/fall)   1–0
F. M. Hall (1893)   0–1
John Heisman (1895)   1–0
Billy Watkins (1900–1901)   2–0
Robert Kent (1902)   1–0
Billy Bates (1903)   0–1
Mike Donahue (1904–1906)   1–2
W. S. Kienholz (1907)   0–0–1
Earl Brown (1948–50)   1–2
Ralph "Shug" Jordan (1951–75)   9–16
Doug Barfield (1976–80)   0–5
Pat Dye (1981–92)   6–6
Terry Bowden (1993–97)   3–2
Bill Oliver (1998)   0–1
Tommy Tuberville (1999–2000)   1–1

SERIES NOTES

There have been 22 shutouts in the rivalry. The Tide has won 14 of those, most recently in 1992 (17–0).

The most points scored is 55 (Alabama, 1948) in the series renewal. The most combined points is 75, in Auburn's 49–26 win in 1969.

The team leading at halftime has won 71 percent of the time (47 of 65). The game has been tied at the half on seven occasions, with Alabama winning six of those.

There have been five one–point games, with Auburn winning four: 1949 (Auburn, 14–13); 1972 (Auburn, 17–16); 1982 (Auburn, 23–22); 1996 (Alabama, 24–23); 1997 (Auburn, 18–17).

Auburn and Alabama have never had losing records in the same season.

Since 1956, at least one of the two teams has been ranked in the final Associated Press poll.

ALABAMA–AUBURN RECORDS

MOST RUSHES: 42 by Johnny Musso, Alabama, 1970

MOST YARDS RUSHING: 256 by Bo Jackson, Auburn, 1983

MOST PASS ATTEMPTS: 55 by Scott Hunter, Alabama, 1969

MOST PASS COMPLETIONS: 30 by Scott Hunter, Alabama, 1969

MOST YARDS PASSING: 484 by Scott Hunter, Alabama, 1969

MOST TOUCHDOWN PASSES: 3 by Steve Sloan, Alabama, 1971; Jeff Rutledge, Alabama, 1978

MOST RECEPTIONS: 9 by Terry Beasley, Auburn, 1970; David Bailey, Alabama, 1969

MOST YARDS RECEIVING: 187 by David Bailey, Alabama, 1969

MOST FIELD GOALS: 4 by Van Tiffin, Alabama, 1985

LONGEST RUSH: 85, Joe Cribbs, Auburn, 1977

LONGEST PASS: 74, Charlie Trotman to Byron Franklin, Auburn, 1977

LONGEST PUNT: 71, Tank Williamson, Alabama, 1991

LONGEST FIELD GOAL: 52, Van Tiffin, Alabama, 1984 and 1985; Al Del Greco, Auburn, 1980

LONGEST KICKOFF RETURN: 100, George Ranager, Alabama, 1969; Ray Ogden, Alabama, 1964

LONGEST INTERCEPTION RETURN: 79, Tommy Lorino, Auburn, 1957

10 MOST ELECTRIFYING MOMENTS
IN IRON BOWL HISTORY

10. 1971 No. 3, unbeaten Alabama routs No. 5, unbeaten Auburn, 31–7, two days after Tigers quarterback Pat Sullivan won the Heisman Trophy.

9. 1986 Lawyer Tillman runs around end late in the game to give No. 14 Auburn a 21–17 upset of No. 7 Alabama.

8. 1996 Dennis Riddle catches a touchdown pass in the waning seconds and Alabama edges Auburn 24–23. After the game, Tide coach Gene Stallings announces his retirement.

7. 1984 Brent Fullwood fails to score from the 1-yard line when blockers Bo Jackson and Tommie Agee go the wrong way and 4–6 Alabama upsets 8–2 Auburn, 17–15.

6. 1982 Pat Dye's first victory over Alabama is the last defeat of his mentor, Paul "Bear" Bryant, 23–22.

5. 1967 Ken Stabler's 47-yard dash down the left sideline in the mud gives Alabama a 7–3 victory in a driving rainstorm.

4. 1949 In the second year of the rivalry after a 41-year hiatus, Auburn, which has won only one of its last 17 games, upsets Alabama, 14–13.

3. 1989 After an emotional Tiger Walk, Auburn scores on its first possession and never trails in a 30–20 victory, spoiling No. 2, unbeaten Alabama's first visit to Jordan–Hare Stadium.

2. 1985 Van Tiffin's 52-yard field goal as time expired, the fourth lead change of the fourth quarter, gives Alabama a 25–23 win.

1. 1972 David Langer's two blocked punt returns for touchdowns to lead No. 9 Auburn to shocking 17–16 upset of No. 2, unbeaten Alabama.